Don't Turn Your Back in the Barn

Also by David Perrin

Dr. Dave's Stallside Manner

Don't Turn Your Back in the Barn

Adventures of a Country Vet

Dr. David Perrin

**Andrews McMeel
Publishing**

Kansas City

Interior page design by Pete Lippincott

02 03 04 05 06 QUF 10 9 8 7 6 5 4 3 2 1

Library of Congress Cataloging-in-Publication Data

Perrin, David, Dr.
    Don't turn your back in the barn : adventures of a country vet / David Perrin.
        p. cm.
    ISBN 0-7407-2350-2
    1. Perrin, David, Dr. 2. Veterinarians—British Columbia—Biography.
    3. Animals—British Columbia—Anecdotes. I. Title.

SF613.P47 A3 2002
636.089'092—dc21
[B]
                                                                    2001053666

To all the Dorises of my life

CONTENTS

FOREWORD viii

ACKNOWLEDGMENTS ix

SWEET WILLIAM 1

"STAR LIGHT, STAR BRIGHT" 12

FERRY CONTRARY 26

POOR WEE THING 38

PARTY LINE BLUES 45

DORIS 50

MOVING IN 65

THE YAHK CIRCUS 69

VIRGIN TERRITORY 85

LADIES' MAN 93

A DAY AT THE BEACH 106

MY KIDS 128

THIS LITTLE PIGGY 142

PLUM '72 152

MEINE BESTE FREUNDIN 174

BLOOD BROTHERS 186

THE TROUBLE WITH COWS 193

MY NEW CAR 212

THE FREELOADER 220

MOUSE 229

SUCH A GOOD GIRL 234

THE CRUEL MONTH 243

FOREWORD

I HAVE KNOWN DAVE PERRIN first as his employee, then as his partner, and now as a reader of his first book. He has recorded these real-life adventures with the same vigor he showed in his twenty-six years of veterinary practice in the Creston Valley.

Don't Turn Your Back in the Barn follows his year as a rookie country vet—from early summer of 1973 through a striking Kootenay autumn and miserable winter to the prospect of spring. His narratives are an accurate portrayal of the life of a rural practitioner—one filled with challenges, frustrations, and great rewards.

You will find tales of victory and failure, pathos and humor, as Dr. Perrin experiences the rigors of a practice that balances the full range of creatures from kittens to cows. While the science of veterinary medicine has advanced over the years, how people and their animals interact has not changed. Dave's stories highlight the people who rejoice and anguish as their pets and farm animals give birth or succumb to illness or rally to become more vital and productive.

This book should be required reading for aspiring veterinarians. Anyone who has ever cared about an animal will empathize with the main characters, whether those characters walk on two legs or four. Anyone who thrives on the chaos of life will take pleasure from this read.

Dave Perrin is not afraid to display his emotion in his writing nor reveal his own frailties. But the element that runs through each story is his passion—for his work, for his patients, and for the mountains and fertile lands that surround the Kootenay River in the southeast corner of British Columbia.

—DR. ROB MCLEOD, CRESTON, B.C.

ACKNOWLEDGMENTS

SITTING HERE THINKING about all the wonderful people who have helped me over the years, I wonder how I could have been so fortunate. When I was in practice, they worked side by side with me at all hours of the day and night. I owe them so much. They were the ones who made the task bearable and kept me going when my reserves ran low. All too often, they were not given the credit due them, by either my clients or myself.

Thank you, Doris Currie, Shirley Shopa, Linda Roth, Margaret Rogers, Maragret Berg, Faith Clayton, Alan Clayton, Dorothy McKenzie, Helen Turner, Jan Horsnell, Sheila Wilson, Lynne Hornslien, Roxane Schmalz, Jennifer McCartney, Sheila Reynolds, Katerina Hegerova, Lesley Lorencz, Delilah Milne, Terry Mattison, Rebecca Huscroft, and Annie Wile.

Gordon and Ruth Veitch helped me so much in my first years of practice. Thank you, Ruth, for treating me as one of the family. My memories of Gordon, who taught me the meaning of friendship, are alive and well.

Tackling this book was not much easier than starting my own practice, and once again I was blessed with supportive people who encouraged me and helped me to carry on. Thank you, Betsey Brierley and Gary Katz, for your tireless efforts in editing. Wendy Liddle, you are not only an incredible artist but a great human being, and your efforts have helped bring my stories to life. Bill Blakely, Christopher Hart, Rob McLeod, and Bruno Schiefer, you have been great critics; your comments and questions have helped me shape my narratives.

This book is essentially a work of nonfiction. Many of the people are very real and just as rich and full in character as they appear. Most of them have been good clients throughout the years and have been the best friends a man could ask for. In some cases, I have changed names and altered details to protect people's identities.

Again and again, I was pulled from school concerts and family events to fulfill my duties. My family tolerated me and supported me throughout that time. Thank you, Ruth, Joan, Marshall, Gordon, and Alicia. I love you all.

SWEET WILLIAM

WEET WILLIAM AT STUD read the bold print. Beneath, in ordinary script, was *Purebred Nubian Goat available for service. $50 breed fee.*

The ad in the local newspaper caught my attention. I smiled. He might not be the only old goat in town available for stud, but he was probably the only one worthy of a fifty-dollar fee.

I was looking at the classifieds in the *Creston Valley Advance* to try and come up with a notice of my own. As soon as I got a phone installed, I was going to have to get my name out there.

"Hello, anyone here?"

"Yes, just a minute." I tucked in my shirt and headed for the back door.

A slight woman in her twenties stepped back as I opened the screen door. She wore tight blue jeans, a red plaid wool jacket, and well-worn men's hiking boots. Her cascading dark brown hair framed a pleasant, if discerning face. She had a confident, no-nonsense air about her.

"Are you the new vet?"

"Yes, I'm Dave Perrin."

"Hello, Dr. Perrin, I'm Jean Melba." As she extended her hand, I could detect an unusual combination of fragrances—the musk that was popular with the hippies of my era and just the faintest trace of garlic, but what else?

"I was visiting one of your neighbors down the road. She told me that the MacKays said you're starting a new practice in the valley."

"That's right. I just arrived a few days ago; haven't exactly gotten things off the ground yet."

"Well, we're new to the area, too. We just moved up here from the Fraser Valley with a herd of Nubian goats. We wanted to introduce the breed locally and are hoping to sell our stock. So far, I've been disappointed in the attitude of a lot of the breeders."

"Why is that?" I really didn't want to get into a discussion about another breeder. They could be a difficult lot.

"I was talking to one of them about her deworming program—she uses garlic once a month. I have a healthy respect for garlic, but I maintain a regular deworming program as well."

"I certainly agree with you, Mrs. Melba. I'm a big proponent of preventive medicine."

"Would you have time to deworm my goats?"

"Sure thing. It's getting a bit late tonight, but I'd be happy to pop by tomorrow morning."

Mrs. Melba wrote out the directions to her home on a piece of paper, and I watched her retreat down the driveway to her pickup. I smiled as she turned and waved—a real live client!

I settled in to rummaging through the boxes of drugs and miscellaneous household goods that were scattered throughout the house.

It didn't occur to me to question why I was here. Why, after spending seven years at university in an ivory tower with the best of equipment, would I even consider establishing my own practice here—in Creston, British Columbia, with an old log house as a facility and only a few cardboard boxes full of drugs and equipment? I was determined not to tie myself to a telephone, not to lose sight of my personal life. So why was I so bent on establishing a one-man practice that couldn't possibly succeed without my twenty-four-hour attention?

Was it the overwhelming beauty of the Creston Valley, the relationships I had already established with some local farmers, or the failed negotiations to buy Dr. Marling's practice?

Whatever the reason—fate, enchantment, or stubbornness—I was ready to give this venture one hell of a try!

Sitting in front of the kitchen window, I sorted through the medications, looked up prices that Cathy Morganthaler had put on the invoice, and marked the individual prices on the bottles. Many of the drug names were completely foreign to me and, only by finding their generic names, could I decide what they were for. It would take time to get used to all the new names.

The fact that I had no previously established links with any of the drug companies had been a worry. I hadn't the slightest notion which of them produced what and no idea where to start ordering my supplies.

It was Dr. Morganthaler in Trail who came to my rescue. When I stopped at his office to discuss my plans with him, he provided me with both phone numbers and catalogs. I was on my way out the door to leave for Creston when he said, "Tell you what, I'll give you a bit of a stake to get started—you pay me when you get the chance."

That led to a whirlwind trip through his clinic, with his wife, Cath, following in his wake.

"You'll need six or eight grams of Biotal, maybe a couple of the five-gram size for horses."

"What about some atropine and Demerol," Cath prompted, "and probably some Atravet."

So it was that a couple of hours later I departed from the West Kootenay Animal Hospital with everything I was likely to require during the coming weeks.

As I marked the last bottle of injectable vitamin ADE, the kittens distracted me. Perched on a rickety old washstand, they paused in their pursuit of an elusive bat that led them from one end of the building to the other. I had chosen them from a litter at my parent's home in Casino.

The two mischievous felines had spent the better part of the last half hour chasing the creature, and they were now exhausted. I had to admit that this structure was better suited to a bat than it was to a veterinarian.

Poor Grandma would roll over in her grave to see the condition of her once picturesque home. I thought back to the last time I had visited my grandparents in this house—it was their final day in West Creston. Grampa had just been hospitalized with rampant high blood pressure that launched him into fits of rage and left him unconscious for ever longer periods of time. Poor old Granny, her huge frame no longer able to support her weight, was being loaded into our waiting car. Her eyes brimmed with tears as my parents plunked her on the seat and struggled to squeeze first one leg, then the other, into a space that was too cramped to accommodate her.

She sat stoically looking out the window as my father locked the doors to a part of her life that she would never revisit. As we drove away, she turned to gaze at the log cabin that had been a refuge for the last twenty years of her life. I could only imagine how she felt, knowing that she would never lay eyes on it again. That had been eight years ago; since that time the house had been left to a stream of vagrant renters, and it had been more than a year since the last of them had vacated.

A leaky roof had left plasterboard and paper dangling from the ceiling and walls, but a myriad of spiders had done its best to weave a matrix to hold the structure together. Everything, including the kitchen sink and the movable parts of the cupboards, had disappeared with the last renters; the furniture that I managed to scrounge from my parents did little to fill the void.

The kittens curled up in the box of blankets at my feet. "You girls have had enough too, haven't you? It's time to call it a day—I'd better get the light going, or we'll soon be groping in the dark."

With lantern and matches in hand, I collapsed in a chair in front of the living room window. Pumping away at the lamp, I was about to light it, when the view brought me to a halt. The valley below lay like a picture glued to the wall—peaceful and captivating.

Four years of flat, expansive prairie landscape had left me with an insatiable thirst for rugged mountain splendor; like a drunk with sudden access to booze, I strained to get my fill.

I threw open the screen door and stepped down to the veranda that ran the full length of the old house. At the far end, I straddled the rail and focused on the untamed beauty of the Kootenays.

The yellows, greens, and browns of the flatlands blended into the darker greens and blues of the surrounding mountains. The Kootenay River, whose lavish dumps of silty loam had created the Creston plateau, meandered its way from the south to the north end of the valley, its large, lazy S-shaped curves reflecting like a mirror in the fading light.

The road that crossed the flats in a north to south direction lay like a ribbon along the river's length. An irrigation canal running parallel to it sent out perpendicular ditches to carve the land into the blocks of a patchwork quilt—the light green of the pastures dotted with grazing cattle, the lusher green of alfalfa fields, the dark brown of freshly plowed earth, the green-tinged brown of newly sprouted barley and oats.

Gazing across the valley, I knew what had kept my grandfather captive for the twenty years he had lived in his house on the hill. Nightly, he would sit on this same veranda in his rocking chair watching this very scene unfold before him. Watch, as the lights of Creston and Erickson blinked on. Watch, as the benches above the flats and below the massive Thompson Mountain became a beacon in the enveloping darkness.

A pickup truck appeared at the southern end of the flats and, in deliberate, antlike fashion, crawled its way in a northerly direction. At Rogers' landing on the south side of the river, it stopped. Within a few minutes, the mirrored surface of the Kootenay was disrupted by the lights of the ferry as it left the north shore and cut its way toward the waiting vehicle.

A dog barked in the distance, and the fat old gelding in my neighbor's pasture below the road turned his head. Assured that the noise was without consequences, he returned to grazing.

I watched until the darkness stole the last of the mountains, the entire valley floor, and the sprawling river. Drinking in the tranquillity, the croaking of the frogs, the chirping of the crickets, and the soft wooing of the nighthawks, I remained transfixed on my perch.

The chill of the evening eventually broke the spell. A shiver originating from the base of my skull rippled throughout my body—time for bed.

I felt my way through the living room clutter into the bedroom. Shedding my clothing, I crawled into my sleeping bag and stared into the darkness. I don't know what it was that made me feel so good about what I was doing. Yet, I was assured that I had made the right decision about starting on my own.

Mrs. Melba met me at her gate the following morning. She was relaxed and in a bubbly mood.

"Good morning, Dr. Perrin. You get to meet all of my children this morning. I have eight of them." She chuckled, as if responding to a well-told joke. "Six of them are goats, one's a cat, and there goes the other one."

I turned just in time to see a sheltie dog disappear around the corner of the log house. Introductions complete, I reached into the backseat of my car and retrieved my stainless steel bucket.

"Can I have this about half full of warm water please, Mrs. Melba?"

"Certainly." She walked briskly up the path and disappeared into her house. Typical of the homes that had been raised in the early part of the century, hers was one of the first built in Arrow Creek. The logs had been hewn with a broad ax and placed upon large rocks at each of the corners. Over the years the house had settled, so now the bottom logs showed rot where they were exposed to ground moisture. Many of the cedar shakes were missing from the roof, and others were rotting. Large chunks of the sand and mortar chinking had broken out to be replaced with mud or rags. A layer of ivy covered everything.

I rummaged through the back of the car to come up with a dose syringe and the enema tube that was so handy for administering fluids to calves and goats. Supplies in hand, I strode down the worn dirt path in search of Mrs. Melba.

When she didn't appear, I settled on a rock in the backyard to wait. What a gorgeous setting! Sandwiched in a draw between two ridges, we were removed from the noise of the highway and of human activity in general. The surrounding mountains were rolling, wooded, and green to the very top. I glanced at my watch. Mrs. Melba was taking her time with the water.

"Everything all right?" I called, knocking at the screen door.

"Oh yes, fine. There's no hot water in this house so we'll have to wait for it to heat on the stove."

"That's all right, just bring what you have. I'm sure the girls won't mind getting a chaser of cold water."

She grabbed the bucket. "Living here is really special. It's so peaceful and perfect for the goats, but it's not without its drawbacks. It's harder living without hot running water than I thought it would be, and the house is literally crawling with mice."

We walked to a small listing shed surrounded by a temporary-looking corral constructed of newly cut rails. They hadn't been peeled before they were put up, and the goats were busily working at the task.

Mrs. Melba was attentive as I mixed the thiabendazole powder with water. I had eyeballed several of the goats as they came up to nuzzle her hand through the makeshift bars of the shed. In excellent condition, they were probably the least wormy goats I was likely to encounter.

"This beautiful little girl is Lizzy. You're my favorite baby, aren't you, sweetie?" She gave the floppy-eared goat a big hug. Talking as though to a child, Mrs. Melba stroked the animal's sleek head, repeating to her what a pretty girl she was.

Lizzy soaked up every morsel of Mrs. Melba's attention, staring back at her with big brown eyes. Occasionally, she stretched her Roman nose to nibble on the lapel of her owner's jacket.

"So you want to be first, do you, Lizzy?" I squeezed between the rails on the front of the shed. Ducking the rafters, I continued to rub Lizzy's forehead until her "mother" stepped into the pen to help. As if searching for treats, the goats circled around me, pulling at first a sleeve, then a pocket, then a pant leg.

With Lizzy still competing for attention, we backed her into the corner. Before she realized what was going on, I introduced the tube into her nostril. She reared back, her eyes bulging in horror. She uttered a mournful little blat, like the sound of a baby crying for its mother, and the other goats scattered to the far end of the corral.

"Take it easy, sweetie," soothed Mrs. Melba. "You know that Mom wouldn't do anything to harm you. This won't hurt a bit. It'll just feel funny when this nice man puts a tube into your tummy. We'll kill off all those nasty worms that are hiding down there."

Her body rigid, Lizzy stared straight ahead as I passed the tube through her nasal cavity and into her pharynx. Moving it back and forth, I turned the tip upward and pushed forward until she swallowed. To dilate the esophagus, I puffed on the tube and passed it down her throat into the stomach. After delivering the thiabendazole mixture, I followed with a syringe full of water as a chaser. With a puff of air, I emptied the tube and withdrew it.

"See how easy that was, Lizzy; that didn't hurt at all. All those disgusting worms are going to die now, and you're going to feel so much better." Mrs. Melba continued placating Lizzy, but the look in the goat's eyes made it evident she wasn't buying it. The moment we released her, she scurried away to hide amid the rest of the herd.

Catching and handling the remaining four animals was far more difficult than it had been with Lizzy but, after a small rodeo, I tubed the last of them. We crawled out between the rails.

"I thought you mentioned you had six nannies to deworm, Mrs. Melba."

"I hope you don't mind my telling you, Dr. Perrin," she said in a disapproving tone, "that we goat breeders find it a sign of ignorance on the part of people who don't know goats, when they talk about 'nanny' goats and 'billy' goats. We much prefer to call a female goat a 'doe' and a male goat a 'buck.'"

"I'm sorry, Mrs. Melba, but didn't you mention that you had six 'does' to deworm?"

Her smile was almost sinister. Whether it was in acceptance of my admission of ignorance or in anticipation of what was to follow, I wasn't sure.

"We are finished with the does, Dr. Perrin! All we have left is Sweet William."

"Sweet William?"

"Yes, Sweet William is my buck."

Nearing the log shelter that housed William, I became aware of why I wouldn't strive for a large volume of goat work in my practice. Cuddly, nibbly, attention-loving nanny goats were one thing; stinky, obnoxious, unmanageable billies were another.

Why the hell hadn't it dawned on me that I would be dealing with the notorious Sweet William? My feet dragged as I followed Mrs. Melba to his pen.

As we got closer, the odor intensified. Between the rails on the front of the enclosure, I could make out the form of an enormous goat. He had a massive forehead that extended into a prominent Roman nose. His forelock was shaggy, his beard thick and greasy. Large floppy ears hung on either side of his face; his neck was broad and muscular. Comparing Sweet William to the delicate, gentle nannies, I wondered if he could possibly be a member of the same species.

Standing in front of his paddock, I closed my eyes and focused on drawing in air. After four or five wimpy attempts, I was finally able to force in enough to call it a breath.

William strained against the corral rails to reach us, peeling back his upper lip. As if frustrated by our lack of attentiveness, he went through the routine that characterizes a billy goat "in rut." Bending his head to his underbelly, he squirted jets of urine first onto his beard and then onto his forelock. Not content with that, he rubbed the poll of his head and his beard on both his sides, taking care to massage the urine into his hair. Excited now, he achieved an erection and ejaculated into his mouth and beard.

Mrs. Melba expelled a long sigh. "He's really a dream to handle when he's not in mating season. When he's like this, I don't handle him much, and I certainly don't turn my back on him."

As if to punctuate her statement, William returned to the depth of his log shack and first butted then mounted the rubber tire that had been hung there for his gratification.

I summoned the courage to do what had to be done. Why was I contemplating this, anyway? If this woman had a skunk in a cage and wanted me to go in and wrestle it, would I feel obligated to do so? Was I looking for a gold star or a badge of honor? By the time I had made up my mind to crawl into the pen, my olfactory senses had faded, and I was almost able to draw normal breaths without the desire to gag.

"Hand me the medication as soon as I have the tube in." I drew up the thiabendazole in the dose syringe and looked at it absently.

Determined to get the job over with, I squeezed through the rails and entered William's domain. More curious than aggressive, he rubbed his forehead on my elbow. I pushed him aside, and he nibbled playfully at my coveralls.

Desperate to avoid intimacy with William, I wondered how I could possibly hold the goat tightly enough to control him and get the tube into him without that wretched smell permeating my clothes and skin? I would have to burn these coveralls.

I determined that the only way to proceed was to grasp William firmly by the neck and ears and force him to the back of the shelter. I moved toward him, and he backed obligingly into the corner. It was now or never. Grabbing him by the neck, I pushed my hip against his shoulder and forced him to the wall.

William's neck was massive, and I was glad he didn't resist. He was still more curious than frightened. He was wondering, as I was, just what I would do next. The smell was so intense that I wanted to retch! How could he live with that stench?

"Okay, Mrs. Melba, give me the tube."

I was keenly cognizant of the fact that Mrs. Melba went through great pains to deliver the materials to me without entering the corral, and without coming into contact with Sweet William.

Bloody woman didn't care what I smelled like! But she knew enough to stay outside. How did she talk me into this? I bet she had never found a vet fool enough to deworm William before.

Stretching from the top rail of the corral, she tried to pass me the stomach tube. I reached as far as I dared without losing control of the goat and grasped the very tip of the tube with two fingers. As I brought the end to my mouth to hold on to it, it slipped and fell to the ground. Holding William against the wall with my arm, I stooped to pick up the tube. It was then that William made his move.

"Look out!" screeched Mrs. Melba. "He's going to mount you!"

The warning came too late. With a toss of his head, Sweet William freed himself from my grip and lunged forward. His front legs arched over my back, and the weight of his chest forced me to my knees. He lurched ahead, pushing my face to the ground. I felt a wet sensation as he slid his penis beneath my shirt collar and ejaculated over my neck and upper back. I struggled to get up but found myself pinned, as William rubbed his beard and scent gland into the small of my back.

I positioned my hands under his chest and flung him over backward. In a blind fury, I was no longer wary of his smell. As he scrambled to his feet, I pushed him into the corner.

"Don't hurt him!" Mrs. Melba squealed in panic. "Maybe we should forget about him for today."

"Forget about him? Never! Just get in here with that syringe full of medication!"

I crammed the tube into his nose and through his pharynx. He swallowed quickly, and I passed it on down. As though sensing the gravity of the moment, he stood stock-still, his eyes riveted straight ahead.

"The syringe, Mrs. Melba!"

Scrambling through the rails, she flushed the thiabendazole into the end of the tube that I held out for her.

"The chaser, Mrs. Melba!"

She hurriedly produced the water and flushed the remaining dewormer into Sweet William. With a quick puff into the tube, I pulled it from his nose and released him. Shaking his head, William retired to the back of his pen, screwed up his lip, and watched me climb through the rails.

I was regaining my composure by the time I reached the car and pulled off my coveralls. Mrs. Melba scurried behind me carrying my bucket and dose syringe.

"Are you all right, Dr. Perrin?"

All right! Why shouldn't I be all right? I always go around smelling like a billy goat; the back of my shirt was frequently saturated with semen.

"Yes, Mrs. Melba . . . I'm just fine. Now I understand where the old saying 'hornier than a billy goat' comes from."

Without a trace of a smile, she replied, "Buck, Dr. Perrin. William is a buck, not a billy goat!"

"Star Light, Star Bright"

FOR HOURS ON END, I stared into the clear, starlit night thinking, hoping, dreaming about what the future held in store. Several times I gazed upon the brightest star and made my wish.

Finally, I closed my eyes to visualize a well-appointed concrete block building on the edge of town. Its spacious waiting room brimmed with healthy flowering plants—on the reception desk, the window ledges, the counters. Two cozy examination rooms exited from the waiting room. The surgery sparkled of stainless steel complete with surgery lights, heart monitors, and gas anesthetic machines. The entire facility glowed, as natural light streamed in windows and skylights. The lab was the heart of the hospital; central to all stations, its counters were laden with microscopes, blood counting machines, and incubators. The kennel room was spacious with two sections of kennels—one for dogs and one for cats.

At the rear of the hospital was a large-animal facility. From an unloading chute, an animal could be moved along an alley to a squeeze where it could be restrained and treated without endangering either the animal or the handler. In the center was a surgery table used only for the occasional procedure on a horse or a bull. Next to it was the padded room for recovering patients. Its walls and floor were cushioned with so much foam rubber that I imagined floating on air when I stepped in.

"Star light, star bright" . . . If only I could remember the rest of the incantation, maybe my fairy godmother or Gepetto's blue fairy would appear before me and wave her wand. I could see it all so clearly as I walked from room to room adding a counter here, a closet there, moving a telephone from one area to the next. Stopping at the reception desk, I browsed through drawer after drawer of patient files.

When I opened my eyes, I was sitting on the top rail of the old veranda of an antiquated log house that I didn't even own. Although I was still without power, things had improved substantially over the last few days. The local dairymen and beef growers had confirmed their offer of a subsidy to establish my practice and provide reliable service for large animals. One of the dairymen, Phil Kemle, had volunteered to act as a temporary answering service, and the word spread throughout the valley that a new vet was in town and could be reached through the Kemles.

A trip to Veitch Realty had been both depressing and uplifting. Depressing in that everything listed for purchase or for lease was more than what I wanted to pay. Uplifting because Gordon Veitch invited me to his home in Erickson for supper and a very enjoyable evening with his family.

We had just finished eating when the telephone rang. Ruth answered it in her usual brusque tone. "Veitch residence, Ruth speaking . . . Yes. Yes, I do. As a matter of fact, he's here right now."

Holding the phone out, she smiled, "For you, Doctor."

"Dr. Perrin speaking." I was mystified by the unexpected call.

"Dr. Perrin," said the woman, "I'm sorry to bother you after hours like this, but Gordon mentioned to me you were in town, and my dog just got hit by a car. He looks pretty bright and is able to walk, but he's bleeding all over from where he's banged up. There's a cut on the hind leg and a big hunk of skin missing from his front one, too—the wound on his hind leg looks pretty bad to me. I took a quick look at it but it grossed me right out."

"Can you take a look at his gums?"

"There's nothing wrong with his mouth!" She was taken aback by my stupid question. "It's his legs he's bleeding from."

"I realize that. What I wanted you to do was check the color of his gums to see if they're nice and pink, or if they've turned a real pale color. It's a way of evaluating how much blood he's actually lost."

"Oh, just a second, I'll go have a look."

She was back in a few moments. "They're all black! Is that bad?"

"Have a look higher up or farther back in the mouth. The black color is just pigment. If you look on both sides, you'll probably find a spot where the gums are not dark. When you do, just push on them so they blanch and see how long it takes for the color to come back to pink again."

I waited as she set down the phone and returned to the dog.

"You're right. There's some pink at the back of his mouth, and when I push on the gums, they go pink right away."

"That's good. That means he's not in shock, and it's very unlikely that he's bleeding internally."

"Oh, good. Will you be able to come and have a look at him?"

"I'll come over right away. Can you give me directions on how to get there? And by the way, what's your name?"

"My name's Deb Anson, and I'm staying in unit three at Hi-way Cabins. How long do you think you'll be?"

"I shouldn't be more than ten minutes."

I returned to the table. Gordon had monitored the conversation and was smiling as if he'd just sold the half of main street that he didn't already own.

Smirking at Ruth, he droned, "Deb sure didn't waste any time. This morning, when I had coffee with her, she said she was going to have to snare that big new vet in town. Looks like she's at it already."

"Come on, Gordon," Ruth interjected. "She wouldn't run over her own dog just to get to meet Dave."

"The hell she wouldn't! This morning, she didn't even have a dog. She said she was going to have to go out and get one so she could snag her long, tall vet."

"You've got to be kidding," Ruth replied. "No one would go to that much trouble to meet somebody. She was probably joking when she said that!"

"Tonight, she magically has a wounded dog! What more proof do you need? Deb's a very determined girl. She's over six feet tall and doesn't run into many guys that are taller than her."

"I better go and have a look at the dog and see if there really is something wrong with him. Do you want to come along, Gordon? I may be in need of a chaperone."

"I better not come." Gordon put on a deadpan look. "You haven't seen Deb when she gets mad."

"Go with him, Gordon," Ruth interjected. "You've got the poor guy scared spitless."

Within a few minutes, I was parking my Volkswagen in front of the Hi-way Cabins store.

"The cabins are just around back on the lower level," Gordon volunteered. "Here comes Deb now." He pointed to the tall, solidly built woman who was climbing the hill to greet us. "She's closing in for the kill."

"Hey, Gord," she shouted as she got closer, "if I'd known you were coming too, I'd have sold tickets to see the pair of you—the two biggest dudes in Creston—crawling out of a Volkswagen!"

"Probably lots of room for you in there too, Deb," Gordon retorted with a mischievous grin.

She opened her mouth as if to reply, but instead walked around the vehicle and addressed me. "I'm Deb Anson, Dr. Perrin." She extended her hand and grasped mine in a hearty shake.

"Glad to meet you. How're you making out with our patient?"

"He's really been super! I just got him today from a fellow who had to leave town. I was taking him for a walk, trying to get him used to me, and he ran out in front of a car. The guy never had a chance to miss him. Can't blame him for hitting him . . . but the bugger never stopped—just kept on driving like nothing had happened. I'd like to get my hands on him! Can you imagine having something like that happen and just driving away?"

I shook my head and turned toward the crowd of boys who were milling around in front of one of the small log cabins. At the center of their circle lay a large tan dog with floppy ears. His build and facial characteristics boasted of Doberman parentage, but the long, rough hair coat was a testament to his lack of purity.

"Hey there, fellow, you sure look like you came out second best." I bent down and gently rumpled his ears. "Would you mind holding his head, Deb, while I check him out?"

"His name's Theo," she informed me, as she held him firmly against her knee. Theo sported a silly grin, holding out his left front foot as if he wanted to shake a paw.

"There's a boy." I lifted his leg and inspected the massive area that was now devoid of skin. "It looks as if this foot dragged along the pavement. There's not a bit of skin left to suture; I'm afraid we won't be able to do much more than bandage this one."

"Will it heal? There's such a large bare spot. Looks like it'd take forever."

"It'll heal, but unless we do some skin grafting, we'll have to put a lot of time into changing bandages."

"Ohhh." She glanced at Gordon with a wicked little smile. Suddenly, her face took on a more serious expression. "Will that be expensive?"

15

"Let's have a better look at the rest of the damage." I lifted his hind leg to examine the gaping wound in his thigh. "It looks like there's enough skin to close the wound here as long as the blood supply's still intact."

"What do you think?"

"I can't see anything that time won't heal. There's no question it'll take a while for some of the areas where the skin's totally missing to granulate in, but if you have the patience with him, he'll heal. He's going to have quite a scar on the front leg, so there'll be a patch without hair."

"Well, you do the best you can for now. I'll follow your instructions later."

"Okay." I wrapped my arms around the dog and carefully lifted him up.

Deb brought a blanket from her cabin to cover the backseat of my car and, as Gordon held the front seat forward, I settled Theo down on his side.

We'd barely pulled out of the lane when Gordon started his banter.

"Boy, she's really got her talons sharpened for your behind. Did you see her eyes light up when you said he'd need a lot of aftercare?"

"You've got an overactive imagination, Gordon. She just wants her dog looked after."

"Bullcrap to that! Deb's hormones are more overworked than my imagination. You just wait and see."

It was almost dark by the time we pulled up in front of Grampa's house. I unlocked the door to the back porch.

"Could you hold the door open while I get him out, Gord?" Wrapping the blanket around Theo, I pulled his head firmly against my shoulder and lifted him into my arms. He whimpered as his hind legs were pulled under him but made no move to resist as I maneuvered him through the car door. Gordon rushed to open the outside door, took a few hesitant steps into the porch, and halted. He lit his lighter and fumbled for the kitchen doorknob. Following him into the black void, I deposited Theo on what I was sure must be the kitchen table.

"Could you hold him steady here, while I see to lighting up the surgery?"

Gordon chuckled as he stumbled hesitantly through the darkened room toward the table.

I found a flashlight and quickly retrieved the lantern from the bedroom. After a few hearty pumps and a couple of wasted matches, we were treated to the gentle hiss and soft flickering light of the Coleman lamp. Gordon surveyed the room, his face betraying his utter disbelief.

"Oh, man! How'd you end up in a place like this?"

"This was my grampa's house; my aunts own it now. It's somewhere to start from, and besides, the price is right."

"It better be!"

I chuckled. "You're not afraid of bats, are you?"

"Not particularly, but they're not my favorite creatures either."

"Well, I guess we'd better get looking after this beast." I ladled a few dippers of water from the bucket on the counter into the plastic hand basin that sat beside it. Digging through one of the boxes in the corner, I produced a bottle of Bridine surgical scrub and poured a healthy glug into the basin. I found a syringe and drew up first Atravet and then atropine.

"I'll just give him this cocktail to get him ready for his anesthetic. It'll settle him down a bit and prevent him from salivating."

Gordon nodded as he watched me administer the concoction.

"Let's get a better look at those wounds. Do you think you can hold him flat out so I can get at him a little easier?"

Theo struggled briefly as Gordon forced him onto his side. The skin on his forehead wrinkled, and he emitted a pathetic little whine. There was a look of anticipation in his big brown eyes.

"Good fellow. We're not going to hurt you, boy. Just relax now."

I looked over at Gordon. A few beads of sweat had formed on his brow; the lock of hair that hung over his forehead was glued to his skin. His eyes were focused on the dog's groin, where the inner portion of his right hind leg had been skinned as neatly as if it had been done with a knife. A flap larger than my hand gaped open to reveal the flesh beneath.

"You'd think he had been stripped down for an anatomy lesson, wouldn't you? Everything's dissected as nicely as any specimen I've seen in school. This muscle sticking up here's called the pectineus. The two vessels running over the bottom of it are the femoral artery and femoral vein. If you look closely, you can see that one pulsate . . . that's the artery. This is the gracilis muscle and here are the adductors."

"I'm glad you recognize all of the parts. Can you make a dog out of them again?"

"I guess we better find out, hadn't we?"

Wandering from box to box, I accumulated what I needed for the job at hand. Drawing up twenty milliliters of distilled water, I injected it into the bottle containing Biotal. With vigorous shaking, the powder dissolved to yield a clear yellowish liquid. Drawing twelve milliliters of the solution into my syringe, I laid it on the table next to Theo and repositioned the lantern for better light. I grasped his good leg, blocked the vein, and rhythmically stroked the upper surface of his leg with an alcohol swab until I could plainly detect the outline of the cephalic vein.

"Hold his head against your shoulder for a moment, Gord, just in case he tries to struggle."

I positioned the needle over the vein and drove it through the skin into the ropelike structure of the vessel. I drew back on the plunger and a jet of dark venous blood gushed into the Biotal solution.

"Good shot!"

Releasing the vein, I slid my left hand down to support the leg, then rapidly injected half of the solution.

"How long does it take for this stuff to work, Dave?"

As if in response, Theo relaxed in his arms, closed his eyes, and gave a big yawn.

"You're kidding! It can't be that fast."

"You can let go of him now." I touched the corner of his eye with a finger and got a slow blink in response. I pried open his mouth to determine the tone of his jaw. Theo yawned again, sticking out his long pink tongue and exposing pearly white teeth. Slowly, I injected more Biotal, checked his tone again, and injected the remainder.

Drawing up more Biotal, I reconnected to the needle and taped the syringe to Theo's foreleg. By this time he was totally relaxed, and I was able to roll him onto his side and lift his good leg out of the way to better expose his injury.

"Could you hold this for me, Gord?"

Thhhhhhhhhhhhhhhh . . . Thhhhhhhhhhhhhh . . .

"Whooie! Is this dog ever rotten." Gordon held his nose, then gasped as he grabbed the foot. Opening and closing his mouth like a big goldfish, he backed up to arm's length. "Does an anesthetic always make them fart like that?"

"Not really, but it relaxes them; if they happen to have gas, they'll not have any control over it."

Thhhhhhhhhhhhhhhhhhh . . . Thhhhhhhhhhhhhhhhhhh.

"Man, he keeps passing wind like that and you're going to need a new hind end man!"

"Just hold that leg up, and I'll get this over with."

Pouring the surgical soap into the open wound, I pulled back the skin margins and scrubbed at the underlying tissue.

"Look at all the gravel he's got in that wound. How're you ever going to get that cleaned out?"

"Most of the wound isn't too bad. It's only along this edge that there's a lot of debris."

I poured fresh water into the basin. After finishing my scrub, I peeled back the flap of skin and trimmed away the subcutaneous tissue that was heavily embedded with gravel.

"He doesn't need that?"

"Nope. That's why I've always hated working on machines; the parts all have to fit too precisely. When you're doing surgery, you can do a lot of trimming and still make things fit together. If in doubt, throw it out—unless there's only one of them, of course."

I continued trimming back the wound margins and removing all signs of devitalized tissue. Bringing the wound edges together with single sutures in different locations, I was able to close it in such a way as to minimize the tension on any one suture. Inserting a pair of sharp-nosed forceps under the skin, I moved in three inches from the wound margin and poked them upward to form a tent. With a scalpel blade, I cut the skin to allow the forceps to poke through.

"Hasn't this dog got enough holes in him that you have to be making more?"

"With this much skin undermined, I have to put in some drainage or we'll get an accumulation of fluid that could force its way out between the sutures and keep the wound from healing."

Gord opened the package containing the Penrose drain, and I withdrew the long rubber tube. Spreading the forceps that poked through the skin, I grasped the drain, pulled it through, and sutured it to the skin.

"Hey, your patient's running away!"

Sure enough, Theo made a determined effort to flex his leg. "Looks like he needs more goof." I slowly chased another three milliliters down the needle into the dog's vein. Pausing for a few moments, I checked his jaw tone for signs of resistance. "That should hold you, fellow." I gave him one more milliliter, removed the tape, and pulled out the needle. After scrubbing up again, I returned to sew between the tack sutures that had been placed earlier. When I was done, the wound was closed with neat, evenly placed stitches.

"Sort of looks like he ran into a porcupine," Gordon quipped. "What do you plan on doing—charging Deb by the stitch?"

Thhhhhh . . . Thhhhhhhhhhhhhhhhh.

"Oh no, there he goes again. Thank heavens we're almost finished! I can't take much more of that!"

"I've got to admit, he's pretty ripe. All the way out here in the car, I thought it was you I was smelling."

"Humph!" Gordon snorted.

"Let's get a look at that front leg now." I manipulated Theo's front paw back and forth, checking for abnormal movement or grinding sensations. "It's amazing the amount of abuse a limb can take without breaking. Look at all the skin that was dragged off without injuring the deeper structures."

Sticking Theo's entire foreleg in the basin of soapy water, I scrubbed the wound and removed most of the dirt and hair. As Gordon held the lantern closer, I picked out the worst of the gravel, slathered it with antibiotic ointment, and bandaged it.

After rattling through my boxes to come up with another syringe and needle, I grabbed the flashlight and headed for the door.

"Where are you going?"

"Have to run downstairs for some penicillin. I've got all the medications that have to be kept cool down in the root cellar."

With Gordon minding Theo, I carefully felt my way down the shaky stairwell. Placing each foot deliberately on the creaky treads, I ducked my head to avoid the floor joists. Spiders had been busily at work since my last passage, and I had to continually shield my face in a futile effort to avoid their webs. I grabbed a bottle from the shelf and navigated up the stairs.

"Dave, this dump could be used as a movie setting for the Munsters!" Gordon looked on in disgust as I picked the cobwebs from the front of my shirt. "We've got to find you a better place to work out of. This is ridiculous!"

Theo was already beginning to wake up and, as I administered the injection, he moved his hind leg and raised his head to look around. He tried to focus, but gave up and surrendered to sleep.

I wandered to the spare bedroom with the flashlight, spread an old sleeping bag on the floor, and covered it with Deb's blanket. Rearranging boxes full of unpacked clothing and bedding in a circle to keep the dog confined, I fashioned a bit of a corral, then placed Theo in the center of it.

"Come on, son, time to wake up." I thumped him a few times over the rib cage. "It's all over now. There's a boy. There's a boy."

He rolled onto his sternum, lifted his head, and made a feeble attempt to stand. Shifting unsteadily from one side to the other, he seemed exhausted by his efforts. With a deep sigh, he crumpled, rested his head on his bandaged paw, and went back to sleep.

"Well, Gord, looks like he's safe enough to leave. Maybe I can give you a ride home now." I shut off the lantern and we picked our way to the car with the flashlight.

"You just have to find a decent place to practice out of, Dave. I can see your staying here while you make arrangements for something else, but you have to make a move right away."

All the way to Erickson, Gordon droned on about finding a better location—one that was central and visible to the people of Creston. I listened on the way in and stewed on the way home—he was right and I knew it. I had to intensify the search!

The sky was clear again, and the stars were as bright as they had been earlier in the week. I tipped my head back in search of the brilliant star that had held my focus the night before—the one that would certainly grant my wish and deliver me from these dingy surroundings.

The air was still without the slightest trace of a breeze. Crickets chirped incessantly; frogs worked diligently to drown them out. Off in the bush I could hear the hoot, hoot, hoot of an owl, overhead the droning of the ever-present nighthawks. These were the sounds of silence—the sounds that every country-bred person loves but soon doesn't even notice. I lay on the grass in the backyard and searched for my elusive benefactor. Why was it so difficult to locate tonight, when the night before it had so dominated the heavens?

I stumbled into the house to check on Theo. He was stretched out in a relaxed pose, his breathing soft and regular. He raised his head briefly when the light shone in his eyes, then sighed and returned to sleep.

He was on his feet and stumbling around the room when I arrived to check him in the morning. He limped toward me and thrust his nose into my out-stretched hand. His tail was wagging so briskly that it took his whole body with him, thrusting his hind quarters back and forth from side to side.

"Well, good morning to you too, Theo! You sure look chipper this morning!"

He wandered off through the kitchen, shoving his nose in one box after the other in search of something to eat.

"Pretty slim pickings around here, boy. I should know—it's not any better for me!"

I rummaged through one of the boxes in the corner and found a large can of dog food. I held a heaping tablespoon in front of the eager mutt and watched as it disappeared in a single gulp. Other bites followed until nothing remained but the licking of the spoon. Theo continued to stare hopefully, certain that there must be more where that came from. When nothing was forthcoming, he wan-dered off to continue his snooping.

I passed a length of nylon rope through the ring in Theo's collar and fastened it on with a bowline.

"Time for a pee, boy."

He lunged through the doorway and out into the sunlight. Pulling me to the car, he gingerly lifted his sore hind leg and sent a jet of urine splashing over the tire. After watering every standing structure in the backyard and tak-ing a good long drink from the creek, he indicated he wanted to wander off and do some exploring on his own.

"Enough of this, boy. It's time to take you back to Mama."

I boosted Theo onto the backseat of my car. "I'll be back as soon as I get your blanket." I rolled the window partway down to give him some fresh air, then closed the car door and walked to the house. Rummaging through the kitchen for something that could pass for breakfast, my mind flashed back to the days when these cupboards were laden with food. In Grandma's day, can-ning jars brimmed with goodies of all descriptions. I could see the beans, peas, beets, dills, asparagus, tomatoes, trout, and chicken.

What I wouldn't do for a nice big jar of Grandma's canned chicken. I visualized popping the lid and thrusting a fork through the jelly to fish out a juicy, tender leg or thigh. My mouth watered at the thought!

I found the remains of a bag of whole wheat bread and gave it a quick once-over for signs of mold. Nothing was obvious, so I scraped the bottom and sides of the peanut butter jar for enough to spread a thin layer on a crust. I folded it, took a bite, located Deb's blanket, and headed out.

Munching absently on my less-than-appetizing breakfast, I stopped to lock the door and pick one of Theo's hairs from the last bite of my sandwich. I wandered to the car and opened the passenger door to throw the blanket on the seat.

A shiver ran up my spine. I flung the seat forward. Theo was gone!

"Oh God!" How could this be happening? How could a gibbled-up dog the size of Theo possibly crawl out of a little crack like that? I backed up and examined the half-open window in utter dismay. It was impossible! He couldn't have squeezed through there!

I searched quickly around the yard and out toward the array of weeds where my grandparents once had their garden—he couldn't have gone very far! I turned to the north, took a few indecisive steps up the outhouse path, and stopped.

"Theo! Theo! Come on, boy! Theo! Where are you? Theo! Theeeeeooooo!"

Retracing my steps, I ran to the brow of the hill. "Theeeooo! Theeeooooo! Theo, where are you?"

Not a sign of him. What if he just headed out into the bush and died? I could just hear it now . . . Everyone in town would know about this before the week was out. Where in the world would a crippled dog go?

"Theo! Theeoo! Theeeeeooooooo!"

I returned to the house. Damn it anyway! Maybe I should just pack up my stuff and leave. I always had to be different from the crowd. The rest of the class just went out and worked for an established practice. Why couldn't I?

"Theo! Theeoo!"

I walked briskly down the driveway, scanning the horizon for the faintest glimpse of my escaped patient.

"Theeeeooooo!"

A wave of panic struck me, and I broke into a jog. By the time I arrived at the picket gate of my neighbors, Bea and Fred MacKay, I was on a dead run and almost out of breath. I stumbled onto the porch and pounded on their door.

Bea flung it open. "My lands, Dave, what in the world's the matter? You look like you've seen a ghost!"

"The problem is more that I've lost a ghost! I brought a big brown Doberman-type dog home last night and sewed him up. This morning, I loaded him into my car and left him for just a few seconds. By the time I got back, he'd jumped out the window and disappeared. He has two injured legs, but he's running around here somewhere. If you see him, could you give me a holler?"

"I tell you what; I'll throw on some shoes and a jacket and see if I can help you find him."

"Thanks, Bea, I'd appreciate it. Wouldn't you know it? The first bloody dog I get to work on, and he runs off on me!"

"Well, he couldn't have gone far. What's his name?"

"Theo, but he doesn't appear to answer to it."

"I'll get right out there, Dave, and I'll give Fred a holler and tell him to keep an eye out. He's gone out to get the cows in."

"Thanks, Bea!" I was already halfway up the walk. "I'm heading into the bush above Grampa's old garden site if you see anything of him . . . Theo! Theeooo!"

I made a quick pass through the underbrush at the edge of the garden without finding a trace of him.

"Theeeeooooo!"

Like an echo from across the road came Bea's voice. "Theo! Theeooo! Here, Theo . . . Come, Theo."

"Theo! Damn!" Wandering along and peering off into the bushes, I hadn't paid attention to the ground. Before I knew it, I was up to my ankles in mud.

"Oh, Mother! How did I get into such a mess?"

For the next hour, I crawled through the underbrush, calling, cursing, praying, crying. I was ready to admit defeat when I dragged myself back to the house and collapsed on the lawn. Bea's voice had long since petered out, replaced with an ominous silence.

Tears were welling in my eyes, and I had a horrendous feeling of despair deep in my breast. How could I have let this happen? How could I have been so stupid?

I lay for a long time staring into the bright blue of the morning sky. The tears had stopped and the vise that gripped my chest was starting to ease. The movie projector that had been playing one awful film of misery after another in my mind finally ceased running, and I was possessed by an eerie calm.

I played a game that I had invented as a child, while lying alone in the back field of our home in Casino. Staring intensely at the open sky without blinking, I was soon seeing millions of blips of light, which flicked across the blue of the heavens. Swirling, darting, and jumping from one place to the other, they danced their way across the sky and through the full arc of my vision.

The trick of the game was not only to concentrate until you were able to see the blips of light, but to focus on one of them for as long as you could. I had been playing for a while and had watched one fleeting dynamo for so long that my eyes began to burn and water. I was just about to give in and blink, when the incantation started running through my mind. "Star light, star bright, the first star I see tonight . . ."

Fred's voice cracked like a rifle shot, "Get out of here, you good-for-nothing critter! You useless, chicken-killing hound!"

I sprang to my feet and ran in Fred's direction—sure enough, it was Theo! Running for everything he was worth, he galloped up the driveway. He ran to me like a long-lost friend, certain that I would protect him from the devil who was hot on his tail. Licking his lips as if to remove the telltale feathers from the corner of his mouth, he hid behind my legs and peered back down the drive toward Fred.

"Oh, thank you, Lord," I moaned, as my hand closed on the plastic rope that trailed along behind Theo. "Thank you!"

FERRY CONTRARY

ICK DOUMA WAS PACING up and down in front of the milk house when I arrived. I was a couple of minutes late for a routine herd health appointment at his Canyon farm, but Dick was acting as if I had kept him waiting for hours.

"I'm in big trouble with a heifer."

"What's going on?" I shook out my coveralls and stepped into them.

"When I first noticed her, she just looked uncomfortable. She was getting up and down and kicking at her belly occasionally, but when I was in there a few minutes ago, she couldn't even stand up."

"How old is she?"

"Got to be around eight to ten weeks. Her mother's already milking over a hundred and ten pounds a day."

I slipped into my rubber boots while Dick fidgeted and shuffled his feet. Plucking my stethoscope from the dash and a thermometer from the ashtray, I followed him into the milk house.

"Have the calves been bothered with diarrhea?"

"Not a bit. My hired hand, Alex, has been doing a great job with them; we haven't had a sick one for months."

Dick turned into the calf barn, and I followed him down a row of neatly strawed pens.

"This calf's been doing well, then?"

"Yeah, up till this morning, I would've said she was the healthiest calf on the farm. Fed her myself last night, and she cleaned everything up and was looking for more. Don't know about this morning, but Alex watches the calves like a hawk, and he'd have mentioned something if she hadn't taken her milk."

As we walked down the aisle in front of the calves, they bucked and played. Several stuck their heads out through the front slats and bawled in anticipation of another feeding.

"She's looking worse by the minute!" Dick lamented, stopping in front of the second pen from the wall.

The calf was lying on her tummy with her nose jammed firmly into her flank. Her hair coat was rough and standing on end. Her breathing was fast and labored, each expiration ending in a pronounced grunt.

"You haven't had a problem with bloat?" I asked, eyeing the fine green alfalfa hay that sat untouched on the rack at the front of the pen. "She certainly looks full."

"No, we've been feeding them the same second-cut hay for months and haven't had a problem."

I climbed over the pen wall and ran my hands over the heifer's body. She lay stoically, giving no indication that she even noticed my presence. I inserted the thermometer into her rectum. Her tailhead was dry and completely clean aside from a small amount of fecal material clinging to the surrounding hairs.

"She doesn't seem to have a problem with diarrhea," I observed.

I straightened her neck and examined her face. Her ears drooped pathetically, and her eyes had sunk deeply into her head, revealing the pink of the tissue that lined the socket and covered the globe.

"Look at these eyes! This calf is severely dehydrated."

Forcing her mouth open, I took a quick look inside, then let her have her head. She gave a deep-throated groan and made a feeble attempt to bawl.

"Her mouth feels as cold as ice." I retrieved the thermometer. "Hm-m-m, ninety-eight point six, almost a degree and a half below normal."

I grasped the hair on her sides and lifted her from the back corner to the center of the stall. She made no effort to support herself and, when released, crumpled in a heap on the straw. Grunting with each breath, she turned around and jammed her head firmly back into her flank.

"This calf's at death's door," I mumbled.

"Wouldn't you know it!" Dick groaned. "She's out of my best cow and sired by the top bull in North America. I had a lot of hope for her."

Taking the stethoscope from my back pocket, I listened to the rapid pounding of the heifer's heart.

"Could a pneumonia bring her down this fast?"

"It can occasionally, but I don't think the problem's in her chest. It looks to me like she has a blockage somewhere and the grunting's just a result of pain."

Shifting my examination to the abdomen, I systematically moved the stethoscope, listened for sound, then thumped with my finger in search of a distended bowel. A hollow, high-pitched ringing answered my thumping.

"There's a lot of gas under pressure here. I'd be willing to bet we have a torsion of some sort."

With both hands and the stethoscope under the calf's belly, I lifted up and down rapidly, literally shaking her abdomen. Tremendous tinkling and slopping sounds emanated, like water sloshing around in a mostly empty container.

"My God!" Dick exclaimed. "You don't need that thing; I can hear it from up here. So what's a torsion in farmer's language?"

"The gut's supported by a structure called the mesentery with vessels that fan out to all the various parts of the bowel. Sometimes things twist to interfere with blood flow and the movement of stomach contents."

"So what do we do with her? I don't want to lose her."

"She's a long shot by the look of her, but if you want to try to save her, we better do surgery."

"So what'll you need?"

"We'll need to get her out of here. Have you got somewhere out of the flies where the light's better? How about the milk house?"

"The light would be best over in the meat shop. I'll go get the tractor and the front-end loader. We can put her in the bucket to get her there."

By the time we had the heifer unloaded at the meat shop, she was even more despondent. Her head hung limply as we slid her onto the cutting table. While Dick stood beside her, I clipped the hair over her jugular vein. The black and white hair peeled off to fall in clumps on the floor, leaving a pink and gray mosaic pattern on the soft, smooth skin beneath.

"Just press your finger in here." I directed Dick's fingers to the crease at the base of the calf's neck.

With a gauze soaked in alcohol, I rubbed vigorously toward his fingers. The vessel was there—not well defined the way it would be on a healthy calf, but I could see it. Again and again, I stroked toward his fingers, trying to build pressure behind the dam. Finally, I peeled a catheter open and plunged it into the ripple that I hoped was the vein. Nothing!

"Just keep your fingers in place a bit longer. I think I've gone through it."

I slowly eased the plastic portion of the catheter back until I was rewarded with a flow of dark, blue-red blood. I pushed forward to thread it up the vein and started the fluids running. I wrapped a piece of tape around the indwelling catheter and sutured it to the skin.

The heifer lay quietly on her side, her breathing slow, regular, and punctuated with that same pronounced grunt. She made no response when I turned on the clippers and began stripping the hair from her abdomen and flank.

"Are you going to put her to sleep to do this?"

"She's in no shape for a general anesthetic. I'll give her a high epidural to paralyze her hind legs and use a regional block to keep her from feeling pain from the incision."

I was ready to block her for surgery when I realized I didn't have my instruments. I had washed, packed, and put them through the pressure cooker after I got home the previous night. I remembered taking them out and setting them on the counter. After uttering a few choice words, I turned to Dick.

"Wouldn't you know it, I have to go to West Creston to get my instruments."

I slowed the IV and ran for my car. I had clear sailing to the Canyon bridge and was able to speed along quite nicely until I came upon Grandma Moses. Following the thirty-five-mile-an-hour speed limit, the elderly lady had three cars backed up behind her. I grumbled along behind the procession until I reached the Erickson back road. Taking the short cut, I was able to avoid most of the traffic and was soon tearing along the gravel road to the ferry.

Fortune was smiling on me for the moment. I arrived at the top of the knoll above the Kootenay River, and there sat the ferry waiting for me. The operator waved me on board. He was a slight man with graying hair in his late fifties. He always seemed preoccupied with poking around the ferry, and I often felt he was doing me a big favor to give me a ride. He glumly nodded as I proceeded down the ramp and onto the deck. I heard the rattle of the chain against the metal flooring as he lifted it and locked it in place as a barrier at the back of the ferry. In less than a minute, the motor revved. The cable that lay submerged beneath the water tightened and reared as it propelled us along.

I slumped back against the seat and watched the far bank of the river grow closer, the cable slicing through the water like a serpent after its prey. We landed on the opposite shore, and the operator idled the engine. He sauntered past me and lowered the forward chain. I nodded my thanks, drove over it and up the ramp.

It didn't take long to get to the house, grab the instruments, and drive back to the ferry landing. I was patting myself on the back as I approached the top of the dike. This was going to work out just right; it was probably best for the calf to be at least partially rehydrated before I started surgery anyway.

I just had to learn to take things as they came. After all, this was no more than a minor inconvenience and probably wouldn't be detrimental to my patient.

"Well," I muttered, as I pulled to a stop, "it looks like my luck's run out."

The ferry was parked on the other side this time.

Determined to be patient, I leaned my head back. The ferry operator had surely seen me and would soon be on his way. I closed my eyes and took a deep breath. I relished the warmth of the sun beating through the window. It was a beautiful day, and there was no reason why I shouldn't enjoy this peaceful setting.

I gazed down at the river and, for a few moments, forgot about the calf. What beautiful country this was—a massive river meandering through majestic mountains that would soon be sporting caps of snow. This time of year, the Kootenay was the picture of serenity. The greens and yellows of late summer lined her quiet, calm waters. From this vantage point, it was difficult to see that she had any current whatsoever.

Gradually my mind wandered back to the business at hand. I hadn't seen many animals with twisted guts during my time at the veterinary college. There had been two that I could remember, and neither of them had survived. Time was of the essence with this type of bowel blockage and had played a role in both of those previous cases. One died because an indecisive farmer had waited too long to bring the calf in and the other because a dithering clinician couldn't convince himself to start cutting. I wasn't anxious to see my patient die because I didn't get things corrected soon enough.

What could be taking so long? I suddenly found myself very much focused on the passage of time. A few minutes can feel like hours when you're anxious to get going, but this was ridiculous.

I got out of the car and peered across the river at the motionless vessel. Why hadn't it fired up? Was that the operator at the back?

There he was lying on the hood of the engine behind the cabin. Surely he couldn't be asleep. I strained my ears to hear if the ferry's engine was running. The only sound I could detect was the distant rumble of a tractor working in the field on the Rogers' farm.

"Hey!" I bellowed. "Over here!"

Not a hint of movement from across the water—there had to be something wrong. Maybe he was seriously injured! I had myself talked into going to the Rogers' to phone across when I saw him move. His hand casually meandered from his side to his face. There it was again. He moved his arm again.

"Damn," I fumed. "He's lying in the sun eating his bloody lunch!"

I leaned on the horn. The pathetic bleat that came forth from under the hood aggravated me at the best of times, but today it enraged me. What in the world were those Germans thinking when they put a horn like that into a vehicle?

Running to the landing, I jumped up and down, waving and hollering at the top of my lungs. I took a deep breath, paused, and stared across the water. There it was again—the rhythmic movement of his right arm.

"Hell, I've got a calf dying, and he's stretched out in the sun stuffing his face!"

The next ten minutes were a blur. I must have seemed an absolute idiot, running up and down the embankment of the ramp, hollering, cursing, waving my arms. Not once did the ferry operator indicate that he knew such a performance was going on within earshot on the other side of the river. Not once did he signal that he would stir from his perch in the sun.

In desperation, I headed back the way I'd come. The bypass at the north end of the valley that would eventually lead to the decommissioning of the ferry was almost complete, and I thought I might be able to get through. Driving north, I followed the edge of the mountain, arriving at the construction site as they stopped for lunch. Huge mounds of blasted rock were stacked along the mountain face, and truckloads of earth were being packed on top of them. Maneuvering between piles of gravel and idle machines, I waved at the workers and passed through as if the road were open for travel.

I arrived back in Canyon still fuming about my ordeal. Dick's wife, Marie, was seated on a chair next to the calf. A good-looking blonde with a slight build, she hardly suited the role of a farmer.

"How're we making out?" I asked, stumbling through the door.

"I don't know; she doesn't exactly look like she wants to live yet."

The poor little critter was struggling to drag in another breath against the pressure of an ever-expanding abdomen. I quickly inspected the drip chamber to make certain that the fluids were still flowing, then filled a syringe with lidocaine and stuffed it in my coveralls pocket.

The calf lay stoically as I clipped and scrubbed her. She didn't even react to the injections of anesthetic.

"By the look of all those needles," shuddered Marie, "you must be getting ready to open her up. I'm going to run over to the barn and get Dick. I don't think he knows you're back yet, and I'd rather have him here when you start cutting."

I finished the final scrub on the calf and laid out my materials.

Dick rushed through the door. "So we're ready to start?" The look on his face told me he had a dozen other things he'd rather be doing. "Do you think we'll have this all wrapped up in a couple hours? If not, I better call Alex for help."

"No problem. If you'll just give me some of this soap, I'll get on with my scrub." I handed him the bottle of Bridine and extended my hands.

I had finished lathering a second time and was offering my hands for the final scrub, when Dick spoke out. "Boy, I can sure see what the guys have been saying about you; you spend more time washing than you do cutting."

"I'm glad to hear that! I'd rather be spending my time washing than doing postmortems and lancing abscesses. Better to have farmers talking about my washing habits than the critters that died from the lack of it."

"Yeah, guess you're right. Don't get me wrong. Wash as much as you like."

Gowned and gloved, I clamped a disposable drape to the heifer and exposed a line of pink flesh down her side. I sliced through the muscle layer beneath. As I approached the last, semitransparent layer called the peritoneum, I picked it up with forceps and made a stab incision with the scalpel. Then with scissors, I extended it generously in both directions. Coils of gas-distended bowel boiled up through the incision.

"Boy, I can see why you didn't just whack through that with the scalpel!"

Retracting the bowels as much as possible, I slid my gloved hand forward and toward the bottom of her spine. The heifer moaned in anguish and started breathing rapidly, her expiratory grunt more pronounced than ever.

"That's where it hurts, isn't it, girl?" I slipped my hand down to the root of the mesentery. I could feel a hard band of tissue and the pulsating vessels. "See how this part of the bowel is all dark and full of gas? You can see that pale area way down there where it's twisted off; some blood can get out here, but none can go back."

Dick was engrossed and moved around to get a better view. Marie seemed content to view the procedure from where she stood.

Choosing an area with maximum distention, I drove a needle through the gut wall, and gas hissed from the end of it.

"Man, that stinks," Dick protested. "That's absolutely rank!"

After five minutes of repositioning the needle and expressing air, the tension in the bowel diminished dramatically. Finally, I grasped the mass and rotated it in a counterclockwise direction.

"See that?" I gloated, as the bowel returned to its normal position. "See that swollen area where it was twisted off?" I felt a tingle run up my spine as the color of the bowel lightened and took on a pinkish hue. Still holding the loops up out of the abdomen, I poked the tissue with a needle. Blood slowly leaked from the puncture site.

"That's great news!" I was smiling from ear to ear and pointing to the pool that was accumulating. "It definitely looks like the gut's still alive. As long as we treat her shock, she'll have a fighting chance."

Dick opened some suture material for me, and I began the chore of closing her body wall. I placed each suture first, then pushed the intestines back into her tummy before tightening the stitch.

"Are you sure you're going to get all that back into her?"

"It makes you wonder, doesn't it? I'm afraid these are parts she can't do without."

"Now I know where to bring my mending," Dick joked, as I placed the last of the sutures in the bottom of the incision. "You're one hell of a tailor!"

Although the heifer looked as if she might come around, she was a long way from being off the critical list. Her grunt had become decidedly less pronounced, but her breathing was rapid and shallow, and her eyes were still sunken.

We bedded down the corner of the cutting-room floor with straw and made a corral of the table and some well-placed boxes.

"Keep the fluids running for the rest of the day, and I'll leave you another bag for tonight. I've given her antibiotics as a preventive, and I'll bring you more tomorrow."

I drove from the Doumas' yard pondering the emotional fluctuations that had occurred throughout the day. It was amazing how a morning that looked so mundane could become a roller-coaster ride replete with awesome peaks and gut-wrenching hollows. I could still feel the effects of some of the highs, and my gut was feeling woozy from the lows. I was going to discover over the years to come just how often that would be the way with veterinary practice.

The remainder of the day was jam-packed, what with catching up on late appointments and looking after calls relayed to me from one farmer to the next.

A storm blew in during the late afternoon, enveloping the valley in dark, low-hung clouds. After an initial heavy downpour, the rain continued in the form of a steady drizzle.

It was after ten when I pulled my car into Grampa's yard and shut off the engine. I clicked out the lights, leaned my head back, and took a deep breath. It was strangely comforting to sit there all alone and listen to the sound of the rain falling gently on the car roof. I stared into the darkness, thinking of nothing more intense than when to take the next breath. At last, a shiver set me in search of the flashlight and motivated me to move.

The house was dark and uninviting. I shone the light into the box containing my meager rations of food and found nothing remotely interesting. I fished a lonely pickle from a jar and munched on it absently. Popping the last bite into my mouth, I collapsed on the bed and pulled the sleeping bag over me.

I closed my eyes and the scenes of the day flicked before me like slides flashing on a screen. I watched as I cut into the poor dejected calf, saw the needle enter the gut, and heard the gas rush from the end of the needle. I had just straightened the torsion and was ready to get on with the suturing when it struck me. The instruments were still out in the car—just as dirty and bloody as when I put them there in the morning!

Damn, I sure didn't feel like washing instruments and firing up the Coleman stove. Reluctantly, I abandoned the warmth of my bed to retrieve the surgery box. The night was without the slightest trace of a breeze. The only sound was the faint patter of the rain as it settled on the grass and the trees around me. I paused for a moment to drink in the silence—to just stand there alone, to be still and feel the rain settle gently upon my face.

I loved this place, I loved the panoramic view of the valley, I loved the peace and tranquillity of the quiet nights, but I knew it couldn't work. Fall was on its way, and inexorably, winter. The nip in the air was a warning of what was to come. This house would be impossible for me soon. I was hardly ever here, and the thought of coming home to a cold, lonely house was more than I could bear. As much as I hated to think about it, I was going to have to find somewhere else, somewhere closer to town.

I had lowered the instruments into the pressure cooker when a vision of the heifer flashed through my mind. I thought about giving Dick a call to see how he was making out, but glanced at my watch and thought better of it. It was late and dairymen tended not to be coherent at that time of night.

The next morning things seemed to be unfolding nicely. There were a few calls before I left home, but nothing had a ring of urgency about it. My time would be dedicated to doing the herd health at the Doumas' that never got started yesterday.

From the time I got out of bed, my thoughts revolved around the pathetic little creature that we had done surgery on the day before. One minute, I pictured her tearing across the pasture as if nothing had ever been wrong. The next, I jerked myself back to reality and saw her lying there bloated, with her feet in the air. The closer I got to the Douma farm, the more I steeled myself for the moment I would find out that she hadn't made it. There was something about putting your best effort forth and failing that didn't seem fair.

I parked the car in front of the meat shop and took a quick look around. There was no sign of anyone about. Inside, the debris from the surgery had been cleared away, but the corner where we had bedded the calf was still covered with straw. The boxes that had formed the barrier were scattered throughout the room, and a pool of congealed blood lay on the floor.

That must have been where she died, I mused. The way the boxes had been flung about, Dick must have had a real temper tantrum when he found her dead. I didn't see his truck anywhere about and supposed he had made a quick run to the dump with the carcass.

I was downcast as I wandered to the barn. I never was a good sport about losing, and I felt even worse when a creature's life was at stake. I passed through the milk house into the barn to see if either Alex or Dick was about. A metallic screeching and clattering greeted me as the cows turned their heads and stanchions to see who had invaded their domain.

"Hello! Anybody here?"

No one answered. I wandered into the calf barn on the off chance that Dick had moved the heifer over but found her pen empty. I was on my way back to the barn when I heard him call.

"Hello! Are you in here?"

I met him at the corner. He was obviously perplexed; his face was fixed in a scowl.

"We didn't get our shipment of brewer's mash yesterday and the cows have really gone into a tailspin," he grumped. "They dropped almost five hundred pounds this pickup."

I was anxious to get the uncomfortable conversation about the heifer over with. Even though I couldn't think of what else I might have done to save her, I still felt responsible for her death. Maybe if I had brought my instruments with me, that hour would have made the difference.

"So, do you want to have a look at the heifer?" Dick asked in a matter-of-fact tone.

"Yeah, sure." I trailed along in silence, wishing that things could have turned out differently. It would probably be best to get the postmortem over with before we started with herd health.

We rounded the corner of the barn, and there she was—not lying dead as I expected, but picking at green grass along the side of the building! As we approached, she turned to face us and took a step in our direction. She looked a bit rough, what with her bald right side and her sunken flanks, but the improvements overnight were simply amazing.

Her eyes told the story. Where yesterday they had been sunken, today the lids and eyes were a perfect fit. Yesterday they had been filled with pain; today they were bright and attentive.

"Boy, I'm sure glad that ordeal's over," Dick muttered. "Yesterday, when I changed the fluids around five, she was starting to move her back legs a bit and was holding up her head. Her guts must have been really moving; I could hear them rumbling and she had already had a couple big dumps. I was over here about ten last night and she was lying there as quiet as could be.

"Came out this morning at quarter to five and there she was out in the middle of the room! She'd knocked the boxes all over hell's half acre. I just cut all the tubes off her neck and stuffed her out here where there's still some green grass."

I stared at the heifer as she resumed her grazing. She was really alive! The way she was looking right now, I didn't doubt that she would make an uneventful recovery. Who would have dared to predict?

During my years of practice, I continually reminded myself that there were many different ways of receiving payment for the services I rendered. I've long since forgotten what I charged to do the surgery on that calf, but there's no way I'll ever forget the feeling of satisfaction that gripped me as we got on with the morning's work.

POOR WEE THING

WAS ON MY WAY to the car when Evelyn Hurford came running from the house. "A lady's on the phone about a sick cat. I'm not sure how she knew you were here, but she wants to talk to you. She sounds rather anxious."

"Thanks, Ev. I'll take it."

The voice on the phone was rich and lyrical. As Elspeth McSeveney ran on in her Scottish brogue, I focused intently to keep from losing her. "Dr. Perrin, I was talking to Ruth Veitch on the street during my lunch break. She told me you'd been to her place for supper last night, and that you were going to be at Hurfords' this morning."

"I see. Yes." It was amazing how people could track me down. "Mrs. Hurford was mentioning you had a sick cat."

"Yes . . . It's our little Tikkie. The poor wee thing has wasted away before our eyes; we can't seem to do a thing about it."

"So this has been going on for some time, Mrs. McSeveney?"

"It's been months, it has. I've had her checked out a number of times, but we just can't find out what's wrong with her."

"What exactly are her symptoms? Has she had vomiting or diarrhea?"

"Her stools have been a bit off from time to time, but it's never anything consistent. She hasn't had a movement in days now, but that's not surprising. She hasn't eaten either—she's so weak, she can hardly get around."

"I can stop over right now, if you'd like me to look at her."

I took directions to the McSeveney residence and headed for Erickson, the orchard community east of Creston. I arrived at the ferry ramp moments after it had departed—it was a hundred feet out. I watched the cables slice through the water as it pulled itself toward the north shore of the river. A car and a pickup were on board; a grain truck waited on the opposite side.

I craned my neck to make out the operator. I was sure it was the same guy who had ignored me last week. I felt foolish using the ferry when he was operating. I still wanted to wring his neck for stranding me. Although he'd given no indication he had witnessed my temper tantrum, I couldn't shake the feeling that he was chuckling behind my back.

The group America finished the song "A Horse with No Name," and Black Sabbath began pounding out the chords of some god-awful heavy metal. I shut off the ignition and welcomed the ensuing silence. The sunlight shimmered on the river. An osprey swooped to the surface. I saw a flash as the bird hit the water, then watched in appreciation as it flapped lazily to a tree on the riverbank, a fish dangling from its talons.

The cable reared once again. Water sprayed from the box end of the ferry and ripples appeared on either side. It was on its way back.

Like some clumsy river animal, it wallowed in the water until finally bumping against the landing. The ramp of the old scow dropped, and the operator strolled to the front deck to lower the forward chain. The grain truck lurched ahead and ground its way slowly up the ramp; the ferry buoyed in relief. Bob Rogers, who operated the farm next to the ferry landing, smiled broadly and waved out the truck window.

I waved in return and drove down the ramp onto the deck. The operator nodded when I passed him; the chain rattled as he lifted it and fixed it in place. I watched in the rearview mirror as he strolled to the cabin. Was that a smirk on his face?

I drove up the steep ramp and was soon meandering through fields of newly growing barley. Driving through Creston, I headed east toward Cranbrook. Within minutes I approached a sharp, checkerboard corner and turned onto Haskin's West. That should be the McSeveneys—the house with the brown-stained wood siding. Elspeth said they lived in the Carmichaels' basement suite. It had to be the place—Groot's Farm was right across the road.

A pleasant-looking woman in her early thirties opened the door. She had long brown hair pulled back from her face and expressive blue eyes framed by wire-rimmed glasses.

"My, aren't you the tall one?" I loved her musical Scottish lilt and was casually wondering how my accent sounded to her. "I thought my husband, Jim, was a big man; he's almost six foot six." She extended her hand for a firm shake. "I'm Elspeth McSeveney."

"Dave Perrin." I rested my arm on the top of the refrigerator and pulled off my shoes. Elspeth chuckled to see her fridge used as a leaning post.

"How tall are you, anyway?"

"I'm six eleven."

A healthy-looking seal-point Siamese circled my legs and vied for attention. She rubbed against me and stared up at me with intense blue eyes that oscillated from side to side in Siamese fashion.

"That's Sheba. She came over with us from Scotland. We bought her in Dunfermline."

"Really? I've never met a Scottish Siamese before. Did you fly her over?"

"Oh no, she came with us on the cruise liner *Empress of Canada*. She was trained to the leash, so we took her for walks on deck. We got meat from the butcher on board; she ate better than we did."

"Aren't you the spoiled one!" I picked her up. She purred vehemently and rubbed her head against my hand.

"She pretty much runs the household. We got Tikkie from Olga Edwards to keep Sheba company. It was so funny to watch that wee little kitten try to gain her affection. She worked at it for weeks, she did. She tore after Sheba to get her attention. Sheba was embarrassed at first, but she finally gave in, and they became the best of friends. Tikkie was the first kitten we ever got for nothing. The others all cost us a bundle."

Turning toward the kennel in the corner of the kitchen, her expression was suddenly sad. "We've all but given up hope for poor little Tikkie." I followed Elspeth across the room to find a dejected-looking specimen lying at my feet. I knelt and wrestled with the catch that held the kennel door fixed.

"I keep hoping she'll just give up and die in her sleep. You know, with all the pets I've had, I've never had one that died on its own. I've always had to have them put to sleep . . . It's just so hard." She removed her glasses to wipe away the tears that welled in her eyes.

Tikkie was indeed in a terrible state. Her light-colored hair was oily and lifeless. Her muscle had wasted and the bones of her face, hips, and spine protruded. I lifted her gently from the kennel and set her next to Elspeth on the kitchen counter. Her eyes opened. Bright and blue, they flicked haphazardly as she tried to focus.

She meowed pitifully and Elspeth looked away. Tears trickled freely down her cheeks.

"There's a girl. Good Tikkie," I crooned.

"She was such an active little thing." Elspeth ran her hands lovingly over Tikkie's bony body. "She was always a bit on the small side, but she was full of life and mischief. I had a heck of a time keeping her from climbing my curtains. She was a tremendous hunter even as a kitten, constantly dragging in mice and birds."

"Her decline has been very gradual then?"

"She was always so playful before. At first I couldn't put my finger on what was wrong. She just didn't look right! I took her in for a checkup, and he couldn't find anything wrong with her. He was sure she had worms, but we dewormed her and it didn't make any difference."

I inserted a thermometer into her rectum and Tikkie squirmed. I palpated her body in search of unusual lumps and bumps but was unable to find anything of interest. Her lips and gums were pale. Grasping the skin at the scruff of her neck, I pulled it into a tent. It remained there as if the skin were bent.

"She's terribly dehydrated."

"I've tried to force fluids into her, but she won't take a thing. She looks at me as if to say, *Just put me out of my misery, Mom.* They seem to know, don't they?"

I removed the thermometer and rotated it in the light to read it—98.6 degrees Farenheit! A degree and a half below normal.

"You mentioned having her examined, Elspeth. Did she ever have blood work done? She looks anemic to me."

"No, never blood work. I'm a lab tech myself, and I would have had her put to sleep some time ago if I'd known why she was sick. It really bothers me to give up when I don't know what's wrong."

"I don't have to tell you how rough she is, Elspeth. She's very dehydrated and anemic. Let's draw blood and see if we can figure out what's going on. If there are signs of regeneration of red cells, she may have a chance. If there's no evidence that she's trying to rally and kick out early red cells, then maybe it would be best to put her to sleep."

"I'd like that. A part of me wants to just put an end to her misery. Another part keeps telling me there's hope—that there's something we've missed!"

I soaked a gauze with alcohol and had Elspeth support Tikkie in an upright position so I could rub down her foreleg and raise a vein. I drove the needle through the skin and the syringe slowly filled with watery, pink fluid. It was hard to even think of it as blood.

"Oh my!" Elspeth watched in horror as the sample trickled from the syringe into the lavender-topped tube that would keep the blood from clotting.

"I'll run right back to West Creston and do a complete blood count on her. I don't have to tell you that something's very much amiss with this sample."

Elspeth was still focused on the tube that rotated in my fingertips. Picking up Tikkie, she cuddled her to her breast and rocked back and forth. Tikkie lay in her arms, lifeless except for the slow rise and fall of her chest.

"I'll call you as soon as I have some results, Elspeth."

She nodded. Tears ran steadily down her face. I departed without looking back. Damn! Some days this job just tore me apart.

I arrived home wondering how I was going to evaluate this sample properly. Clinical pathology had always been one of my strong points in the final years at college; The answer to Tikkie's illness was there for the discovery—somewhere in that tube with the lavender top.

I dug through the box of goodies that I had bought before leaving the college. The hemacytometer for doing a total count of the cells and the stain for evaluation of the individual cells would both give me clues.

Owning a microscope that required power was a major impediment. Microscopes work on the principle of light refraction, and my light source was an electric bulb. I lifted the microscope from its wooden case and set it up on the kitchen table. If I could just wedge the flashlight under the stage in some manner, I was sure I could get enough light to do an evaluation.

I took a glass hematocrit tube and watched pink blood flow into it. I just couldn't believe the color of this sample. There had to be some sort of explanation.

I touched the end of the tube to a microscope slide; fluid flowed onto the glass surface. With another slide, I stroked across the drop to produce a thumbnail-shaped smear. I waved it around in the air to dry it and applied the stain. Setting the slide on a paper towel to dry, I went about trying to figure out a way to use the apparatus.

I removed the light source from beneath the microscope and struggled to position the flashlight in such a manner as to shine the light up through the stage. No matter how I positioned it, I couldn't get enough light to illuminate the slide. I was wishing I had one of the old microscopes that utilized a mirror to reflect light through the lens.

Maybe I could just convert this one. I rustled through the boxes and suitcases in search of a mirror. Other than the big one on the wall, there was none. I looked at it skeptically. There was no way that I'd be able to jam a corner of it under the stage—it was just too big.

I took the mirror off the wall and worked the cardboard backing free. I'd never miss a little corner of it, anyway. I wrapped a towel around the mirror and was poised with the pliers closed over it; just a little piece would do. For several minutes, I pondered the wisdom of this move. The thought of seven years of bad luck starting now was less than appealing.

Crack. "Shoot!" I wanted a bigger piece than that. I looked at the meager scrap that I held in my fingertips and shrugged. I decided to try it. I propped the sliver of glass beneath the microscope stage and shone the flashlight against it. It might be possible; I could see some light.

Setting the microscope outside on the lawn, I ran back inside for my slide. I slipped it onto the stage and rotated the scope into the sunlight, then propped the sliver of mirror under it. I focused the lens on low power and was delighted that I was able to make out cells. This was going to work.

Rotating the lens to a medium power, I surveyed the slide. My God! The entire field was taken up with blue. Mammalian red cells are more highly specialized for the carrying of oxygen than are the red cells of birds and reptiles; in order to cram more hemoglobin into the cell the nucleus is dropped. Normally one would have to look around the slide to see any number of nucleated cells. Tikkie's cells were almost all nucleated; one would think it was chicken blood!

I put a drop of oil in the center of the slide and rotated to the oil emersion lens to get maximum resolution to the cells. I fiddled with the sliver of glass until enough light shone through. Everywhere I looked were cells with huge purple nuclei that looked like early lymphocytes. No wonder poor Tikkie was in such a sad state! She had leukemia.

I moved the slide around, checking cell morphology. No doubt about it! Those cells were of the lymphocytic series—and those sad-looking red cells! The few that were present were sick and punched out. This was a hopeless picture.

Poor Tikkie. Poor Elspeth!

I called my client. "I'm sorry, Elspeth; there's no doubt about it. It's not a common condition, but it certainly explains why she's in such a terrible state."

"Can you come and take her? Jim and I talked this through, and if there's nothing we can do for her, we want to have you put her out of her misery. She was such a fine, wee cat; we just can't watch her like this anymore."

When I arrived to pick Tikkie up, Elspeth was again alone. Her eyes were red and she looked truly exhausted. "Just take the kennel and all; we won't be needing it any longer. Why couldn't she have just gone in her sleep?"

"I can imagine how hard this is for you, Elspeth. I hate it myself—but there's no question that it's best for her." I looked at the miserable creature in the kennel and again at the tenderhearted woman who loved her so.

"I tried to get Jim to stay home and give her to you, but no way. He just can't stand to be around at times like this. He can go fishing and pull the fish out of the water and knock them on the head. He says that it's different."

"I'm sorry I couldn't help, Elspeth."

"You have, Dr. Perrin, you've helped us both find peace. Tikkie will be out of her misery, and I finally know there's nothing more I can do to help her."

PARTY LINE BLUES

I'D NEVER BEEN A PARTICULARLY PATIENT PERSON, but waiting for someone to finish gossiping on a party line had to be the ultimate in pain and suffering. Today, the time seemed like an eternity and my patience had worn very thin before one of the neighbors finally finished her conversation. It was hard to believe that in this day and age I was unable to have a private telephone, but in West Creston a party line was the only service I could get.

When I was finally blessed with a dial tone instead of an agitated "Line's busy!" I checked in with the Kemles for my messages. Vern Petersen had called. He was having problems with pink eye in some newly purchased calves and wanted advice on how to handle the situation. Vern ran a small feedlot on Highway 21 below the town of Creston. I had met him briefly at a beef growers' meeting and was anxiously awaiting an opportunity to set foot on his farm.

The first time I called, his wife informed me that he was out working a few of the worst calves through the chute. She assured me that he would return my call in a few minutes and that he was anxious to resolve his problem.

While I waited, I built a salami sandwich. I had wandered through the Creston Valley Cooperative last thing the day before; it was a treat to have some real groceries for a change. I finished my sandwich and a second one. I glanced at my watch. It had been over half an hour since I'd talked to Mrs. Petersen, and I didn't think it should take that long for her to find her husband.

On a whim, I picked up the phone. Sure enough, it was busy again! This time it was humming with voices I didn't recognize; surely to God there wasn't yet another family that shared this line. What a hell of a way to run a business— with a phone that constantly rang busy not because I was overworked, but because I had neighbors who loved to talk.

After five minutes of checking the phone at regular intervals and dealing with the anger of the lady on the line, it was free. I hated pestering someone to get off the phone, but what else was I to do? Vern answered on the first ring—his aggravation was evident.

"Was about ready to give up on you and get back to treating those calves," he snorted. "I've been trying to phone you every five minutes and your phone's been ringin' busy!"

"I'm sorry about that, but I'm on a party line out here, and it's worth your life to try and get on. So you're having some problems with pink eye in your feedlot?"

"God, yes! Have never had it like this. It started with one calf the day they came off the truck. Its right eye was watering and half closed. I thought he'd just bumped it on the truck during the trip over here, but the next day both eyes were closed and a couple of the other calves were in trouble. I'm trying to treat eight of them in the chute right now; the first ones are looking worse than ever."

"Have you run them right into the head gate and opened the eyes to get a good look?"

"Yeah. You get one good look at them before you spray them; after that, they won't open their eyes for anything."

"And you're treating them with pink eye spray and nothing else?"

"Didn't know there was anything else I could do. That's why I'm callin' you for help!"

"How do their eyes look before you spray them? Is there a little white spot in the very middle of the eye? Do the ones you've been treating for a long time develop a pink cone in the center?"

"That's exactly how they look. The first calf I told you about is completely blind now and has pink cones like that in both eyes."

"What are the flies like right now? Have they been worse than normal for this time of year?"

"Yeah . . . Yeah, I'd say they're worse than I've had for some time. Do you think that has something to do with it?"

"Yes, undoubtedly with its spreading, but you probably imported the first case on the load."

"What do you suggest we do about it? I'm about sick of runnin' those calves through and there are new cases every day."

"How about keeping those calves in the chute until I get there. I'll give them an injection under the lining of the eye. That's about the best way I . . . ."

"Dave! Dave!" came a breathless voice over the phone. "It's Blaze! He's stuck upside down in the drainage ditch over in the pasture!"

The booming voice was obviously Bea's.

"I was just down there, and he was flailing around on his back and fighting to get up! The way he's thrashing, he's bound to hurt himself. His head looks pretty bashed up already. Fred's off to town and I don't know what to do with him! Can you come and help?"

"Keep the calves in, Vern!" I blurted. "I'll get there as soon as I can!"

"Oh, Vern, it's you!" Bea shouted. "Sorry to butt into your conversation like this, but I didn't know what else to do."

Slamming down the receiver, I rushed out of the house and rummaged through the car. I grabbed my lariat and a twenty-five-foot length of one-inch cotton rope that I had just bought for casting horses. Looping them over my shoulder, I sprinted down the drive.

I reached the road with Bea nowhere in sight; knowing her, she was probably still on the phone apologizing to Vern. I ran down the roadway until I could see the drainage ditch angle off through the pasture. Fred had plowed a trench across the field to help control the direction of the water flowing through his property during spring runoff.

Stepping over the barbed-wire fence, I jogged beside the trench until I came over a rise and spotted the horse. He was lying completely motionless, his feet pointing into the air and his backbone lodged in the trench. His head was hanging back, all but out of sight in the depths of the ditch. As I approached, I wondered if the horse was dead. It wasn't until I got closer that I could see the rapid expansion and contraction of his chest.

Climbing into the ditch some distance from his head, I crawled forward until I could touch him and examine him without being injured by the thrashing of either his head or his feet. He was pointed downhill, and his head was lodged in a portion of the ditch that was somewhat deeper than the rest. The bridge of his nose was resting on a boulder that had been washed clean by runoff waters. It was now covered with blood and dirt from the constant thrashing and banging of Blaze's head.

Blood trickled from a gash at the corner of his muzzle. His eyes were puffy and partly swollen shut. There were abrasions on the bridge of his nose and a lot of the hair and the surface layer of skin had been rubbed from his forehead. His hair coat was soaked with sweat, the normally gray hair now a shiny black. A frothy lather had accumulated between his hind legs.

Inching my way forward, I pushed up on his head with my right hand and pried on the boulder beneath his forehead with my left. The rock rolled free, but the intervention set Blaze off on a wave of frantic struggling. His forehead struck the ground with a sickening thud, and the tip of one of his flailing front feet struck my shoulder and knocked me over backward.

I broke out in a cold sweat as I picked myself up and realized how close I had come to serious injury. I had foolishly allowed myself to get in range of those feet and felt fortunate to have come away unscathed.

I crawled out of the ditch as Fred and Bea came running across the pasture.

"Fred just pulled up as I was coming down!" Bea gasped. "Land sakes, how'd he ever get himself in such a predicament?"

"We need to get something under his head so he doesn't do himself any more injury!" I hollered as they approached. "If we build his head up a bit higher so that he can bridge with his neck, I'm sure he can help flip himself over. A few flakes of hay or straw and a blanket would do just fine."

Fred ran off to the barn as I attached ropes to Blaze's legs to prepare for an attempt at righting him. Several times, the horse erupted in a fit of panic, and his hooves lashed wildly in all directions. His bouts were unpredictable and seemed to have little bearing on what I happened to be doing at the moment. By the time Fred arrived with a bale of straw and a saddle blanket, I had the ropes secured.

I crammed several flakes of straw under Blaze's head and covered them with the saddle blanket. As if on cue, the horse thrashed and flailed about. We pulled sideways on the ropes and flipped him over. Exhausted by his efforts, he lay on his side, his chest heaving and his nostrils flared.

We allowed him to rest in that position for several minutes, then Fred knelt down beside him and slipped on a halter. I pulled the ropes off his feet, and we waited for the horse's breathing to settle down.

I gave him a sharp smack on the rump with the flat of my hand, and he struggled to right himself. I pulled on his tail as Fred pulled on the halter shank. With a desperate heave, the horse got his feet under him and took a few unsteady steps toward level ground. Every muscle in his body quivered, and he stood there swaying back and forth. Like a drunken sailor, he took the odd step forward and an occasional step to the side. It was ten minutes before I dared to release his tail and allow him to navigate on his own steam.

Blaze was a woeful site to behold. His muzzle only inches from the ground, he looked as if he had gone the distance in a heavyweight boxing match.

I pried his eyes open one at a time, looking for serious injury. Aside from an accumulation of mud on the corners of his lids, there was little damage to the eyes themselves. His forehead was a raw mass of oozing tissue, and a small gash was still weeping blood.

"I can't see anything that actually needs stitching, but I better give you some medication to put into those eyes."

I was talking to myself all the way to the house and wondering if veterinary practice would always be so unpredictable. I returned with a bottle of penicillin, an injection of Butazone, and a tube of eye ointment.

"This should help keep his muscles from cramping up." I drove the needle into his jugular vein and slowly injected the yellowish liquid. "You'll need to give him a shot of penicillin every day for a while too, Fred. None of those abrasions can be sewn, but the whole thing could turn into an infected mess if you aren't careful."

After showing Fred how to apply the eye ointment, I released Blaze's halter shank and let him go. I felt good about the way things had gone. It wasn't until I was climbing the stairs to the veranda that Vern Petersen again came to mind. I was anxious to get on my way before he got impatient and let those calves out of the corral.

I washed up, changed my clothes, and decided to give him a call to let him know I was coming. I picked up the receiver and was beginning to dial when I heard it—the familiar sound of my neighbor's voice, " . . . and there he was upside down in the ditch . . . Sorry! Line's busy!"

DORIS

MY GOD, this place is even worse than Grampa's," I groaned, as Gordon parked his car in front of the dilapidated gray building at the south end of Canyon Street.

"I gotta agree it's not the best, but right at the moment it's the only place in town I know that's available and in your price range. Come on, let's go in and have a look. Looking doesn't hurt."

"Are you sure? My eyes are sore already!" I gazed at the old false front of the building with the huge flakes of paint peeling from its surface.

"It used to be Gunnar Larsen's Photo Studio." Gordon stepped around a wizened old man leaning against the corner of the building. A native Indian, he appeared to have survived some rough times. His stature was stooped, his clothing disheveled, his unkempt hair as white as snow. A scar ran diagonally across his face, and his left eye was a shrunken mass of scar tissue.

"Hello, George." Gordon acknowledged the old man, then opened the right-hand door to an alcove that housed two entrances. "That one's Anthony's Barbershop." He pointed to the half of the building that had the word Barber painted across the glass window front. George turned to view us with his good eye, then shuffled off down the street.

"Watch it." Gordon took a giant stride to avoid the broken boards in the threshold. "The landlord promised me last week he was going to fix those."

Following Gord's lead, I entered a tiny room that was chopped in half by a partition wall. On the inside of the wall, cabinets jutted out to claim another three feet of available floor. Bending down, I grasped the faceted glass knob and gave it a pull. The top of the door sprang out two to three inches before the catch at the bottom released.

"They never spared on expense when they built things back in the thirties."

"Nothing but the best." Gordon sported the impish smirk that I would come to know so well.

50

"Isn't that about the sickest color you've ever seen? Why would anyone paint wallpaper such a washed-out green and match it with a red carpet?"

"I don't think that's actually wallpaper. If you look closer, you'll see that it's roofing paper glued onto the wall."

I scraped at it with my fingernail. "That's exactly what it is. What's back here?" I wandered through a doorway into a confined little room.

"That's where Gunnar used to develop his pictures."

Fumbling along the walls, I tried to locate a light switch. "There has to be a light in here somewhere. No one would have a room—even a darkroom—without some kind of light."

"I'm sure there's one somewhere, but I wouldn't bet the farm on it."

"Where's the bathroom?"

"There's one out the darkroom door. It's shared by the barbershop."

"You mean there's another door in that black hole somewhere? I sure didn't notice it."

"Yeah, there's a maze back there you wouldn't believe, with a set of stairs going to an apartment and another doorway into a storage room and the rest room."

"I can imagine how restful that room is, if it's anything like the rest of this dump."

Returning to the darkroom, I reached the far wall and groped about until I finally felt a doorknob. Fumbling with one rickety door after the other, I picked my way to the back room.

"Oh man, Gordon, has the fire inspector ever been invited into this pit?"

"I wouldn't be trying to rent it to you if he had been."

The portion of the building that we now entered was obviously a lean-to that had been added on. I cautiously entered the room, stooping more with each step.

"This place certainly wasn't designed with someone of your height in mind."

"Hardly," I groaned.

Reaching to the bulb over his head, Gordon pulled a chain and turned on the light.

"Maybe that's why I was having so much trouble finding a light switch in the other room. There's probably a string dangling from the ceiling somewhere."

The room was of two-by-four construction and no attempt had been made to insulate it or in any way cover the bare boards that lined the outside walls.

"I thought you said there was a bathroom back here."

"There is." Gordon pointed to the far end of the lean-to where the ceiling was barely four feet from the floor.

"You have to be kidding! How am I supposed to get through that door?"

"I'm not really sure. But when you decide to try it, let me know. I can think of a few people who would want to buy tickets for that performance."

Ducking my head still farther, I pushed the door inward and turned the light on by pulling the string.

"I'd have to drop my drawers out here to be able to get onto this throne. Even then, that fool lightbulb would whack me on the head."

We returned to the front in silence, closing each rickety door behind us. I had been down in the dumps before we got here. Everything seemed to be taking so long, and I was constantly nagged by worries about the image I was portraying to my clientele. Moving into this place would do nothing to improve my image, and the last few minutes had done little to lift my spirits.

"You really think that people would come to visit someone in a dive like this and not be afraid to leave their pet behind?"

"Someone, maybe not. You, yes. For some reason, you seem to have a lot of people thinking you're all right. You keep people happy and stay busy enough, and you won't have to be in this building for long. Besides, you'd be surprised what a bit of paint and some wallpaper could do to fix it up."

"I'm afraid it'll take more than wallpaper and paint to make me happy with this dump."

"What're you going to do for a receptionist?" Gordon asked, as we pulled into the parking lot behind Veitch Realty.

"Hadn't given it too much thought really. I've been delaying the inevitable as long as possible. It's one thing to keep from starving to death when I'm just worrying about myself. It'll be a different story if I have to earn enough to pay staff as well."

"Once you become more visible and people can get to you without having to call all over town, you're going to have more to do than you can handle. You'll need someone good to organize you, someone who isn't afraid of work and who'll keep busy without being asked."

"You sound as if you have someone in mind. Are you in the personnel business as well?"

"Not really." That sneaky smile crept onto his face. "But I do."

"Who?"

"Her name's Doris Currie. Her husband died a few months ago. He was on a kidney machine for years and she ran it—she's not the least bit scared of blood."

"How do you know she wants to work?"

"I chatted with her the other day, and she said she was going to have to find a job. I think you should talk to her right away before she gets one somewhere else."

"I don't know. I'm not sure I'm ready for an employee yet."

"I'm not trying to knock what you're doing right now. You've got to admit though, when you're doing everything, you're not working efficiently. With a good employee like Doris and an office in town, you'll get twice as much accomplished and not feel so pressed for time."

"You may be right . . . You may be right."

"So do you want to meet her tonight? I'll take you over and introduce you to her if you want."

"Let me think on it. Things are moving just a little too fast for me at the moment."

"Well, you let me know. You could sure do a lot worse than hiring Doris; and if you rent that spot for even six months, it'll get you started."

I was in a pensive mood when I called in for messages. Maybe it was time to move on. The Kemles were certain to tire of fielding my calls—after all, they were just clients trying to help out. There was no question that I needed an assistant off and on, and I was sick of going home at the end of a long day with the prospect of sterilizing instruments for the morning. Gordon was right. Something had to give!

"Werner Beier has a cat with a broken leg. He sounded quite upset and was hoping to have it looked at right away. He just barely hung up the phone. He's waiting in his office for your call."

"Thanks, Donna."

I soon had a very worried Mr. Beier on the phone.

"Sorry to be so worked up, but I've never seen anything quite this gross before! His leg's just hanging there, and the bone's poking out and all covered with dirt."

"Does the wound look fresh, or has it been like that for a while?"

"It's been like that for a while; it's a mess! Something has to be done."

After taking directions on how to find the Beiers' farm, I called Gordon.

"Why don't you set up a time to meet with this lady tonight? It's obvious that I'm going to need someone I can depend on to help me with cases. You may as well phone Norman Husband and tell him I'll rent his building, too."

"Okay, I'll see what I can do."

Werner's instructions had been good, and I had no problem whatsoever finding his poultry farm. I turned off the Erickson back road onto Beier's lane. A pungent odor invaded the car as I proceeded down the drive. Pulling into the yard, I was met by a tall, slender, blond man in his early twenties. Planted near the entrance to the barn, he stood as rigid as a statue. I could hardly see the kitten he clutched tightly to his chest.

"I'm Werner Beier. This is Albert."

I was more than a little surprised that this man was actually Mr. Beier himself. Until he introduced himself, I assumed that he was, in fact, a hired hand—he was no older than I was.

"Hello, Werner, I'm Dave Perrin."

"This happened yesterday." Werner gazed at the rumpled ball of black fur that he cuddled in his arms. "Albert's such an affectionate little guy—he follows me around everywhere. I was working out in the yard with the one-ton, and he was sitting on the frame. I chased him away and got back into the truck to lower the box. Albert must have jumped right back up on the frame. The box came down on his leg . . . I heard him screech and lifted it right away. He took off . . . I just found him again a few minutes ago."

"How old is he?"

I gently stroked his head with my finger. Albert opened one eye just a slit, shot a disinterested glance in my direction, then immediately closed it.

"He's four months. This is not like him at all—he's usually a perpetual motion machine."

"Have you seen him move his back end at all?"

"Yeah, he crawled out from under one of the big fan units."

The kitten lay motionless while I examined him. From the vibration of his head and chest, I could tell that he was managing to carry on with a feeble purr. There was a sizable gash over the base of his tail and, for a moment, I wondered if the spine might be fractured. I squeezed his tail and could feel him shift his body to avoid the discomfort.

His good foreleg was uppermost and, with the exception of a few broken claws and the skin missing from his outer pad, it seemed to be intact. The leg flexed smoothly without causing him pain, and a firm pinch of his good toes revealed a normal withdrawal reflex. Manipulation of his hind end didn't seem to distress him.

"Let's shift him around so I can get a better look at the bad leg."

Carefully turning him over in his arms, Werner gave him an anxious look, then focused his gaze on the horizon. Albert's right front leg was an entanglement of jagged bone and sinew. The leg had been broken in several locations and almost completely stripped of skin to an area well above the foreleg. The elbow was dislocated, leaving the foot dangling by tissue that was stiff and dried out. The humerus was broken and sticking through near his shoulder. As the kitten shifted his weight to get more comfortable, the end of the bone slashed through the air, then buried itself again beneath the muscles of his upper leg. Feathers and fragments of grain clung randomly to the exposed flesh.

"Do you think you can save him?"

"I think we can save him, but that leg's definitely beyond hope."

"I figured that. Would it be cruel to let him live with just three legs? I can baby him a bit, but there are other cats here, and he'll have to fend for himself."

"Cats are capable of doing very well with one leg missing."

I rolled back his lip to check his color; although his gums were pale, they still had a pinkish hue. Grabbing the skin at the scruff of his neck, I pulled upward, then released it. It maintained a peak, only very slowly flattening at the margins.

"He's dehydrated. We'll have to get some fluids into him before doing surgery."

Werner hesitated. "I like this critter, but he is a barn cat. If you think this is going to be really expensive, I may have you put him to sleep."

"I'll keep that in mind. Do you have a counter or desk where we can work on him? He has a small vein, so you're going to have to hold him very still."

"I have a desk in my office."

I gathered the necessary materials from the car, then followed Werner into the little alcove that functioned as his office. Albert lay quietly in Werner's hands as I clipped the hair from the paw to the elbow. I was nervous about trying to start an intravenous on such a small kitten.

Grasping the cat above the elbow, I aggressively rubbed down the foreleg with an alcohol swab. The small but firm blue string that materialized meandered from the inside of the foreleg to disappear beneath my finger at the elbow. Closing my eyes, I pictured the apparatus installed and the drip running at a slow, steady pace. Nothing to it—just a bit of simple plumbing.

I drove the catheter through the skin and advanced it. It looked good; I was certain I was in! I removed the metal stilette and blood crept up the catheter. "Hallelujah!"

Werner cuddled the kitten to his chest as I injected him with antibiotics. He watched apprehensively as I settled him in a cat carrier in the back of my car.

It was after six by the time I finished my last helping of Chinese food at the Club Café. I had made arrangements to meet Gordon at his home in Erickson at six-thirty and was already feeling nervous about meeting this woman. What would I say if I didn't think she was suitable for the job? A litany of one-liners flashed to mind. "I'm sorry, you're definitely not the person I want to hire." "Not a chance!" "I'm not really ready to hire someone yet, but I'll give you a ring when I am." Or maybe, "I have several interviews set up with other people, and I'll let you know after I've met with them."

I got back to the car and took a quick look at Albert. He was curled up on his blanket, his mutilated leg under him, his head tucked inside the crook of his hind leg. It always amazed me that animals so frequently lie with their injured limb under them. Was it to portray to the world: I'm fine! Nothing wrong with me. Find a meal somewhere else? Or was there something about lying on an injury that suppressed the pain?

Whatever the reason, I couldn't imagine my wanting to lie on that tangled mass of flesh. He was looking much brighter now. I stroked his head and he opened his eyes to give a pitiful meow. He purred and pressed his head into my palm as if asking for more. When I lifted a pinch of skin on the scruff of his neck and released it, it returned to its normal position.

"That's what we want to see, Albert. You're feeling better too, aren't you?"

I pulled into Veitch's driveway, still rehearsing what I was going to say to this lady if I didn't like her. I was certainly not going to put myself in this situation again! From now on, any interviews would be on my own turf. Gordon was nowhere to be seen, so I knocked on the door. I was met by Ruth, who had been busy in the kitchen.

"Come on in and have some dessert. Gord's in the living room watching the news."

I found Gordon stretched out like a walrus, his expansive belly on the carpeted floor, a great stuffed cushion under his chest. On the floor before him was a huge bowl of trifle cake smothered in whipped cream.

"Ah, *Doctauri's* here! You're just in time for supper."

"No thanks, I'm stuffed. I just had Chinese food at Mae's, and I couldn't eat another thing."

"Well, you certainly have room for dessert," Ruth insisted, handing me a bowl of cake and whipped cream that was piled every bit as high as Gordon's. The focus of the news was the same as every other night. They just couldn't get enough of Nixon and Watergate! They had him by the throat and weren't about to let go.

"Are you sure that this lady's going to work out all right?" I asked, as we jumped into his car.

"Madame C! Oh yeah, don't worry about her; she's a real trouper. She's exactly what you need."

I felt like an expectant groom at an arranged marriage waiting to see the woman he would spend the rest of his life with.

I was more than a little nervous by the time Gordon pointed to the house a half mile up the road from his and chirped, "That's Madame C's right there. The one with the white siding."

I followed him up the walk, feeling somewhat like the proverbial schoolboy. He rang the buzzer; I stood nervously behind him staring at my feet.

We were met by a tall, gray-haired, very proper-looking woman in her mid-fifties. She was immaculately dressed; her hair looked as if she had just left the beauty parlor.

My God, what had I gotten myself into? This woman looked like she could pass for a matron in a reform school. Maybe I could see her as a receptionist in an accounting firm, but I couldn't imagine her wrestling a dog in a veterinary clinic.

"Come on in," she invited cordially.

"Doris, this is Dr. Dave Perrin, the new veterinarian in town. Dave, this is my friend, Doris Currie."

"Glad to meet you, Dr. Perrin." Doris was nervous. She extended her hand, and I was surprised by the firmness of her grip.

"Good to meet you too, Doris." I was lying. All I wanted to do was get out of there!

"Come on in and sit down," she invited, showing us into a living room that was as orderly and well groomed as she was.

"Would you like something to eat—coffee perhaps?"

"No, thank you," I responded. "I just stuffed myself on a huge piece of Ruth's trifle cake."

"Speak for yourself, Dr. Perrin," Gordon groused. "I'd love a coffee."

Doris returned with coffee for Gordon. She carried his cup on a serving tray next to a cream pitcher, a sugar bowl, and a plate of chocolate chip cookies.

Gordon smiled. Holding the coffee cup in his right hand, he grabbed a few cookies with his left. "Just set the cookies over here," he smirked. "Dr. Perrin's obviously not interested in them!"

We all chuckled nervously, then the room fell silent and Doris and Gordon looked at me expectantly.

"How long have you lived in Creston, Doris?"

"My parents moved here from Woodstock, Ontario, when I was only a year and a half. I've lived here ever since."

"Have you worked on the farm all of that time? Or have you had any other job experience?"

Doris smiled and there was reverence to her tone when she continued. "I went to school with Stu; we got married in 1941. We lived in a little house up the road a bit, and when they upped the rent to ten dollars a month we built here. Stu bought this farm from his dad after he was discharged from the air force in 1945. He was wounded in the war and treated with sulfonamides.

That landed him with chronic nephritis, and he lived with it for twenty-odd years before he finally went on dialysis."

Doris stopped and tears welled up. She took a deep breath, then continued with resolve. "I guess I've been pretty much a housewife, a farmer, and a mother for my three children. In the later years, I spent my time looking after Stu. At first we went back and forth to Trail for dialysis. When they came up with the home units, I took training as a renal technician, and we started doing it here."

She stopped for a moment to stare out the window. "Stu died in March."

Listening to her talk, I began to lose my reservations about hiring her. She had not had an easy life and had stuck with caring for a family and operating this farm. Maybe she'd be just as loyal and hardworking an employee as she had been a wife and mother.

"So when do you think you'd be able to start?" I asked, breaking an uneasy silence.

"Well, I don't have anything keeping me from starting right away." There was a hint of surprise and excitement in her voice. "I think it's time to get on with my life and quit moping around this house."

"Good, would you like to start tonight or tomorrow morning?"

"Pardon me?"

"I know this is Saturday night, but it just so happens that I have a surgery that has to be done fairly soon. It's a kitten that got his front leg badly mutilated, and I'm afraid I'm going to have to amputate it."

"Oh." Doris gave Gordon a nervous look. "Well, I'm planning to go to church in the morning, but I guess we could do it tonight."

"Okay, we'll give it a try." I slowly rose from the sofa. "If this surgery doesn't bother you and we don't have to scrape you off the floor, it's not likely any of the others will either. I'm not sure how busy we're going to be at the start—it may be just part-time. If it gets slow, you can always bring your knitting."

I felt strangely relieved with the decision to hire Doris. She had a presence about her that I found reassuring. It would be good to have her on board.

"I have nothing set up in town yet for surgeries, but if you don't mind driving out to West Creston, we can make do there."

"Could you do it here?" Doris offered.

Gordon shot me an I-told-you-so look.

"I don't see why not, if you don't mind. I could do it right over there on the countertop."

"Well, you know, I have the sink and everything set up in the spare room where we used to do Stu's dialysis. How about there?"

"Sounds good to me."

By the time Gordon had given me a ride back to his place and I had returned with Albert, Doris had completely cleared the counter.

"I'm afraid I don't have much of an idea of what to expect. I guess if this were in an old western movie, I'd be boiling water and ripping up bedsheets for bandages."

"To be honest with you, you're not the only one who doesn't know quite what to expect! This is the first leg I've ever amputated, and it'll be the first time I've done a major surgery like this with just an injectable anesthetic. At the vet college, there'd be no way this cat would be done without an endotracheal tube and a gas anesthetic machine."

"Oh dear." Doris gave me a meek smile and wrung her hands. "This is going to be quite the evening, isn't it?"

"If it's any consolation, almost every surgery I do is breaking new ground. It's truly amazing how well things have been turning out!"

"That's reassuring to hear."

Doris grabbed a dishcloth and began scrubbing at a counter that was already sparkling clean, while I rummaged in the car and returned with all my anesthetic and surgical supplies.

"We'll premed Albert first."

"Oh my," Doris groaned, when she saw the wound. "I can see why you have to amputate it—that's plain disgusting!"

Albert was obviously feeling better, and the moment he was on the counter, turned to lick gently at the gash at the base of his tail.

"There's a boy, Albert." I grasped his hind leg and administered the premedication.

"Why, he never even felt that! He kept right on washing himself."

I diluted a bottle of Pentothal with saline. Taking up three milliliters, I diluted it once again and set it on the counter. Placing the pack of instruments on the end of the table, I instructed Doris on how she was to open it without reaching over and possibly contaminating them. I explained that she would have to open the gloves and the drapes in a similar fashion.

"It's not as if this is a sterile surgery site by any means, but the cleaner we are, the less chance we have of ending up with an infection. When we're dealing with bone surgery, we're extremely careful. There aren't many things uglier than working with an infected bone."

Within twenty minutes, Albert was very obviously sedated. His eyes were once again reduced to slits; his head rested fully on his forepaw.

"We'll do everything we can with just sedation before I inject the Pentothal. That way, we'll be able to cut down considerably on how much anesthetic we have to use. It'll be less dangerous for Albert."

I cautiously turned him over so that his mutilated leg was uppermost. This time, he just lay there. Applying surgical scrub to the dried edges of the wound, I gently worked loose some of the debris and smeared more soap over the fur adjacent to the wounds. I flexed the double-edged razor blade to a slightly bowed position, then ran it down both edges of the wound by his tail, shaving the hair cleanly away.

"I've never seen anyone use a razor blade that way," Doris exclaimed.

"I learned this trick from Dr. Croxall, the veterinarian from Nelson. It gives you a cleaner wound edge, and all the hair sticks together so that you can remove it easily. If you try doing this with the clippers, you end up with little hair fragments all over your wound that are almost impossible to pick out."

Within a matter of minutes, the kitten was denuded of hair over the base of his tail and over his right shoulder. I positioned him next to the sink, and with the tap running warm water, kept picking debris from the wound and rinsing it with gauze.

"Doris, could you squirt on soap whenever I ask for it?"

She was getting into the cleaning of the wound with a great deal of interest.

"There's something sticking out of the hole up there by the end of the bone. Yes, that's it. You've got it."

I pulled a long whitish object from deep beneath the bone and held it up to the light.

"My word, what's that?"

"It's a feather," I replied, after closer scrutiny. "His owner found him under a fan in his chicken barn."

"Imagine that—the poor thing."

"We've done about all we're going to do without the anesthetic." I picked aggressively at some debris that stuck tenaciously to the wound margins. In his tranquilized state, Albert had been tolerant of my endeavors, but I had now reached the point of needing instruments.

"I'm going to give him the first injection, Doris. But after I get scrubbed up, if he needs more anesthetic, you'll have to give it to him. I made this up so it's very dilute—that'll give us a wider margin for error, and we'll be less likely to overdose him. Make sure you inject it gradually and only a little at a time."

I began a slow, deliberate administration of the Pentothal. Albert clenched then slackened his jaw. His body relaxed. I waited a few moments, then firmly squeezed the toes of his hind leg. His reaction was detached, but he had definitely felt discomfort and been able to move.

I forced open his jaw and pulled out his tongue. His mouth was dry and clear of mucous and the color was much pinker than it had been earlier. His breathing was regular. I injected just a bit more Pentothal. Waiting a moment, I gave his toes another firm squeeze—no reaction.

"Doris, how about you scrubbing the area where I'm going to make the incision? We'll get rid of as much of this contaminated debris as possible, then work toward making it a cleaner environment."

She grasped the kitten's foot and began scrubbing as if she'd been at it all her life. "How aggressive do you want me to get with the stuff that's really caked on?"

"He can't feel what you're doing. Everything you're holding on to is going to be gone after the amputation, so just do the best you can to get down to bare flesh—even if you have to scrape it off with a fingernail."

Without a moment's hesitation, Doris continued her task, alternately squirting the reddish-brown soap over the leg and working at the debris. Watching her progress out of the corner of my eye, I carefully opened the surgery pack.

"Make sure you remember not to touch the instruments, Doris. It's amazing how often you'll feel like reaching over and handing me something. In most surgeries, we try to avoid even bending over them. For routine procedures where we're not dealing with contaminated wounds, I use a mask and a cap as well. But when you pick feathers from your wound, you can forget the possibility of sterile surgery."

"How does this look?"

"That's probably as good as you're going to get it. How about lifting the leg up just a little more and scrubbing it better underneath? I'll have to cut through the skin under there as well."

While Doris finished her scrub, I opened a pair of gloves and a package of cotton corner drapes. I laid them on the counter next to a spool of gut and a spool of synthetic suture.

I gave Albert's foot one final squeeze. Donning my gloves, I spread out my instruments so that I could see them at a glance. I applied the drapes so that the haired portion of Albert's upper body was covered. I wrapped the mangled remains of the lower leg to prevent further contact with it and flexed the leg toward the inside to expose the fractured end of the humerus. On closer inspection, I could see the bone was fractured lengthwise for a considerable distance up the leg. Although the fragments were still attached, they were quite unstable.

"We'll amputate the bone up here." I wiggled the end of the humerus to show Doris the line of the fracture.

She moved in closer to get a better view. "Are you going to cut the whole leg off up there?" she asked, obviously not the least distressed by the sight of the exposed tissues.

"No, we'll want the muscles to be quite a bit longer so we can fold them down over the end of the bone to act as a cushion for the stump."

I flexed the fragment, and it easily broke away from the remaining bone leaving a sharp, jagged end. With a pair of forceps, I continually broke off small pieces until the bone stump was blunted.

"Do you see the vessel that's pulsating down there? That's the brachial artery. And that's the vein and this little white string over here's the radial nerve."

"That's pretty neat."

"I'm going to need a package of that three 0 gut, Doris . . . That's the one in the gold package," I prompted. "Just slip your fingers between the two layers and fold back until I can grab the inner package."

I pulled the suture material free and ran it through my fingers to straighten the kinks. Guesstimating the length of the muscle tissue that I would require to cover the bone fragment, I passed the needle under the artery and vein and through a portion of muscle and carefully tied them off. Repeating the procedure, I placed another ligature about a half-inch lower and cut the vessels between them. With a pair of curved scissors, I isolated and severed one muscle at a time.

"Why isn't there more bleeding? I was expecting to see blood spurting all over."

"It's surprising how little the muscle tissue actually bleeds when it's cut. Usually, it doesn't do much more than ooze unless you tackle a major vessel."

"Amazing."

"There's one that would bleed." I pointed out a vein and tied it off.

Soon, all that kept the end of the leg attached was the skin on the under part. Leaving it as long as possible, I trimmed through the attached portion and tossed the amputated limb aside. I folded the muscles beneath the end of the bone and sutured them in place.

"I need some of the other suture now, Doris, if you don't mind." I pointed to the spool of Vetafil on the counter. "Pop off the lid, then grab the suture material and pull it straight up."

Doris did as she was instructed and when she had pulled a couple of inches from the spool I grabbed it and cut it below her fingertips. Pulling out another few feet, I cut it off and threaded it through a needle. I draped the skin over the exposed muscle tissue, trimmed the excess away, and tacked it together.

"He just twitched his ear," Doris volunteered. "Should I give him some more anesthetic?"

"No, I'll be just a couple of minutes. That's almost perfect timing."

As I finished suturing the stump wound, Albert was indeed starting to recover. He made a few feeble attempts to move first his front, then his hind legs. I could feel a smile coming on as I pulled off my gloves.

Albert was going to be just fine. And better still, so was Doris!

Moving In

"O H DEAR," MOANED DORIS, as she surveyed the dingy little room. "Talk about your fixer-upper!"

"Pretty depressing, isn't it? Do you think there's any hope?"

Doris didn't say a thing. We walked to the center of the room and paused under a lonely, flickering fluorescent light fixture. The walls and ceiling had been tastefully covered with rolled roofing and painted an institutional green. Its surface rippled and bulged in waves depending on where the glue had been applied. The indoor-outdoor carpeting, a reddish-brown color reminiscent of bargain-brand catsup, was covered with debris and stained by a filthy traffic pattern.

"You know," Doris started, "I came into this building dozens of times when it was Gunnar Larsen's Photo Studio, and I never got the impression it was such a dump. It's amazing how much different I feel now that I'm faced with the prospect of spending a lot of time here. I never gave it a thought when I dropped off a roll of film."

"Any brilliant ideas?"

"Well, when Stu and I moved into our first house in Erickson, the walls were covered with this same stuff, and we just plastered it all with wallpaper—it hides a multitude of sins." Doris's eyes sparkled as she shifted her gaze from one corner of the room to the other. She had the look of a woman about to head off on a shopping spree, and I could almost hear the wheels turning.

I gazed around the room, fighting a tremendous urge to pack up and run. After all, no one was keeping score. If I disappeared right now, no more than a couple dozen people would even know . . .

Doris interrupted my train of thought. "Maybe we should go down to Creston Hardware and look at the wallpaper. I was in there just the other day and noticed they had a new selection in. I looked at some to put up in my bedroom, but decided against it."

Creston Hardware was a hallmark family business run by Jack Barnes and his two sons, Morley and Bob. It occupied an old concrete building that had been poured in the late twenties and had a selection of everything from brass screws to living room sofas. It was only half a block from the office, and I was beginning to envision wear patterns in the sidewalk from our location to theirs.

Within the hour, Doris and I returned so laden with provisions that Bob Barnes trailed along behind us carrying a mop, a bucket, and a myriad of cleaning supplies.

"Watch your step," I warned Bob as he approached the threshold. "My landlord has a few boards to replace."

Bob stood back, drinking in the glory of the ratty old building. "We just happen to have a sale on paint coming up," he mused, looking up at the huge scrolls of gray paint that were peeling from the false front. "It looks as if you're going to need a few gallons."

"I'll keep that in mind." I relieved him of his burden and threw it in the corner.

"Well, Doris, I'm going to have to leave you with this for a while. I have an appointment at the bank in five minutes."

Doris looked at me helplessly. It was truly difficult to know where to start!

I stood outside the bank building for several moments gathering my thoughts. Up until now, I hadn't really made much of a financial commitment to the establishment of my practice. Other than the few supplies that I'd been able to pay for with cash, the only other thing I was out was my time. At this point in my career, I still had great difficulty putting a lot of value on that— after all, it wasn't long ago that I had been a lowly student, and everyone knows what they're worth! Borrowing money was going to change things in a big way.

I felt conspicuous as I walked into the cavernous room where tellers worked diligently along the right side and long lines of customers waited. I was certain that everyone was staring at the tall, lanky newcomer approaching the reception desk. I was grateful when the manager's secretary acknowledged my presence and showed me to an oak door with a frosted glass panel in the center of it. Across the width was stenciled T. M. Hall, Manager. She knocked and immediately opened the door for me.

The manager was on the phone when I entered. He was a slight, white-haired, balding man with hawkish features that for all the world suited the role he was playing. I stood there a few moments, feeling very much like I was back in high school standing before the principal. He looked up for a moment, plucked off his wire-rimmed glasses, and by extending them, pointed me to a chair. He carried on with his conversation as if I weren't there.

My mind was whirling as I rehearsed my pitch. It hadn't occurred to me to put my plans down on paper, to actually have numbers beside the things that I wanted to buy. I certainly could have, because over the past few days I had ordered most of the things I would require to open my office doors.

"So what can I do for you, young man?" he asked, hanging up the phone.

Pushing his short legs out from the desk, he leaned back into a large swivel chair that engulfed his slight frame. He plunked his glasses onto the end of his nose and peered over them at me. The tone of his voice and the way he emphasized the words young man made me uneasy.

"My name is Dave Perrin," I began hesitantly. "I'm starting a veterinary practice in town, and I'm interested in borrowing enough money to get things off the ground. My plans aren't elaborate but I need a new car, some equipment, and some basic instruments."

"And what, Mr. Perrin, do you plan on offering the bank for collateral?" He was making no attempt whatsoever to put me at ease. I was surprised that he hadn't even bothered to introduce himself.

"The majority of the loan would be for the car, and I assume you would have a lien on that," I started, "and the remainder would be for equipment that the bank could market if necessary. I've just spent the last seven years as a student, so you can appreciate that I don't have a lot of assets to put up for collateral."

"I assumed that might be the case, Mr. Perrin," he replied matter-of-factly.

"Look, I could see that if I came in here with an airy-fairy proposal for thousands of dollars' worth of equipment, you could question my chances of success, but I'm talking about starting small. I'm a professional person who has already invested a lot of time and money in my future, and I have every intention of being successful. I have more than enough cash flow to cover the amount that I need to borrow, and I'm certainly not one to live extravagantly."

"I'm sorry, Mr. Perrin," he said, with a self-congratulatory smile. "But I'm not prepared to offer you any hope of a loan with our bank. I'm afraid that I personally don't put a lot of value on university degrees."

"Well, that was short and sweet!" I vaulted to my feet. "And I have to say from what I've seen of you, that if you were the last banker on earth, I wouldn't deal here."

I was through the door when he calmly added, "It has been a pleasure dealing with you, Mr. Perrin."

I wheeled around to catch his smug smile. His insolent eyes peered over the same silly glasses.

"Look, Mr. Hall," I snarled, "to you it's Dr. Perrin!"

I slammed the door. I'd taken half a step toward the exit when I heard the crash. Turning with a start, I could see that the oak door no longer had a frosted glass panel, and although Mr. Hall still peered from behind the wire-rimmed glasses, he was no longer smiling.

I stomped from the bank, aware that every eye in the place was focused on my retreating figure. My face burning with humiliation, and my heart pounding, I walked up the block to Veitch Realty. I was still furious when I sat down to tell my story to Gordon and Ruth.

"Well, I could have told you not to go there," Gordon blurted with a hearty laugh. "This is Creston—your opposition banks there!"

THE YAHK CIRCUS

E HAD ALMOST FINISHED a long morning of rectal palpations at the Partington dairy farm when the call came through. The telephone company had yet to install a phone in my office, and this was another of those miraculous calls that was passed from one farmer to the next until I was finally located.

"It's for you, Dave," Jean yelled over the high-pitched whine of the compressors.

"Dr. Perrin, this is Mrs. Lennard from out to Yahk. I got a little horse that's bin hurt. The kids found 'im layin' down all caught in his tether chain. When we got 'im up, his leg was stickin' out funny. He can't walk on it and just hops 'round on his good legs."

"Where does the leg change angles—at the top or at the bottom?" I was trying to visualize where the leg was fractured.

"Halfway up—near where it bends in the middle."

"Near the hock?"

"I guess—don't know the parts of a horse too good. Kin you come right now?"

"I'll be leaving here shortly; we're all but finished."

After getting directions from Mrs. Lennard on how to find her house, I returned to the Partingtons and a cow that I was treating for a uterine infection.

I was ecstatic that many of the dairymen in the Creston Valley had embraced the idea of a routine herd health program for their cattle. On a monthly basis, the farmer would pick out cows that had calved recently, been bred more than thirty-five days, or had multiple breedings. I would examine them by inserting my gloved hand into their rectums to check their reproductive tracts for signs of abnormalities or pregnancy. Cows that were sick or just not performing up to expectation were also examined.

The goal was to pick up problems early and enhance the likelihood that the cows would perform well and calve on a regular basis. This made it possible to increase the amount of milk a cow yielded in her lifetime and reduce the amount of money that it cost to produce it.

At the end of every herd health, the cows that were found to have uterine infections were infused with antibiotics. Scrubbing the vaginal region of the last cow, I held her tail to one side and passed the tip of a two-foot infusion pipette through the vulva to the os of the cervix. Pushing through the rectum with my other hand, I expelled jets of manure to the barn floor. Once the stool was evacuated, the rectal wall fit like a glove. I was then able to grab the cervix, which lay directly below, and thread the pipette through the cervical rings and into the uterus.

"Okay, Jean." I held the end of the pipette so she could flush in the syringe full of tetracyclines. "I guess that's it for today."

"Thanks, Dave. Hope we don't have to see you before next month."

The half-hour drive to Yahk gave me the opportunity to reflect on my limited experience in equine orthopedics. I had gone to veterinary college thinking that I might want to work exclusively with horses. After the first two years, I gradually changed my mind. Observation had convinced me that horses as patients were the most cantankerous of any of the species that I would be called to work on. They were totally without patience for their own inabilities and extremely difficult to reason with.

I thought back to an incident when I was still a third-year student at the Western College of Veterinary Medicine at Saskatoon. A thoroughbred filly had broken her right hind leg midshaft through the cannon bone, and Dr. Larry Kramer had just finished an arduous session of surgery to repair it when I arrived on the scene. His face was a portrait of concern as he viewed before and after X rays of a fracture site that had been carefully girded by bone plates. The plates were secured meticulously by chains of screws on both ends of the fracture, a repair that would have satisfied any orthopedic surgeon. Perusing those radiographs with a half-dozen other students, I felt proud to be a part of a profession that could accomplish such a fantastic feat. Truly proud!

We peered through the crack in the recovery room door as the filly made her first movements. When she was able to support herself on her sternum, the observers hushed in anticipation. Within minutes, she would be on her feet and everyone would know whether or not the repair could hold up to that first crucial test.

When it became obvious that she was ready to stand, two interns ventured onto the spongy surface of the recovery room floor, ready to support her. Suddenly, she lurched to her feet. Bearing most of the weight on her good hind leg, she steadied herself. Five minutes passed and everything was looking great.

The filly appeared determined to try out her injured limb. She began with a peculiar rocking motion, shifting weight from her good leg to her repaired one. She tried part of her weight, then almost all of it. Finally, she lifted her good one off the ground about six inches and held it. The repair appeared to be holding up to her test. Then as we all looked on in horror it bowed and collapsed. The injury was considered to be irreparable, and the filly was euthanized.

Her leg was on display during pathology rounds the next afternoon. Beside a view box with before and after radiographs, lay two ends of bones still held by one twisted plate.

Following the directions that I had jotted down on a scrap of paper, I drove through the village of Yahk, past the gas station, and over a bridge. Immediately after crossing the river, in the midst of a grove of old cotton-woods, was the white house that Mrs. Lennard had described—an old building of clapboard construction. The roof had once been cedar shingles, but now it was patched with an array of materials ranging from tar paper to oil cans, which had been cut open and spread flat. The white paint on the siding was checked and peeling, exposing the gray of the boards beneath it.

The narrow driveway that led up to the house had been plucked of stones, but the surrounding area was a sea of boulders. Wherever the mounds of rock were thin, an automobile had been parked and scavenged. Some cars lay on their wheels, some on their roofs, some on their sides. Nowhere was there a vehicle that appeared to be in running condition.

I pulled up in front of the house and Mrs. Lennard appeared. She was a pleasant-looking woman in her forties.

"The pony's over to the pasture," she said, leading me through piles of stones toward the riverbank.

Pasture indeed! I stumbled over boulders the size of my head and walked around others that would weigh over a ton. The Lennard pasture was no more than the Moyie riverbed at low tide.

71

As we neared the river, I could see a pony surrounded by a half-dozen children. Sitting on a rock not far from the group was a portly, gray-haired fellow I presumed to be Mr. Lennard. His right arm was suspended in a sling fashioned from part of a well-worn bedsheet.

"He's a prince of a pony, that one," Mrs. Lennard was saying. "The kids kin do absolutely anythin' with 'im. He was fine when we put 'im out here at nine this mornin'. The kids come over to fetch 'im and found 'im just layin' with his broken leg under 'im and the chain wrapped 'round. We got 'im untangled but the leg just kinda hangs there and dangles funny—shur hope that he's gonna be all right or them kids'll be some upset."

"The chain saw!" yelled Mr. Lennard, as we came within earshot.

"Pardon me?"

"The chain saw!" he repeated with agitation. "I cut my damned cords with the chain saw. Just got back to work too—only my second day. Can't wiggle the damned things yet." He thrust the arm in front of my face to show me the motionless fingers.

"First me, now the bloody horse!" Mr. Lennard walked away shaking his head, then turned on his heel. "Bloody hell, it makes ya wonder what'll happen next. It always comes in threes, ya know."

As I stooped to examine the horse's leg, Mrs. Lennard and the children crowded close in an effort not to miss a thing. Mr. Lennard stood back, oblivious to what I was doing, and droned on about his miseries with the compensation board.

Gently manipulating the flopping end of the leg, I could see that the problem was not a fracture at all but a dislocation at the level of the tibial tarsal joint.

Not quite what I had expected; not what I had expected at all! I had never seen or heard of a situation similar to this, but nonetheless, here we were.

At this point in my career, my bedside (or should I say stallside) manner was in its infantile stage. An acquired gift, it is that intangible something that allows an open rapport and makes everyone—patient, client, and doctor—feel more at ease.

"The problem is a dislocation. The pony must have gotten the chain wrapped around his hock; then he fell over sideways. He didn't break a bone, but he tore the ligaments that hold the bones together. They pulled apart and are now badly overlapped."

The whole family by this time was peering over my shoulder. As no one spoke up or questioned me, I continued, "This is the joint where most of the movement in the hock takes place, so an arthritis here would be very serious!"

No one commented. I soon felt obligated to resume talking. "There's not much doubt that even if it were possible to repair this dislocation, the pony would end up with arthritis in the joint and not be good for riding."

Silence. Damn it—someone could make a comment, ask a question. They all just stared at the pony's dangling leg. Not one of the family moved from his position at my elbow. I was engulfed by an overwhelming feeling of frustration; after all, I had known from the beginning that this was going to be a euthanasia. Surely, they weren't expecting me to repair it! Hadn't I told Mrs. Lennard on the phone that there probably wasn't much I could do with it? Why didn't someone say something?

I took yet another run at it. "I'm afraid he'll have to be put to sleep."

I was met with the same impassive stares that I had received previously. Pressing on, I addressed Mrs. Lennard directly. "Is that what you would like me to do? Would you like me to put him to sleep?"

Without displaying the slightest emotion, she nodded her head and responded simply, "Okay."

Baffled by her lack of emotion—by everyone's lack of emotion—I picked my way through the boulders to my car. I dug through the box of syringes until I found a sixty-milliliter size, slipped on a fourteen-gauge needle, and drew it full of euthanasia solution. After drenching a swab in alcohol, I trekked back to the others.

As I approached, I noted that the family was more talkative when I wasn't around. I assumed they had been discussing my diagnosis, but no one appeared the least bit disturbed that their pony was soon to be lying dead at their feet.

"Wouldn't it be better for the children if they were to go back to the house?" I asked Mrs. Lennard, thinking that surely to God they had some feelings for the horse.

She answered me with her own question, "They won't be in yer way, will they?"

Taking this as permission for them to stay, I asked the children to stand back, blocked the jugular vein at the bottom of the horse's neck, and wiped with the alcohol swab.

Just as I was about to drive the needle into the vein, Mrs. Lennard spoke. "What're you gonna do with Freckles when he's sleepin'?"

A cold shiver ran up my spine as I realized that the Lennards and I had not been speaking the same language. No one had the faintest idea that the solution I was about to inject would kill Freckles.

Stepping back, I turned to Mrs. Lennard. "You obviously don't understand what I was suggesting. What I meant was that I don't think the pony has much of a chance for a normal life, and that he should be put to sleep permanently—destroyed!"

"Kill 'im?"

As I nodded, the entire family burst into tears. Not one of the children was left with dry eyes. Mrs. Lennard had her head on the pony's mane and was weeping uncontrollably. Desperate for justification and moral support, I turned to Mr. Lennard.

"I doubt if there's any way I'd be able to fix it even if I tried," I stammered.

It was to no avail; Mr. Lennard was crying in harmony with the rest of his family. Had I the sense that the Lord gave the lowest of creatures, I would have quietly listened until they could appreciate the wisdom of my advice and then performed my terrible duty.

I blathered on. "There's such little chance that he would be normal even if I could get it back in place. You wouldn't want to see him crippled and limping around for the rest of his life?"

Pausing again, I hoped that someone would say something to make it easier—something that would take the responsibility for their grief from my shoulders. It wasn't to be. Sobs from one and all.

Justifying their tears as much to myself as to them, I muttered, "The only thing we could possibly do would be to anesthetize him and see how well it would reduce, but it may never stay in place."

The trap was sprung! Even though I was sure no one had listened to a single thing I'd said all day, they stopped crying in unison, and Mrs. Lennard said, "Okay."

74

Okay! Okay what? What in hell had I gotten myself into now? Why had Mrs. Lennard chosen that particular moment to pay attention to my ramblings?

"Where'll ya want to do it?" asked Mr. Lennard. "Do ya want 'im over to the house? I think he kin hop that far."

Stunned by the rapid train of events, all I could manage was a nod. As I had come prepared for little more than a euthanasia, it was necessary to return to the office for the materials that I'd need to perform this minor miracle.

My inner voice harangued me all the way to town. This was a fool's errand. I probably wouldn't get the damned leg back in place to start with; even if I did get good reduction, he was bound to get so much arthritic change that he'd be permanently lame. Besides that, it was obvious that the Lennards couldn't afford to be spending money on that horse. They looked as if their ends were a long way from meeting already.

When I arrived back in Creston, Doris was still chipping away at the filth in the back room. Wandering around with a trouble light in one hand and a scrub rag in the other, she had the arborite on the countertop gleaming. From the look of the improvements, it was obvious she had had little time for knitting.

"I found a light switch under the sink, but I can't find anything that it turns on."

Ignoring the mystery of the hidden light switch, I got working on the problem at hand. The drug salesman from Clarke Cote had left me a couple of packages of a muscle relaxant called glycerol guacoate, and I busied myself with preparing it.

I juggled the plastic pouch of the medication back and forth over the narrow neck of a bottle of saline in an attempt to empty the icing sugar–like material inside with a minimal chance of contaminating it. After ten minutes of patient manipulation and a two- or three-minute temper tantrum, the final lumps of glycerol guacoate passed into the bottle.

Getting the material through the bottleneck was one thing; putting it into solution was yet another. I shook that bottle until my arm was sore but was only able to decrease the sludge layer from an inch and a half to a half-inch plus lumps. No manner of contortion, no burning glare, no discharge of four-letter words was the key to getting that product into solution.

Certain that using saline rather than sterile water had led to poor solubility, I poured the concoction down the drain and started over with the second bag of muscle relaxant and my one and only bottle of sterile water. Transferring the glycerol guacoate from bag to bottle went no smoother than it had the first time and, to my dismay, the lumps and the sludge that sat in the bottom were no more soluble in distilled water than they were in saline.

"Doris! Could you come and shake this damned bottle while I hunt up the rest of the stuff I need?"

Doris had wisely stayed as far away from the commotion in the back room as possible and surrendered her dust rag with considerable reluctance. Leaving her to deal with the sludge, I busied myself digging through boxes for the potions that would be required for my "magic hock" routine.

A general walk-through of a procedure in my mind had become a very useful technique and the more detailed my imaging, the less likely I was to forget something vital. First the tranquilizer—I already had Atravet in the car. Two grams of Biotal to mix with the sludge should put the horse down. I placed two bottles of Biotal in a cardboard box and returned to the visualizing. The horse was now stretched out on the ground. I had a rope pulling on the bottom of the leg, a rope anchoring his hip, and either a tug-of-war team or a come-along stretching his leg out.

Along with the image of the chain block appeared a picture of Gordon. Surely he'd know where I could come up with one on short notice.

Okay, the horse's leg was repaired and back in position. I'd wrapped it with padding and was now applying a cast. A bag of cast padding and a carton of Velroc went into the box.

"I'm going down to Gordon's to see if he can come up with a chain block, Doris!" She was still in the back room, vigorously agitating the bottle of sludge.

An hour later, my Volkswagen was on its way to Yahk with Gordon in front, a chain block at his feet, and Doris in the back beside a box of materials.

"I'm sure glad you warmed that bottle of glycerol guacoate and got it into solution, Doris. I would really have been up the creek without that stuff."

The trip passed quickly with my giving Doris and Gordon a description of what was about to happen with the horse: how it was likely to be a very difficult case. How horses were troublesome patients. I had finished telling my story of the filly with the broken leg when we drove through Yahk. Passing over the little bridge, I was met with a sight that sent shivers up my spine. I pulled over to the side of the road and buried my head in my hands. My whole body shook as though I had suddenly been thrown naked into a prairie snow-drift.

"Holy . . . ," muttered Gordon. "The whole town is here."

The whole town indeed! The driveway was plugged with vehicles. People were coming and going from the yard. A car pulled up and two women got out carrying plates of sandwiches and an assortment of other goodies.

"They've turned this into a bloody carnival," I moaned. "There's no way I'm going in there. This is just plain ridiculous!"

"You have to!" Doris interjected. "What about the pony?"

"What about me? I can't work with a bunch of idiots running everywhere. I'm supposed to go out there and anesthetize a horse for the first time in front of all those people." I was on the verge of tears.

The comment about anesthetizing my first horse unnerved both my companions, and I noticed them exchange a worried glance.

Before I could give further consideration to running, Mr. Lennard appeared in his driveway madly waving his left arm.

"Make way! Make way! The vet's here!"

Taking a deep breath, I drove up the narrow path he had cleared through the vehicles and bystanders until we stopped next to the pony. Freckles stood on his good leg, his head and neck cuddled by a swarm of children.

I did my best to shoot an accusing eye at Mr. Lennard. I felt like wringing the old fool's neck. What right had he to turn this surgery into a circus sideshow? The last thing I needed was a big audience.

My glare was totally lost on Mr. Lennard. He had prepared a show for all of Yahk, and he wasn't about to fade from the spotlight for even a moment.

"What can we get for ya, Doc?" he asked. "Where do ya want to do him?"

Where did I want to do him? Probably about where any other rookie vet-erinarian would want to anesthetize his first horse—miles from all these rocks and people and old car bodies. How about the veterinary college on their padded recovery room floor, with Larry Kramer sitting at my elbow?

"Is there an area somewhere around the house that's free of rocks?" I finally asked him.

"Not really."

"Well, let's clear one then." I stooped to pick up the end of an old car bumper.

A half hour passed with Mr. Lennard diligently supervising the cleanup of his front yard. When we had most of the boulders plucked from a twenty-by-twenty-foot area around the horse, I could stall no longer.

"Bring Freckles ahead a couple more steps while I get the anesthetic."

The kids scattered as I approached, their eyes focused on the huge syringe I cradled in my hand. "Okay, guys, you back up now; it's time for Freckles to go to sleep. Gordon, could you hold the horse's head while I give the anesthetic?" My friend looked aghast as he realized his role was changing from spectator to participant and exchanged a nervous smile with Doris. He stepped up to grasp the halter shank.

"Hold him tight and support his weight until the last moment." I adjusted Gordon's hand on the halter, then stroked the jugular vein with an alcohol swab. "Remember that when he goes down, we want the bad side up."

Taking a deep breath, I thrust the needle into the vein, drew back the plunger until a jet of blood shot into the clear solution, then delivered the contents in one rapid, smooth injection.

Freckles stood with a bewildered look for a few seconds, then leaned back on the rope and sank to the ground. As he went down, a clamor rose from the crowd that by now completely encircled us.

"Boy, did you see that?"

"Is he ever good. Look at the way he put that horse to sleep!"

Freckles had gone down in a perfect position. His bad leg was uppermost, as was the needle, which sent a steady trickle of blood down his neck and onto the ground. He had been down for almost a minute and still hadn't taken a breath! I watched the steady rhythmic vibration of his thorax, which was a testament to the beating of his heart, and willed him to take a breath.

"Come on, you son of a b . . . breathe!" I muttered to myself. "Ahh, there he goes!"

The inspiration was deep—long, deliberate, almost dramatic. Feeling more confident now, I ran the air out of the intravenous tube and connected the glycerol guacoate solution to the needle that still protruded from the jugular vein.

The second, third, and fourth breaths followed the first with regularity. Allowing the muscle relaxant to flow at a steady rate, I passed the bottle to Gordon.

"Run about half in at this speed, Gord, then stop it. I'll let you know when we need some more."

I ran two loops of a one-inch cotton rope around the horse's upper thigh and tied the end to a nearby cottonwood tree. With a second rope, I placed a half hitch above and below the fetlock joint.

In need of another anchor point, I yelled into the crowd, "Who owns the blue four-wheel-drive pickup?"

A heavyset fellow on the edge of the crowd replied, "I do."

"Could you back it over here to give us something to pull against?" I continued stretching the rope out and hooked it to one end of the chain block.

With directions from the crowd, the driver maneuvered among the boulders until he had backed within about eight feet of the pony's leg.

"That should be fine!" I shouted, connecting the other hook of the chain block to the clevis on the truck hitch.

Hopping from the vehicle, the fellow grabbed the apparatus and let it be known that he was ready to go.

"Just snug it up," I directed, as he started the chains rattling. To Gordon I said, "Give him about half of what's left; he doesn't want to be feeling this."

The circle of spectators got closer and closer. My newly recruited assistant had a look of determination, and his hand lay poised on the chain awaiting my instruction.

"Okay, put more tension on."

As the pressure on the end of the leg was increased, the pony slid over the dirt toward the pickup until the rope in his groin held him firm.

"Hold it for a bit!" The leg was now as tight as a fiddle string, suspending the pony between the cottonwood tree and the pickup truck. To my amazement, the overlap of the tibial tarsal bone and the central tarsal bone was still almost three inches.

"Some more."

The tension on the leg was tremendous and the skin adjacent to the half hitches was taut and blanched. It was hard to believe that the contraction of the leg muscles could hold out against such force. Bracing my feet, I pulled backward on the hock, trying to replace its natural curvature.

"Some more yet." I held my breath and strained against the hock. I could feel beads of sweat trickling down the back of my neck.

"Almost, almost." The joint edges were almost in apposition. "A little more."

He increased the tension again, but it suddenly slackened as the truck slid forward.

"I'm out of purchase!" Sure enough, he had pulled the hook right up to the block itself.

"Okay, we better release it and try again. Can you drive the truck ahead a bit and park it more on an angle?"

He maneuvered his truck back and forth in the tight confines. If the vehicle were to slide now, it would have to be pulled almost sideways over the rock-strewn ground.

Stretching the leg again, we paused for four or five minutes with a constant pressure as I strained to put a curvature in the hock.

"Again." I wiped sweat from my forehead with the back of one hand while continuing to pull with the other. With the chain rattling and the body part stretching, the scene had a flavor of medieval torture. At this point, it wouldn't have surprised me if the leg had pulled in two.

"Again!"

This time when I heaved, the leg gave way with a resounding clunk and slid into place.

"Wow, look at that!" came a voice from the crowd. "I didn't think they were ever gonna get it."

"Neither did I," I muttered under my breath.

I felt my way around the outside of the joint. "Try releasing the pressure."

As the operator slackened the pressure on the chain block, I untied the leg and carefully flexed the hock.

"I'll be damned." The limb flexed freely—no crunching, no grinding. It even felt fairly stable. "Better give him the rest of the bottle, Gordon!" I pointed to the pony's head. "His eye's twitching. We aren't going to have much time left for the anesthetic."

As Gordon ran the rest of the muscle relaxer in, I brought casting material from the car and asked Mrs. Lennard for some warm water.

I measured enough stockinet to reach well above the hock. Sliding it over the pony's hoof, I pulled it tight and began making passes over top of it with cast padding. I reminded myself not to overdo it, as I remembered the first one we had applied in medical exercises back at college. Too much cotton had allowed our dog to literally step out of his cast before he had gone a dozen strides.

"Doris!" I was applying my last turn of cast padding. "See what Mrs. Lennard is doing about the water. She must have gotten lost!"

As Doris went searching, the pony made his first attempt to move. It wasn't much to worry about, merely a twitch of the front leg, but it was a warning that I was running out of time. Just as I was thinking of going in search of Doris, she appeared with my stainless steel bucket filled to the brim.

"Sorry it took so long. They don't have running water here, and Mrs. Lennard had to go to the neighbor's house to get it."

I plunged a roll of cast padding into the warm water, squeezed it several times to drain off the excess, and began applying the cast in a roundabout fashion.

The box of casting material was half gone before I realized I was in trouble. There wasn't enough here to put an acceptable cast on a large dog, never mind a horse!

"Doris! Could you head into town and see if you can bum some casting material from the hospital? I'll need at least another full box to finish this properly."

"I'll run you in," said the man with the blue truck. They jumped into the vehicle, and Gordon cleared a path through the crowd.

"What's the holdup? What's the holdup?" An abrasive red-haired man ventured from the crowd to see what was delaying the show. I gritted my teeth and tried to ignore him. It was only after another "What's the holdup?" that I replied tersely, "I've run out of casting material!"

"I've got lots of plaster of Paris at home."

"This isn't just plaster of Paris! It's special casting material—I'm sure you wouldn't have any at home."

"Do so!" He headed off in the direction of the highway.

The casting material had already hardened to a thin but flexible shell by the time he returned.

"There you go. Same as yours!" He dropped a box at my feet. "Got another one at the house if you need it."

Sure enough, Velroc green—extra fast-setting. Exactly the same as the one I had just used. Almost as if to look at the box of casting material, the pony raised his head and tried to sit.

"Easy, fellow, we're not quite finished with you yet." Hopping over the pony's body, I grabbed his halter, knelt on his neck, and held his head at right angles to the ground.

"Can you hold him like this, Gordon? I'm going to need at least fifteen minutes more before we can let him up." Gordon grabbed the halter and planted himself on Freckles's neck, anchoring him firmly to the ground.

"Just lean back a little more, Gord, in case he tries to strike with his front foot. If he struggles, just pull his head up toward you and lean back a little harder."

The pony behaved himself as if he knew what was good for him; the cast was applied and nicely hardening by the time he started moving again. This time, rather than holding him down, I folded his front legs under his body and propped him in a sitting position.

"What in the world are you doing with all that casting material, Paul?" Gordon asked the fellow who had miraculously produced the box of Velroc.

"Keep lots of stuff on hand," he replied matter-of-factly. "Broke my foot a couple of years ago when my medical run out. Cost me a fortune! What a rip-off for a cast. If I ever break anything again, I'll just fix it myself."

By the time Doris arrived on the scene with the extra casting material, the Lennards' yard had taken on the air of a carnival ground. A horseshoe pitch was well underway; tables were set up laden with cakes, cookies, and squares.

"You mean, I risked my life driving with this maniac, and you don't even need it!" Doris wailed. She looked as if she had endured a harrowing experience. Her normally well-groomed hair was windblown and hanging over her forehead; her face was drained of color. Her hands hung loosely at the side of her body, and in each she clutched a box of Velroc.

"Sorry, Doris, but look at him." I walked her to the side of the house where Freckles stood nibbling on bits of grass that the Lennard children had gathered. "He looks like he's going to make it."

"If you only knew!" She plunked the boxes down on the top of the car. "You have no idea what it was like."

A few minutes out of the blue truck did wonders for Doris's complexion. By the time the equipment was cleaned up, she was bubbling away about the trip.

"You've never in your life seen anyone drive like him—we passed every car in sight. I bet you can still find my handprints embedded in his dash."

"Let's get something to eat; I'm starved."

Mrs. Lennard offered us a piece of cake. It was a chocolate cake coated with a thick, fluffy layer of white icing, and my mouth watered at the sight of it.

"Just finished icin' it," she said with a smile. "Do you think he's gonna be all right, Dr. Perrin?"

"I sure hope so, Mrs. Lennard." I took a bite of the cake and continued with my mouth half full. "But only time will tell."

"Let me give you and the girls a hand," said Doris. She followed Mrs. Lennard into the kitchen.

Gordon and I had finished a sandwich and were just attacking another piece of Mrs. Lennard's cake when Doris came charging back from the kitchen. Her face was once more ashen, and she had lost her composure again.

"Don't eat it," she said to Gordon, who had the cake halfway into his mouth. "You wouldn't believe the kitchen! You've got to see it; I've never in my entire life seen anything like it." She gagged, suppressing the urge to retch. Clutching Gordon by the arm, she dragged him into the kitchen.

Mrs. Lennard's exit with a plateful of cookies gave us the opportunity to examine the source of Doris's distress. A quick peek said it all. The makeshift counter that held the remaining food at one end was piled with dirty dishes at the other. The table and countertops were buried in layer upon layer of filth. At the corner of the counter, the very tip of a spoon was visible, protruding through years of accumulated grime.

"An archaeologist's delight," I muttered.

"Yeah," Gordon responded. "You could excavate layer by layer to see what they had for supper each year at this time."

Still holding our cake in hand, Gordon and I followed Doris outside.

"I think I'm going to be sick," she said, rushing around the corner.
"What the hell," I declared, holding the cake up as a toast to Gordon.
"Here's looking at you." He devoured his piece whole.
"Good cake," I responded. "Real good cake!"

Virgin Territory

FEW NIGHTS OF WALLPAPERING and painting did wonders for the dreary little rooms that had become the clinic. I argued with Doris over the wallpaper—a black velvet pattern on off-white—but she insisted. Now that it was up, I had to admit that we probably couldn't have found a more appropriate camouflage. Gordon and Ruth showed up one evening as Doris and I were wallpapering in the gloom and, by the next afternoon, Gordon had installed four new fluorescent fixtures. For a Realtor, he was a man of many talents.

He also introduced me to the manager of the other bank in town and, within a few minutes, I had financing approved for the equipment that had already started to arrive. The telephone hookup proceeded more quickly in town than in West Creston, and the phone was beginning to monopolize Doris's time. We had postponed booking elective surgeries until the anesthetic machine and surgery table arrived, but now that they were here, the daybook began to fill with neuters and cat spays.

I never mentioned anything to Doris, but I was surprised and relieved to see no dog spays booked within the first few weeks. Because a spay is such a frequently performed surgery, most people have the misconception that it is easy to carry out—that something is simply snipped. To the contrary, the surgery is far more complicated than many other procedures that are considered major. Only because most veterinarians do large numbers of them do they seem routine.

I had spayed a cat at veterinary college, but had been relegated to the role of anesthetist for the ovariohysterectomy on the dog. While my partner waded around in our surgery dog's abdomen in search of her uterus, I watched the bag of the anesthetic machine expand and contract. My first spay here would be another of those giant steps into virgin territory!

During those first few days, Doris and I had been too preoccupied to pay much attention to what was going on next door. As time went by, however, we began to notice some strange things. Although there was a continual flow of traffic through Anthony's doors, it was rare to actually walk by and see him cutting hair.

"What on earth is that odor?" Doris asked, when I returned one afternoon from a farm call. "I've been smelling it all day. I made a trip to the bathroom about an hour ago, and it was so strong out there that I almost gagged!"

"We really are from a different generation, aren't we, Doris? Someone must be toking up next door."

"What do you mean?"

"That's the smell of weed, whacky tobaccy, marijuana!"

"Noooo!"

"I hope you haven't had any clients in here in the last few minutes; they'll think you were smoking weed in the back between customers."

"I haven't had anyone in lately," she worried, "but what if people actually think we're smoking that stuff? Are you sure?"

Within a few moments, she was wandering around the office with a can of Lysol, spraying for all she was worth.

Doris and I looked up and stared at one another.

"What's that ungodly noise?" I asked.

We had prepared a cat for a neuter. I had just showed Doris how to pluck the hair from his testicles and was finishing the last scrub of the surgery site, when the wailing began. At first, it was hard to determine what the noise was, but eventually we agreed—it had to be an accordion!

"I can't believe this." I laid the gloves out on the table. "Anthony's learning to play the accordion."

I finished the neuter and was waiting for the cat to wake up. The squawking and squealing that came through the wall was really beginning to annoy me. There didn't seem to be much pattern to the sounds.

"Surely he's not trying to play a tune. I haven't heard two notes yet that could possibly belong together!"

"I haven't either," agreed Doris.

"I can manage here. You sneak out and peek in Anthony's window to see what's going on."

Doris feigned a look of shock. "Spying on our neighbors was not part of the job description!"

"Neither was smoking dope, and you've been inhaling that all day!"

Doris snorted and left for the lab in a pretend huff. We were still using an extension cord for light in the back room, and I knew that she wouldn't be likely to stay in there for long.

"When's the landlord going to do something about a light back here?" she hollered. "It's ridiculous to have to drag this thing around."

"There's one there. If you can believe it, it's on the ceiling under that big sheet metal tray. Apparently, the upstairs renters let the bathtub run over and the water wrecked some of Gunnar Larsen's photo equipment. That big galvanized tray over your head was a plumber's answer to the problem."

"You've got to be kidding."

Within a few minutes, Doris returned with her jacket on.

"Can you cover the phone?" It was more a command than a request. "I'm going to slip down and get some more room deodorizer."

The cat was off the anesthetic machine and was beginning to come around. He made faint paddling motions with his front paws and was breathing more rapidly.

"I knew you couldn't resist going next door for a look," I laughed, pulling the cat's tongue out and removing the tube. "You're as curious as I am."

"Don't be silly! I'm no peeping Tom."

I had no sooner opened the kennel door to settle the cat than Doris burst back into the office.

"He looks like he's giving a kid lessons," she blurted, before she was even over the threshold. "There's a boy about ten or twelve sitting there, and Anthony's teaching him how to finger the keyboard."

Sure enough, Anthony was giving music lessons. Over the ensuing weeks, we were treated to about every possible squeak, squawk, and wail that could be manufactured by a man-made instrument. We had never heard evidence that Anthony actually knew how to play an instrument himself, but it wasn't stopping him from trying to teach others.

The pace in the office really began to pick up. We experienced no rude surprises, and I was doing enough of some procedures that they were actually becoming routine. I was surprised how accepting people were of our meager surroundings and how easily we could please them when we expended a bit of effort. One day around closing time, I was hanging a curtain to block off the surgery from the waiting area.

"Oh, by the way," Doris called from the back room, "I've booked a dog spay for tomorrow afternoon. I wasn't sure how long it would take to do one, so I put it down at three. Would you rather do it in the morning from now on, or should I just fit surgeries in where I can find room?"

My heart sank. I knew we were going to book spays sooner or later, but later would sound better than tomorrow! I stood up on the chair attempting nonchalance and managed to start one screw into the ceiling. I took a deep breath, and my heart rate slowed almost to normal.

"It was Max Sneider who called," Doris went on, "and his dog just had a litter of pups three weeks ago. He drowned them all as soon as they were born, and he doesn't want to deal with her getting pregnant again."

"Did he happen to say what kind of dog she was?" I was feeling so insecure about the procedure that I never even commented on the distasteful manner Mr. Sneider had chosen to dispose of the puppies.

"He lives just up the road from my place. I see her in the orchard all the time. She's one of those tan-colored hunting dogs—a little bit on the fat side."

A little bit on the fat side was putting it mildly! Mandy, the Sneiders' golden retriever, was obese; perched upside down on the tabletop, she looked more like a walrus than a dog.

I took more than the usual amount of time clipping and shaving the area for surgery; to tell the truth, I was stalling. Finally, I motivated myself to get on with it. The site was prepped, the drapes were in place, and the blade was fixed into the scalpel handle. The scalpel was poised over the most forward part of the incision.

Anthony couldn't have timed it better if he had been peeking through a hole in the wall! Just as I started my incision, there came the most unnerving blast on a horn.

"Oh no," Doris groaned, as the pitch changed. "Someone is practicing his scales."

As I made my incision through the skin and into the subcutaneous tissue, we bantered back and forth, arguing about whether we were being tormented by a trombone, a trumpet, or a French horn. We had finally decided on a trombone, when I got my first bleeder.

"My God, I'm not even into the abdomen yet and look at that sucker bleed." As I waded through the deep layer of fat on Mandy's abdomen, vessels lay like booby traps in a minefield to slow my progress. Anthony's student had finished his scales and we were into the second chorus of "Twinkle, Twinkle, Little Star" by the time I ligated the last vessel in the muscle layer and made my way into Mandy's abdomen.

"Will you look at that, Doris! She's got to be the fattest dog that I've ever seen on a surgery table."

"It makes me want to get started on a diet," Doris said, surveying the scrolls of fat that billowed forth from the dog's tummy.

Working my finger down the right side of Mandy's peritoneal cavity, I fished repeatedly for something that would fit the description of her uterus. Just when I was certain that the ligament I had applied traction to would produce the uterus for me, up popped a round pink blob that I recognized as the bladder. Our student next door was into the final throes of what I decided was "The Star-Spangled Banner."

"*Son of a bitch!*" My right foot found its way to the wall with four or five well-planted kicks. Doris froze, a look of horror on her face, then quietly made her way to the front and locked the door.

"The Star-Spangled Banner" came to an abrupt end, and an eerie silence pervaded the room. Now the only distracting noises were those of the traffic outside and the rhythmic click, click of the valves on the anesthetic machine as Mandy breathed in and out.

My incision had been lengthened a third and fourth time. The entire contents of Mandy's abdomen were displayed on the drapes in front of me before I finally found the pink strip of uterus floating in that ocean of blubber.

By this time, my gloves were slippery and gleaming with fat, and I was having a great deal of difficulty holding on to the tissues. My surgery notes and textbook had detailed the process: follow the uterus to its termination at the ovary, grasp the ovary firmly, and apply traction to rupture the uterovarian ligament that attaches it to the body at the level of the kidney.

That all sounded fine if you could see it, but in Mandy all those structures were enshrouded in gobs of fat. I could feel a solid, irregular structure buried deep in the blubber. Assuming it to be the ovary, I grasped it and began to pull. The textbook had mentioned mild traction; I wondered when applying mild traction became pulling like hell.

To me, mild traction occurred when tearing a piece of heavy paper towel or at the very most, when tying a shoe. Well, that was one tight shoelace! It finally ruptured with a pop that made Doris's eyes light up. She had been watching intently as I struggled to bring the ovary up and out of the abdomen. She quickly checked the color of Mandy's tongue in an attempt to conceal her concern.

"Just look at that fat," I whined, trying to imagine how the artery and vein that I was required to ligate would ever see the light of day.

My hands were shaking. I was startled by the fact that such a dramatic rupture could occur without doing permanent damage to the dog herself. I grabbed a sponge and began stripping away at the blubber to try and expose the vessels. My gloves were now so slippery with fat that I could hardly maintain my grip on the ovary. I had just found the vein when an accordion lesson began.

"Can you believe this?" I glanced at Doris in a plea for moral support. "This is supposed to be a routine procedure. Can you believe this?"

Doris shrugged her shoulders and rolled her eyes. The accordion lesson proceeded with the same squawking and squealing as did every other session. I could just see the kid wrenching those bellows back and forth and taunting the keys to scream louder and louder.

Trying to tune it out, I focused on the task of working the gauze back and forth and stripping the fat away to leave nothing but the artery and vein. I applied my clamps and tied off the vessels. Next, I cut the stump, held it with a clamp, and watched for signs of hemorrhage. Gently releasing the ligature, I began tearing through the broad ligament that suspends the uterus. Several vessels were larger than normal due to the recent pregnancy, and they had to be tied off as I went.

By the time I repeated the process on the other side, Doris was a nervous wreck. What with the squawks and squeals that penetrated the wall and my robust cursing as each new vessel sprang a leak, she was having difficulty focusing.

The severing of the uterine stump and closure of the abdomen were relatively uneventful and toward the end of the surgery we almost relaxed. The spay from hell was all but over! Mandy was recovering nicely, and most of the mess had been cleaned up when Doris took her leave.

"Are you all right without me, Dave? I'm sorry, but I've got to go to the bathroom in the worst way." Her body shivered uncontrollably. "I've been holding it for the last hour."

"Sure, I'll be fine."

Peeling off her smock, Doris hurried toward for the back door. I knew this was a rush call because we both worked hard at timing our lavatory breaks away from that dingy little hole that passed for a bathroom. Sharing it with the barbershop annoyed Doris because nobody kept it as clean as she would like.

I rolled Mandy onto her opposite side and gave her a few healthy thumps over her rib cage. She was shivering now and made a weak attempt at swallowing. I had the door to the kennel open and was about to lift her down when I heard Doris.

Her scream was piercing! I headed toward her but quickly retraced my steps as Mandy tried to lift her head. I rushed back to the table and lifted the dog to the floor. She was coughing and gagging on the endotracheal tube and as I pulled it out she responded with a high-pitched whine. I could hear a racket and the sound of doors slamming. I took off in Doris's direction in time to catch her in the back room. She was struggling to slide the bolt in place to lock the door.

"Oh, my God!" she shrieked.

She was shivering convulsively, wave after wave. Her normal composure was in ruins—her hair ruffled, her blouse untucked, and her glasses perched precariously on the end of her nose.

"Never in my life!" she managed to spit out. "Never in my life!"

"What is it, Doris? What's going on?"

"He was in there! He was in the bathroom!"

She didn't speak while she concentrated on straightening her clothes and hair. She was finally settling down, and I could no longer see her trembling. She pulled her glasses off and cleaned them with a Kleenex.

"He was in the bathroom," she began again, with more composure. "The light wasn't on, so I never gave it a second thought—with that damned bathroom back there, not big enough to swing a cat. I was undoing my skirt and squeezing through the door when I turned on the light and saw him sitting there on the toilet."

"Oh no! Who was it?"

"It was that George, the white-haired guy who always hangs out on the corner. The guy with only one eye."

"What did he do?"

"Nothing. He just sat there."

"What did he say when you screamed?" Doris didn't appear to appreciate the broad smile that adorned my face.

"He said, 'Sorry, lady,' " she replied, with the tiniest trace of a smile.

From that day forward, whenever something happened to get Doris upset or off track, I would try to get back in her good graces with the uttering of those same simple words, "Sorry, lady!"

LADIES' MAN

ODAY WAS SHAPING UP to be one of those difficult days. It wasn't that I couldn't keep up with the work or that any of the cases looked particularly hard to handle. The problem was that everyone seemed to want an appointment for the same time of day.

Things really got complicated when Mr. Renz called and wanted me to see Chico as soon as he finished work at four. He insisted there was no other time that he'd be able to come this week, and Chico was in a "bad way."

The dog had been agitated in the morning and had dragged his bum across the white living room carpet just as Mrs. Renz was on her way to the hairdresser. As the carpet had been laid only two weeks previously, Alvira was less than impressed with the smelly, blood-tinged deposit that remained. In fact, she'd called her husband at work and suggested that he deal with Chico today, or both he and his dog could spend the night in the carport.

The fact that my afternoon had already been booked for farm calls was the stickler. When I returned to the office from a herd health at Tsolum Farms, Doris was fit to be tied. She was discovering that being an orchardist had some advantages over being a veterinary receptionist. Today, no one was easy to please, including her boss.

"It's not as if any of these appointments is a matter of life and death," I grumbled, scanning the daybook. "Try and rearrange them so we can fit everything in and keep everyone happy."

"But . . ." stammered Doris, "everyone insisted that the appointments be for the afternoon."

"So that means you have to be persuasive. I don't want to sit around here with nothing to do for the rest of the morning, then rush around all afternoon. Unless you make some changes, I doubt we'll be able to fit everyone in without working all evening."

"Okay," Doris replied with resignation, "I'll call Mabel Stern and see if I can change her appointment. She was very insistent that it be at the end of the day. I told her you like to get finished before too late and suggested that you'd have time this morning. She said there was no way she could arrange it until five or six. I finally talked her into four o'clock."

Doris got busy on the telephone while I removed my coveralls and cleaned myself up. As I came back to the counter, she hung up the receiver.

"I just can't understand people," she said, shaking her head. "This morning when I talked to Mabel, she was absolutely adamant that you had to come out tonight as late as possible. Now when I phone out there, her husband, Jim, says that he'd much rather you come right away—that he'll be able to help you now but won't if you come later."

"Yours is not to reason why, Doris. Remember, the customer's always right."

But Doris was right, too! People were strange, their actions irrational, their reactions unpredictable. Since qualifying as a vet, I'd often thought that veterinary students would benefit tremendously from more classes in psychology and human relations. I'd have loved to trade the classes I suffered through in mathematics and physical chemistry for those that offered insight into the functioning of the human mind. At the same time, it would be worthwhile adding a class or two in astrology so that we could better understand the compulsions of people. Maybe the stars could predict when demands on our services would be greatest, for it's a fact that people always seem to want the same things at the same time.

I pulled on my coveralls and headed to the Stern farm. With any luck at all, I'd be able to get this call done and be back at the office with plenty of time for lunch. As I pulled up the drive, I spotted Jim Stern throwing the last bales onto a pickup load of hay. I parked beside the shed.

Shuffling through the boxes in the car, I gathered together everything that I thought I might need for this case. Doris had taken a rather vague history about a milk cow that was "just not right" so it could be anything. Jim jumped from the tailgate of the pickup. He was a tall, lean man who appeared to be in his early forties. His balding head shone from beneath the battered cowboy hat that he wore well back on his crown. A two-day growth of stubble adorned a face that was furrowed beyond its years.

"Jim Stern," he said, pulling off a stained leather glove and extending his hand. "You may not remember, but I met you at the beef growers' meetin' when you talked on carin' for brood cows."

"Good to see you again," I replied. His grip was firm, his hand warm and sweaty.

"Don't know exactly what's up with Rosie," he grumbled, starting down the path toward the barn. "The wife seems to think that there's somethin' wrong with 'er. Took a look at 'er after your girl phoned, and she looked just fine to me. Called you back to cancel, but you'd already left. Seein's you're here, you may just as well have a look at 'er."

Jim's stride was swift and purposeful, but the uneven wear to the heels of his cowboy boots and the bow to his legs suggested he'd rather be covering the distance on his horse. He pushed open the door to a fenced-in corral that surrounded the barn, and I followed him through. Two cows stood nose to nose at the end of the corral. One looked as if she were a Shorthorn cross and the other, much smaller cow was a Jersey. Standing quietly with their eyes half closed, they were soaking up the morning sun in bovine bliss. As I watched, they each in turn regurgitated and brought up a cud. Chewing contentedly, they swallowed again. Neither cow seemed the least bit disturbed by our presence and it was only after Jim walked between them and cut the Jersey toward me that they even bothered moving.

"This here's Rosie," he clarified, chasing her toward me. "Mabel insists she's off and way down in milk, but I can't see a damn thing wrong with her."

I observed Rosie as Jim whacked her on the flank and herded her toward the barn. She was hesitant, but it was certainly not the slow, painful movement of a cow with hardware. It was the unperturbed, lazy movement of a sleepy cow that didn't want to be separated from her companion. In fact, Rosie looked comely enough to pose as a poster cow on a milk carton. Her confirmation was good and, although dainty, she was plump and well rounded. She had a full, nicely shaped udder and a hair coat that was sleek and glossy.

Rosie had just reached the barn door when the corral gate swung open and Mabel stepped through. I had never been introduced to her, but I recognized her as the slim, long-legged brunette I had seen dancing with Jim at the farmers' ball. I remembered thinking at the time that they seemed a somewhat unlikely couple, Mabel being younger than her husband and not really look-ing the part of a farmer's wife.

"Take it easy now, Jim! You know she's not very fond of you; we don't want to get her all riled up for Dr. Perrin."

"She's not riled up!" Jim retorted tersely. "And how the hell do you know that she doesn't like me?"

Rosie sauntered into the barn and up to the stanchion closest to the wall. Looking for grain, she sniffed the manger. When she found none, she retreated a step and turned to look at us.

"Up you get, Rosie," Jim muttered. Walking up behind the little cow, he gave her a firm pat on the back of her leg. Rosie stepped forward out of the gutter, then turned her head to see if he was bringing her the grain. Jim filled a coffee can with dairy ration and sprinkled it into the manger. As soon as she moved forward, he locked the stanchion. Rosie appeared totally unconcerned about being locked in; her long tongue lapped greedily at the grain.

Jim shook his head in disgust. "Not a damned thing wrong with this bloody cow." Grabbing a square-mouthed shovel, he scraped up the manure and loose straw from the gutter and carried it outside to the manure pile.

Mabel stood by the barn door, glaring at her husband as he returned with the shovel. "She's just not right, I tell you. She was off her milk this morning, and I'm not about to watch my good milk cow go downhill because you're too cheap to get the vet out."

Jim flushed. "I'm goin' to finish loadin' my hay." He turned on his heel and stomped out the door.

"He's so used to looking after his beef cows that he just doesn't appreciate how fragile a cow like Rosie can be."

"Well, dairy cows have their differences from beef cows," I agreed. "That's for certain."

With Jim gone, Mabel's expression softened considerably. She smiled and took a couple of steps closer.

"Has Rosie been fresh for long?" I asked. "Do you think there's a chance she was in heat this morning? That can sure knock a cow's production back badly."

"I hope not. She's supposed to be three or four months along in her pregnancy."

"I'm just going to see if I can get a urine sample from her." I took an empty syringe case from my pocket. "There's a condition called ketosis that can cause a cow to dramatically cut back on her production similar to what you've described."

Reaching under Rosie's tail, I rubbed my hand up and down in a slightly circular fashion under her vagina. As if on command, she stopped chasing after the remaining few kernels of dairy ration, hunched her back, and produced a river of clear, yellow urine. I waited for a moment, then caught a sample mid-flow.

"My, but you're good with those fingers," Mabel purred, smiling seductively.

I flushed as a wave of panic rushed through my body. Pretending not to have heard her comment, I took out a ketone test tablet and set it on the top rail of the stall. Pouring the urine over the tablet, I peered at it intently. I could tell the test was negative almost immediately, but was reluctant to turn around until my face had lost its crimson hue.

Suddenly, a young boy rushed into the barn and hollered, "Mama, Jimmy's got my bridle and won't give it back!"

"I'm goin' to ride Chief, and I need it!" his brother screamed in his defense.

"Shut up, you two!" Mabel bellowed at them. "Can't you see that I'm busy! The vet's looking at Rosie, so just run along and leave us alone."

"Thank you, Lord," I whispered. The cavalry had arrived!

I pulled out my thermometer and inserted it into Rosie's rectum. Grabbing my stethoscope, I listened intently. I was thankful to be able to lose myself in the rumbling sound of hay scraping along the inside of the rumen. Mabel had almost convinced Jimmy and his brother to run outside to play when I gained the upper hand.

"Do you want to have a listen to this, you guys?" I offered, as Mabel was pushing them out the door.

"Yeah, me first!" yelled the oldest boy, pushing past his mother. I hooked the stethoscope in Jimmy's ears. His eyes lit up as he listened to the gurgling and scraping; he was completely oblivious to the dirty looks that his mother shot in his direction. After his brother had had his turn, I continued my examination. Rosie's chest sounds were normal. I lifted my knee into her abdomen repeatedly but was unable to produce pain at any location.

After I had tweaked their interest, the boys were most intent on watching what I was doing, and I was thankful when they refused to leave. I removed the thermometer.

"She read the book," I volunteered. "Her temperature's one hundred one and a half—right on normal."

I palpated her udder and found nothing unusual. Squirting milk from each teat, I filled the wells of my mastitis paddle and added test solution. The milk was perfectly normal and produced a negative test.

Next, I pulled on a palpation sleeve, applied lubricant, and pushed my hand into the cow's rectum. Cleaning manure from her distal colon, I palpated her abdomen. Everything felt completely normal; she was four months pregnant.

"Well," I muttered, peeling off my glove, "I can't see a thing wrong with her. She's indeed pregnant so it's unlikely that she was in heat."

I walked thankfully to the door and pushed it open. Being released from the confines of the barn was a tremendous relief. I hurried through the corral gate and out into the open. I was nearly to the car when Mabel caught up to me.

"What do you suggest we do with her?" she asked, as I deposited my stuff on the seat of the car.

"I'd just keep a close eye on her. If she looks any worse, give me a call and I'll have another look at her. It's not impossible that I missed something, but I don't think so."

"Boy, it's sure going to be nice to be free tonight," she said.

"Pardon me?"

"I'm free tonight! The kids are going to my sister's. Jim's going to Alberta this afternoon and won't be back for two days, and I'm home all by my lonesome."

I felt my ears get hot, and I knew that my face had once again turned beet red.

"Well, I'm sure you'll enjoy it," I stammered. "When you've got kids around all the time, even one night alone would be a real treat."

I rapidly stuffed myself into the car and started it up. As I pulled out of the yard, I looked back into the disappointed face of Mrs. Stern and returned the waves of the children, who came running from the barn to join her.

Back in town, I pondered my close encounter as I waited for my sandwich to arrive. On days like this, when the pressure of dealing with people seemed greater than usual, I liked to escape the office and eat out. It's true that people occasionally asked for free advice when they delivered my food or sat at the next table. Somehow, I never minded that; they didn't try to monopolize my time the way they appeared to when they talked to me across the counter at the office.

I felt somewhat embarrassed about the way I had handled myself at the Sterns' farm this morning. I never was much of a ladies' man, but just thinking about how flushed my face was when Mrs. Stern came on to me made me cringe and glance at the table next to me. I was sure they could see my ears turning red.

"Your sandwich, Dr. Perrin," said the waitress, as she put the plate with my closed Denver down in front of me. Nell was a tall, slim girl with a pleasant face and an easygoing personality. She loved English riding and would frequently camp near me where she could see all her tables and talk about her horse and the ins and outs of training him. Although I usually enjoyed our conversations, today I wanted to be alone.

"Thank you," I mumbled. I looked away from her to avoid a dialogue. She took a few hesitant steps, waiting for me to engage her in conversation. Finally, she drifted off and began refilling sugar containers on the other tables.

I was busy throughout the rest of the afternoon working with a couple of small beef cow operators. It was a treat to be outside on a day like this one, doing something I enjoyed and actually getting paid for it. Small producers were often much more fun to work with; they tended to be less concerned about cost and more appreciative of the information I was able to provide. I arrived back just before four and had plenty of time to get cleaned up before seeing Chico.

Gary Renz and his dog arrived right on time—they usually did. The Renzes were to us what an article in *Veterinary Economics* had referred to as foundation clients—those who made up 15 to 20 percent of our client population but 65 to 70 percent of our income. It wasn't that they came running in about things that were unimportant, but they rarely ignored something significant, and they always came to me for a solution rather than shopping around or trying to handle it themselves.

Gary and Chico were almost inseparable. Whenever I saw the blue GMC pickup that I had come to recognize as Gary's, I was sure to see the head of his big floppy-eared companion peering out from the passenger seat next to him. Chico was a yellow Lab. Big for his breed, he was one of the friendliest and least inhibited dogs in our practice. Where other dogs would drag their owners to the other side of the street when approaching the veterinary clinic, Chico always bounded through the door as if anxious to come in and say hello.

He made his usual animated entry today. With Gary's arm stretched to its full extent and the chain rattling against the doorjamb, the dog lunged into the room. Paying no attention to the choke collar that was restricting his airway, he leapt up on my chest and slurped at my face.

"Chico, for gosh sakes," Gary protested. "Don't you know where you are? He's the only dog I've ever had that just loves to visit the vet. He drags me from the moment we leave the car! The last dog we had in Alberta was terrible; I had to carry him in whenever he had something wrong."

Chico jumped around until he had an opportunity to say hello to everyone. Once he had washed Doris's hands and sniffed at her shoes, he settled down by his master's feet.

"Well, I'm glad that's over with for today. I know you'll find it hard to believe, but he listens about as well as any dog I've ever had except for here—just doesn't make sense to me."

"So I hear you got yourself in trouble with Mom, Chico." His eyes lit up and his tail thumped madly in response to my attention.

"Boy, you want to believe it," Gary winced. "Alvira wasn't the least bit amused. I told her that white was a stupid color for a carpet, but that's what she always wanted."

"You said you noticed some blood?"

"Alvira had the carpet all cleaned up by the time I got home, but she said there was blood."

"Have you noticed him dragging his butt on the ground before this incident?"

"Yeah, he's been doing it once in a while when we're out at the park. As a matter of fact, he did it twice yesterday. I was going to call you about having him dewormed."

"Okay, Chico," I muttered, "let's have a look at you."

Chico leapt to his feet and followed me to the examination room, dragging Gary behind him. I gave the dog a few quick pats, then with an arm around his chest and the other arm around his hind legs, lifted him onto the table.

"Boy, I'm glad you can do that," Gary chuckled, "because I sure can't lift him!"

I raised Chico's tail and inserted the thermometer. He whined and turned his head, lolling his tongue as if to lick his behind.

"He doesn't like that," Gary observed, with a note of concern in his voice.

"I can see why." I took a closer look at the moist, inflamed area below and to the right of the rectum. "It looks like one of his anal glands is abscessed. He's running a bit of a temperature, too," I noted, holding the thermometer up to the light.

I slipped my hand into a rubber glove and eased my finger into his rectum. Chico sat up on his front end and struggled to get away.

"Sorry, Chico, I know that doesn't feel very comfortable."

I explored the anal gland on the left side and expressed a small amount of material from its orifice. On the right, I could feel a large area the size of a walnut that was rock hard and obviously painful to the touch. As I applied a small amount of pressure, a serous blood-tinged liquid oozed from an area just inside the rectum and a watery red material appeared on the surface of the inflamed skin. Chico stood up on the table and strained to get his head around to lick at his rectum.

"Okay, Chico, okay." Doris and Gary were struggling to keep him on the table. "I promise that the worst is over . . . His right anal gland's badly infected and is forming an abscess. We'll get him started on antibiotics right away and hopefully get things under control. Occasionally, when they don't clear up properly, or when they recur, we have to remove them surgically. For the time being though, I'm going to show you how to apply a hot compress; the first day or two you should have a hood at home just in case he decides to lick his behind."

We were able to remove the hair from around the wound and generally clean up the site. After I showed Gary how to apply the compress and gave Chico an injection of antibiotics, Doris counted out the pills. Gary and his dog headed home.

"I guess that's it, then." I was feeling weary and ready to put my feet up to relax.

"Oh," interrupted Doris, "don't leave yet. You've got another farm call to make."

"What now? Why didn't you tell me earlier? I was looking forward to going home."

"I never had the chance to tell you," Doris countered defensively.

I stood there staring in dumb fixation at the name on the page of the day book.

"Mabel Stern called in, and that cow you looked at is doing very poorly."

"Doris, there's no way on God's green earth that I'm going back out there tonight. You've never seen the like of it! Mabel was coming on to me like you wouldn't believe when I was out there this morning."

"Now, Dave," chimed Doris in her motherly way, "you've been listening to Gordon too much. You'll be thinking that half the women in town are coming on to you soon!"

"Doris, there's no doubting this! I tell you, if her kids hadn't showed up when they did today, I may not have escaped the barn with my clothes on."

"Oh, come on! I never thought Mrs. Stern would be the type to carry on like that."

"Well, she may not have been a few years ago, but she's tied down with kids now, and her husband doesn't strike me as the most romantic fellow in the world."

"You've got a point there."

"Just think about it. Didn't you tell me this morning that she insisted I come out as late as possible tonight? Does that make sense, when it would have been easier for her to have her husband deal with a sick cow? He didn't even hesitate when you called this morning. He said to come right out, didn't he?"

"Well, yes he did. And come to think of it, she was very insistent that you go out there tonight."

"That's because she had the whole thing planned. The last thing she said before I escaped was that her husband was leaving this afternoon for Alberta and that he'd be gone two days."

"Well, I'm sure she's not going to try and put the make on another man when she's got the kids in the house," argued Doris, certain that she had shot a hole in my theory.

"You're right there! That's why she told me that her kids are going to be at her sister's tonight and that she's going to be home all by herself."

"Oh, my!" An impish grin spread over Doris's face. "She had this planned to the last detail."

"The last detail indeed! I feel like a caged animal. It's not that she's unattractive or anything, but I don't need to get mixed up in an affair with a married woman. I've heard of veterinarians getting mired down in those sorts of situations. The last thing I need is for the farmers to worry about me around their wives. It's hard enough to gain their trust as it is."

"Well, what are you going to do then? What if the cow really is sick and you refuse to go out?"

"I don't think there's much chance of that, but you're right; it's not impossible that I missed something."

"Do you want me to call her and tell her you can't make it?"

"No," I returned with a smile. "I'll go, but you come with me."

"Don't be silly. You're not getting me mixed up in the middle of this. Besides, I've got bowling tonight!"

"What time do you have to be at the bowling alley?"

Doris sighed. "Eight o'clock."

"It's time to make a deal. You come and chaperone while I look at the cow, and I'll spring for Chinese food at Mae's. If that isn't a win-win deal you've never heard one—you get supper and I don't get raped."

"It never said a darn thing about chaperoning on my job description." Doris choked back a laugh. "But I probably better go. This could be interesting!"

Doris had told Mabel Stern that she would try and have me there shortly after five. By the time we got out of the office, it was quarter to six.

"You know, Dave," Doris lectured, "at times you're such a procrastinator. We could have been out of here darned near an hour ago. Your being an hour late isn't going to change things one bit. You wait and see, we'll get out there and the cow will be sick, and you're going to feel like a damned fool for wasting all this time and making such a fuss. Besides that, if you diddle around much longer, I'm not going to have time to go for Chinese food before bowling."

"Yes, Mother," I chortled. "Mothers are always right."

We drove the rest of the way to the Stern farm in silence. Maybe I was making a big issue out of nothing. I was beginning to think that Doris was right and I was imagining the whole thing. If there was any consolation, I had discussed the situation only with Doris and, by this stage in our relationship, I was getting quite used to making a fool of myself in front of her.

I pulled up in front of the house and knocked on the door.

"Doris," I whispered as loud as I dared, "come out here where she can see you."

I motioned frantically for her to get out of the car and looked through the kitchen window for signs of movement.

"Doris, damn it, come out here!" After knocking a second and then a third time, I started to relax, realizing that Mabel wasn't in the house. The act of coming out here and knocking on the door had me scared spitless. What was I expecting, for God's sake? That she'd come flying to the door in the nude? That she'd stick a shepherd's crook through the door and haul me kicking and screaming into the house?

I felt relieved. Mabel must have been with Rosie and, damn it, I must have missed something on that cow. I literally sprang into the car seat.

"She must be out in the barn," I admitted sheepishly to Doris. "I guess you were right—there really is something wrong with the cow."

I drove right to the barn and shut off the ignition. I was about to get out when I heard Doris gasp.

"Oh, my God!" she whispered.

From around the corner of the barn appeared Mabel. Slowly and deliberately, as if she were a fashion model, she sauntered to my car door. She was attired in a hot-pink see-through negligee and nothing else. No socks, no shoes, no bra, no panties. Nothing! She walked in her bare feet as elegantly as if her stage were carpeted. Her face was relaxed, seductive—yes, sexy—as she meandered toward me.

She was just a few feet away when she saw Doris. Until then, she had only watched me watching her. She put her hand to her mouth as she stifled a scream, then turned and fled to the house. Doris and I sat in silence for several minutes before I started the car.

"The poor thing," Doris murmured, as we drove down the lane.

"Well, Doris, let's look at the bright side. We've got lots of time for supper."

A Day at the Beach

AVE, I'VE BEEN HERE FOR A WEEK, and you've done nothing but work the whole time! Why don't you get away from here and do something fun for a change?"

Those words sounded strange coming from the man who had spent most of our early years together trying to motivate me to be more productive. My father had become quite involved with helping me fix things around the office and took great pride in coming along on farm calls.

It was early Sunday morning, and he had just finished splicing the last of the wires back together on the telephone. The evening before, one of my clients had really gotten under my skin. Most people hated to bother me outside office hours, but there were a few who thought nothing of it. I'd just nicely gotten to sleep when the phone rang. A group of people had been arguing at a party about how much it cost to "fix" a dog. Max knew I wouldn't mind if he called to ask. I hung up the phone with such vigor that it pulled away from the wall, and several of the wires happened to separate.

I didn't sleep well. I had been working day and night for the last few months, and things were starting to get to me. I spent the first half of the night fuming about being woken up with such a dumb question, the last half worrying about missing an emergency call because my telephone was no longer functional. I finally got out of bed, found a screwdriver, and began taking the telephone apart. A stream of profanity woke my father and induced him to take over the interim repairs.

"You've got to start taking more time for yourself, Dave."

"From the way you're talking, you obviously have something in mind."

"Well, the Rayfields did invite us to go down the lake and join them today," Father insisted. "Don't you remember?"

Our final call on Friday had been to the Rayfields, and they invited us to stop for a hamburger with them. David Rayfield had started a glass shop about the same time that I started my practice, and we were constantly commiserating with one another about the rigors of starting a new business in a small town. Over supper he decried not having enough time to enjoy the fruits of his labor. I spent most of the evening nodding my head in agreement.

David was particularly excited about a new boat that he'd recently purchased, and he was bubbling on about how much fun he and Isabel were going to have with it this weekend.

His last words stuck in my mind. "We'll be staying at Mountain Shores Resort if you decide to get away for a bit of a break yourself."

We finished breakfast. The phone, though functional, was mercifully quiet.

"Let's take a drive down to the lake then." I felt strangely empowered by my decision to get away for a few hours. "I'll put a message on the answering service and tell them I'll be gone until later this evening."

By nine o'clock we were passing through Wynndel on our way to Kootenay Lake. We couldn't have picked a more beautiful morning to escape. The sky was blue and there wasn't a cloud in sight. The sun was already sneaking over the mountain peaks and filtering through the roadside trees onto the windshield. It was warm and close in the car; I rolled down the window to relish some cool, fresh air. The radio was tuned to the Canadian Broadcasting Corporation and a panel discussion about whether or not Richard Nixon should be impeached for his actions in Watergate.

"I'm so damned sick of hearing about that break-in," Father moaned. "Do we have to listen to it again? Politicians have been crooked for as long as there's been government, and they're talking as if this is something new."

"Yeah, I know. It's not big news because it happened, but because they were stupid enough to get caught."

I flipped the dial to the Creston station, and we listened to the final throes of "Tie a Yellow Ribbon Round the Old Oak Tree." Father sat back and relaxed as John Denver began crooning his "Rocky Mountain High."

The drive from Creston to the ferry along Kootenay Lake can only be described as spectacular and, today, its scenic beauty added to the euphoria that came from escaping my duties at the office. I was strangely taken by the grandeur of my surroundings, viewing country that I passed on a regular basis as if I were seeing it for the first time. We drove by the last of the open fields of the Creston flats. As we followed the curving ribbon of asphalt, we gazed upon the marshlands of Duck Lake and the Kootenay River drainage. The water surface and the air overhead were speckled with waterfowl that flocked to the preserve for its protection. Pairs of ducks and geese circled constantly. I glanced toward the lake; a pair of trumpeter swans flapped lazily by, heading in the general direction of the Creston Valley.

Further north, marsh grass and cattails made way for the rocky shores and deep blue waters of Kootenay Lake. Stony beaches blended with banks of high rock walls and the occasional stretch of sand. All were encroached upon by pine, fir, and larch trees, which struggled to establish a root system in the rocky ground.

The lake stretched as far as the eye could see, hemmed in on all sides by rugged mountains. Even this late in the summer, white caps of snow graced the highest peaks.

David and Isabel were just leaving the dock when we arrived at Mountain Shores. David was hesitantly backing the big boat from the pier as Isabel, adorned in bathing suit and life jacket, hung nervously over the bow, pushing against a neighboring boat with an oar. Her worried look turned suddenly to a smile as she saw us. She waved, then hollered something to David, who turned and shot us a halfhearted smile.

David idled the engines, and the boat bobbed precariously between the pier and the adjacent craft. He hit the throttle with a short burst; the boat shot forward and rammed rather forcefully into the pier. Isabel extended the oar for me to grab, clutching desperately to the hull of the boat.

"We still aren't much at parking this thing," she hollered over the din of the engines. "I think it's a little bit more than we bargained for!"

"It's a beauty." I grabbed the oar and pulled the boat into the pier. "I've never seen two seventy-five-horse motors on a boat this size."

"The people we bought it from used it for water skiing," Dave shouted, "and does it ever go!"

The look on Isabel's face suggested that it really did go—maybe faster than she would have wanted. As I held the boat next to the pier, Father climbed over the side and settled himself on a backseat. I hopped in and pushed away from the dock. David gave a couple of bursts in reverse, then shifted to forward, and maneuvered smoothly away from the surrounding boats into open water.

"Hallelujah," muttered Isabel. "I can't stand docking this thing."

Dave opened up the engines, and we literally flew across the water toward the rocky shore on the opposite side. The wind whipped against our faces as we listened to the thump, thump, thump of the boat's hull against the choppy surface of the lake.

"Do you want to try water skiing?" Dave yelled over the noise of the racing engines.

"I've only tried once before," I responded, moving to the seat next to him, "and they couldn't get me up out of the water."

"They obviously didn't have enough power to pull you," Dave snorted. "I guarantee you that we won't have the same problem with this boat!"

"We could maybe give it a try later." I displayed a decided lack of enthusiasm. "It would be nice to actually get up on skis."

With that, Dave eased off on the throttle and allowed the boat to coast to a halt.

"You shouldn't have said you'd go," Isabel warned. "He's been dying to find someone to drag around out here!"

Within five minutes, I was bobbing around in the middle of the lake. I watched as Father paid out the loops of tow rope and David idled the boat gently away from me. After a couple of halfhearted attempts in which I allowed the tow rope to be yanked from my grasp, I managed to struggle out of the water and found myself flying effortlessly along in the wake of the boat. I was busy congratulating myself on how well I was doing, when I saw David making circles with his hands as he talked. I knew I was in trouble when he made the first turn. Without slowing down in the least, he turned sharply to send me flying at the end of a wide arc. The speed picked up dramatically as I jumped outside the wake into choppy water. The skis were pounding as I swung at the end of the rope, and all I could think about was how to fall with the least amount of pain.

I survived that first swing and maneuvered once more into the wake. I was even thinking that this could be fun, when Dave turned the boat in the opposite direction.

Oh no, this was it! I thumped over the wake into the chop on the other side. I stared in horror as the boat picked up yet more speed and the waves chattered under my skis. I could see Isabel and Father yelling at Dave, but he seemed determined to make this the ride from hell.

My shoulders were aching from the pull of the rope, and my knees were throbbing from the pounding of the waves. I was at the absolute end of the arc when I decided that I'd had enough! I didn't really fall; I just let go. The sudden loss of momentum made me flip over backward, and I hit the water with my legs outstretched. I felt the skis ripped from my feet and then the impact of my body with the water. My legs burned as though on fire and my colon screamed as it rapidly filled with cold water.

I floated for several minutes before I could even look at the boat. For a while I was certain I had ruptured my colon; the pain had been that intense. But as the minutes passed and the pain subsided, I knew I would likely survive. All I could think of was getting out of the water into the boat and wringing Rayfield's scrawny neck.

"Grab the rope when I come around!" Dave hollered over the sound of the motors.

"I've had enough! I took a ten-gallon enema, and I'm definitely done for the day!"

"Oh, come on!" Dave jeered. "You can't tell me that one little fall's going to put you off. The only way you'll get to shore is if you ski in—we don't give rides to pussies!"

I patiently lay back in the life preserver as the ski rope went by me the first time. He continued to circle, and it became obvious that we were at a standoff. I finally grabbed the line and found myself perching for a takeoff one more time.

The rope was taut and the boat leapt forward. My knees buckled; I almost let go. Throwing up a huge plume of water, I hung on resolutely and finally struggled up. I was apprehensive of David's intentions; I knew he would try and dump me again. As long as I could stay in the wake, I would do just fine. I focused on the opposite shore where we'd started and hoped that he would cool it. We were almost there, and I was congratulating myself on how well I had done, when he cranked it again.

"Rayfield, you SOB!"

I could feel myself accelerating as I got closer to the end of the arc. The skis were chattering over the waves; my legs were rubber. I was having difficulty keeping my balance, sawing back and forth in a desperate attempt to stay erect. I knew my demise was near. The image of my recent enema was still firmly impressed upon my mind; no way was I going to fall ass-first again!

I focused on the water that sped by beneath me. My only hope was getting from here to there with a minimum of pain. I hadn't long to wait; as I wobbled, my ski dug into a passing wave, and my legs splayed widely. I reefed hard on the tow rope, determined to fall face-first. I remember the rope being ripped from my hands and the rude, painful contact with the water. I remember the breath being knocked out of me, the feeling of water invading every portal of my body, the coughing and sputtering for air as I popped to the surface. I became aware of a trickling sensation over the bridge of my nose and, when I pawed at it, my hand came away red with blood.

They circled closely around me. I could see from the looks on their faces that I wouldn't be refused entry again. My head was aching terribly, and my shoulder felt as if someone had tried to rip it off.

As though in a dream, I paddled to a ski some distance away. Everything seemed to be functioning even though I certainly felt worse for wear. Blood was streaming steadily down my face and onto my chest. I fumbled cautiously for the source and decided I had a gash somewhere over my left brow.

By the time I rounded up the other ski, David had maneuvered the boat close enough for me to pass them on board. Father threw over a rope ladder, and I clawed my way up and flopped over the other side. Everyone stared at the blood that flowed down my face to form a puddle on my belly.

"How bad is it?" I asked Dad, as he leaned over to take a closer look.

"Could be worse, but it's going to need a few stitches."

Isabel threw me a towel, and I lay back with it pressed firmly to my face. By the time David managed to dock the boat, I was feeling somewhat perkier, and the bleeding had slowed to a bare trickle.

I glared at him. He gave me a timid smile, then busied himself with tidying up the boat. "You damned near killed me out there—I thought it was supposed to be fun."

"Well, it was! You looked like you were having a good time."

"Yeah, sure! My ass feels like someone drove a truck up it, and I've got a pounding headache."

"I've got just the cure for that!" he declared. "You need to come over to the camper for a couple of stiff drinks of rum."

I returned to the car and slid up in front of the rearview mirror. Father was right; the wound needed to be sutured. After a bit of digging, I found what I was looking for—silk suture with a long, straight needle. I rubbed my hands with alcohol and opened the package.

Taking a deep breath, I peered into the mirror and drove the needle through first the lower side of the wound, then the upper. Tears pooled in my eyes, and blood trickled from the wound once more. Hardly able to see what I was doing, I pulled the wound edges together and knotted the silk.

"Oh, Dave!" Isabel shrieked, as she came around the corner. "What's that dangling from your eye?"

"It's just suture material—haven't gotten around to cutting it yet."

"You mean you're sewing yourself up? I can't believe it!"

"Well, someone has to do it, so I may as well get it over with."

Three more stitches closed the wound and, although it induced tears and sweat, it was over with a minimum of discomfort. We spent the remainder of the afternoon and a good part of the early evening swilling rum and Coke, eating snacks, and playing cards.

Although I had stopped drinking toward the end of the evening and was a long way from being hammered, I wasn't sober either! It was after midnight when Father and I took our leave of the Rayfields and began our trip back to town.

My head was throbbing, but I still felt mellow. All the way home, I could think of nothing other than how great it would feel to hit the pillow. I could almost feel the warmth of the covers.

All of a sudden, I saw lights flashing behind me. "Oh no! That's all I need!"

I pulled over and sat with resignation—the red light of the police car flashed intermittently across the windshield. My heart was pounding as the door of the police cruiser opened and a young officer I had never met sauntered slowly toward us. I suddenly felt weak. I could see the headline in Thursday's paper—LOCAL VET CHARGED WITH DRUNK DRIVING.

I looked across the car at Father and shook my head, then rolled down the window. The officer was tall and lean. He wore the barely visible mustache that branded him a new recruit.

"You're Dr. Perrin, aren't you?"

"Yes," I croaked. I watched as his tongue flicked out and played absently with the tip of the fine blond hair that adorned his upper lip.

"It seems there's a bit of an emergency, and we've been asked to keep an eye out for you. There's a dentist with a sick dog at the Creston Valley Hospital. He's been creating quite a ruckus. Do you think you'll be able to help him out?"

"Yes, sure! I'll head to the office right now if he wants to meet me there."

"Okay, I can tell him to go right down then? The folks at the hospital will be glad to hear that." He smiled, tipped his hat to the back of his head, and returned to his vehicle.

"Thank God," I muttered. "Wouldn't that have been a fitting end to the day?"

"Yeah, wouldn't it just?" Father agreed.

A man waited on the sidewalk outside the office as we drove up to the clinic. "Are you Dr. Perrin?"

"Yes, I am. I hear you're having a problem with your dog."

"Oh, thank heavens, I finally found you," he gushed, on the verge of tears. "Jessie's really in a bad way, and she's getting worse by the minute. I'm Dr. Walker, from Missoula, Montana. I just took a swing up here to drive through the Kootenays and have a look at the country. Jessie was fine until Nelson, then she started acting strange. Over the last couple hours she's been getting worse and worse. When I couldn't get you or the other vet in town, I tried the hospital for someone to examine her—no one was willing."

"Let's have a look at her." I turned to the new Lincoln Continental that was parked in front of the office.

Dr. Walker hustled quickly to the back door and flung it open. There stretched on her side was an old German short-haired pointer. Her head was extended, and she was gasping for air.

"She's been breathing like that for the last hour. I knew she was in big trouble; I just couldn't get anyone to help."

"Not feeling too good, are you, Jessie?" I stroked her head; it was almost totally white with age. She lifted her muzzle slightly, trying to focus her cataract-beleaguered eyes on her master, then shifted her body to find a more comfortable position.

"At first, I wondered if she was having heart trouble, but she's been looking more and more bloated over the last couple of hours."

"Has she tried to vomit?" I gently rubbed my hand over her grossly distended abdomen.

"She retched several times, but never did produce anything."

"This distention is something new, is it? She's normally quite slim through her abdomen?"

"Oh yes. I really work to keep her weight down because of her hips. If anything, I've been having difficulty keeping weight on her lately."

I lifted Jessie and cradled her against my body. She grunted dramatically as I hefted her and continued grunting with each additional breath until I put her down on the examination table.

The dog struggled to right herself, looking around desperately for her master. Dr. Walker grasped her muzzle in his hand and crooned to her in a rhythmic, comforting tone.

"That's a girl, Jessie. That's a girl. The doctor's going to get you fixed up now. That's my girl."

I slipped a thermometer into the dog's rectum and rolled back her lip to examine her color. Her membranes were cool and so pale that I had to look closely when I pressed on her gum to see that there was any return of circulation.

"Jessie's had a rough time the last couple of years. Her hips have been giving out on her and she has a difficult time getting around. My vet has her on Butazone for the pain, but she's never been the same dog since Alice passed on."

Dr. Walker's voice trailed off for a moment then, with a far-off look, he went on. "Neither one of us has been the same since my wife died."

Jessie grunted once again as I ran my hands over her abdomen, then she released a long, agonizing groan that brought tears to her master's eyes.

"Oh, she's in such terrible pain." He looked away so that I wouldn't notice the tears. "Oh, Jessie, you poor, dear girl."

Jessie's belly was as hard as a rock. Thumping with my finger over the bulge in her abdomen, I could hear the resonant tone of a highly compressed organ. I held the thermometer up to the light and rotated it to see the mercury—almost a full degree below normal at 99.7.

"Dr. Walker, it looks as if Jessie has a torsion of her stomach. That's a grim situation for even a young dog. For a dog Jessie's age, the prognosis is very grave indeed! I know that it's my fault that we didn't see her sooner. She certainly would've been a better candidate for surgery a couple of hours ago."

With the serious nature of the old girl's condition and the fact that she had so many other problems, I was almost certain that Dr. Walker would consider euthanasia. Jessie was probably not looking at more than another year or two of life under the best of circumstances.

"You don't think her chances are very good then, Dr. Perrin?" His eyes brimmed with tears, and the corners of his mouth quivered.

"I don't like to be overly pessimistic but, with a lot of cases of gastric torsion, the spleen is involved as well; in some cases that necessitates amputation."

"And you don't think she's up to it?"

"She isn't right now. If I were to get her on intravenous fluids and treat her for shock, we might have a fighting chance. I guess you have to weigh all the odds in your own mind and determine if you think surgery is warranted."

Dr. Walker stared at his dog for several minutes, his tears flowing in a steady stream onto Jessie's coat. Finally, after what seemed an eternity, he turned to me and said in a barely audible voice, "I think I need you to put everything in perspective for me, Dr. Perrin. What would you do if she were your dog?"

"The first thing you have to consider is the quality of her life over the last few months. I notice she has cataracts and doesn't see very well. You mentioned that she has arthritis and has trouble walking. Does she mope around all the time? Does she seem able to get out and enjoy herself, or is she just hanging in there from one day to the next?

"If you're keeping her alive more for you than for her, then I think it would be best to put her to sleep. If you think she's happy, then you have to look at it from the point of view of an investment. You're obviously going to be spending money on surgery and you want to get value for your dollar. She's going to endure pain and suffering and wants to be compensated for that. The reward obviously has to be great enough for both you and Jessie in order to warrant surgery."

"Well then, I think you've answered my question! Jessie's gone downhill over the past couple of years—there's no doubt of that—but she still really enjoys life. If the truth be known, we both have our problems when we first start moving in the morning. It's certainly nothing that we can't live with. She's a very happy dog for the most part.

"As for me, Dr. Perrin, I'm an old man and living all by myself. Jessie's the only company I have. We rattle around in a big house and I've got more money left than I can possibly spend. You do the best you can for her. I know she's in good hands, and I certainly won't blame you if she doesn't pull through. I just think we have to try!"

"We better get started then," I said, with more enthusiasm than I really felt.

It was 2:30 A.M. by the time I got the intravenous started and made the call to Doris. I dialed the number, closed my eyes, and leaned back against the wall. My head was throbbing; I was not looking forward to either the surgery that I was about to tackle or the day that was sure to dawn before I was finished.

"I hate to do this to you, Doris," I began, when she finally croaked hello. "I have an old dog that needs surgery. Do you think you can come and give me a hand?"

"Okay, sure," she responded groggily. "Do I have enough time to shower?"

"We'll have to let her stabilize a bit first anyway. Unless I miss my guess, this'll be your only opportunity to have a shower before you start work in the morning."

"Oh great! And I was having such a good sleep."

Jessie's condition continued to deteriorate as I rushed around getting things laid out for the surgery. Dr. Walker stood by her. His countenance was one of dejection; his body language spelled defeat. His eyes were dull and red from crying. His shoulders were stooped and rounded; he looked very much a tired old man. He peered expectantly toward me as I checked her gums.

I looked him directly in the eyes and shook my head. "Things are not looking good. I was hoping that the fluids and steroids would improve her circulation before we put her under anesthesia."

116

Jessie's abdomen had become tauter over the distended stomach, but there seemed to be distention even in the distal abdomen. I began shaving the hair from her flank. She lay oblivious to the sound of the clippers.

I heard the front door open and the murmur of voices as Doris and Father exchanged greetings in the waiting room. Doris appeared, grabbed the wastebasket, and began collecting Jessie's hair. Dr. Walker introduced himself and apologized profusely for getting her out of bed.

"Doris, could you scrub this area over the left flank for me? I'm going to pop a needle in here to see if we have some bleeding going on."

"What are you looking for?" Dr. Walker's face was strained as he watched me direct the needle into the peritoneal cavity.

"I'm afraid she may be bleeding internally. She's quite distended with fluid as well as gas, and her color isn't improving the way I would expect."

I drew back on the plunger of the syringe, and the barrel quickly filled with blood.

Dr. Walker's voice wavered; his eyes were riveted on the syringe. "What does that mean?"

"It probably means that the spleen got so distended from being twisted off that it ruptured and started to leak blood into the abdomen. We have to get in there quickly; we probably need to do an amputation."

I could see that the old man had reached the limit of his endurance. His hand was trembling as it stroked Jessie's head.

"I think it would be best if you found yourself a motel for the night, Dr. Walker." I motioned for Doris to take over his station at Jessie's head. "I think you've had enough for one day. If we need any more help, my father can come and give us a hand."

He gave Jessie a final caress, then tottered off through the waiting room.

"Give us a call as soon as you check in!" I hollered after him. "We'll want a number to contact you in case we run into more problems."

Jessie had faded so badly that she never even noticed the departure of her faithful master. Unless I was able to make some drastic changes in the dog's favor, we would all soon be able to get some sleep.

"You better get out some transfusion bags, Doris . . . Dad! It looks like you've inherited a job."

After another scrub, I popped the needle for the blood collection bag through the abdominal wall and watched in fascination as it filled far faster than had it been drawn from the jugular vein.

All the literature I was able to find on the correction of gastric torsion stressed the importance of decompression of the stomach as quickly as possible. As much as I wanted to relieve the pressure, I was certain that putting Jessie under anesthesia in her present state would be just another form of euthanasia.

In desperation, I decided to tap some gas. I drove a needle through Jessie's side at the point of maximum distention. Gas hissed from the hub in a torrent and, gradually, the pressure on the old dog's side lessened. Initially there was little change in her demeanor but, as the pressure diminished, her breathing became less labored.

The blood collection bag filled as quickly as I'd ever seen one fill and, as Doris rocked it back and forth to mix in the anticoagulant, it adopted the shape of a grossly swollen tick.

"I know this may sound like a stupid question," Doris began, "but where's this blood coming from?"

"It's coming from her abdominal cavity. This is blood that has leaked from the spleen and is now lost to her as far as her circulatory system is concerned. By the feel of her abdomen, she may well be able to fill a couple more of these bags."

"Well, what good does it do to just take the blood out of there? It's still lost to her, isn't it?"

"It would be if we didn't return it, but we're going to give it back to her as a transfusion."

"You mean it's still good after being dumped out into the abdomen like that?" Doris stared in awe at the bag of blood she held in her hands.

"Sure, when it's as fresh as this blood. There's a filter in the administration set that'll remove any clots and, by using her own blood, we avoid the complications of trying to cross-match a transfusion from a donor."

"I'll be darned," Doris mused. "That's pretty neat, being able to give her back her own blood!"

Within the hour, we had obtained a second bag from Jessie's abdomen and had administered a good portion of the blood from the first transfusion.

Although pressure was again building in the stomach, her color had improved markedly, and I was feeling optimistic about her chances of handling the anesthetic.

"We don't have any more transfusion bags, Dave." Doris pulled off her glasses and polished them nervously. "Do you think we'll need to transfuse more blood?"

"The way she's leaking, we'd better see if we can get some more. Why don't you call the nurse's station and see if we can get a couple just in case. I'd hate to lose her because we couldn't give her one last transfusion."

While Doris drove to the hospital, I gave the dog atropine and Demerol as a premedication and began administering the second bag of blood. By the time Doris returned with additional bags, Dad and I had Jessie stretched out on her side with an induction mask over her muzzle. She had gone to sleep without a struggle and was now snoring deeply. We intubated the dog and connected her to the anesthetic machine.

I pushed a stomach tube over the endotracheal tube and down the esophagus. It slid along easily until it reached the cardiac sphincter, then halted as if butting into a solid object. Maintaining a steady pressure, I continued until it finally advanced and gas came gushing from the end.

"We're making the incision over here, Doris." I pointed to an imaginary line along the margins of the ribs. "We'll want both sides prepared just in case I need to make an incision down the right side too."

"That's a funny place to cut, isn't it? Why aren't you going down the middle like you usually do?"

"The textbook suggests that I'll get better exposure with the paracostal incision and, seeing as this is my first gastric torsion, I think I'll take their word for it."

"Doesn't make sense to me. You're always able to find things when you make an incision down the middle!"

Doris's words were haunting me as I applied the clamps to attach the drapes to the underlying skin. Orientation is so important when doing surgery; it's imperative to feel familiar with the area you've just invaded and know with certainty where everything should be.

The final drops of blood were running into Jessie's vein when I started a third collection. The blood flowed as freely from her abdomen as it had with the others and, by the time I completed my entry, Doris had almost finished collecting the bag.

"We know we're going to have a tummy full of blood here, Doris. Could you get me a sixty-milliliter syringe so that we can collect as much as possible without wasting it."

I soon wished that I had heeded Doris's advice. I realized before starting that the muscle layers would be much thicker here than over the midline, but hadn't given enough thought to what that would do to the abdominal access. It was after I had incised the final layer and could see nothing but an enormous pool of blood that I felt a twinge of panic. I slipped my gloved hand through the incision toward the right side. I could feel the end of the stomach tube and the huge lump that represented the engorged spleen. Putting moderate traction on the massive organ, I tried to maneuver it to the incision; it was so turgid I couldn't move it.

I repositioned the side drapes to expose the rib cage on the right side and cut there as well.

"My Lord," Doris moaned. "Will you look at that blood!"

I could see a steady flow of blood over the edge of the left incision and down the dog's side onto the floor. The front of my gown and the tops of my shoes were already soaked red.

"She's sure cranking it out!" I muttered. "She can't keep that up for long."

I quickly severed one layer after another of the abdominal muscles, then folded the whole flap back to reveal the entire anterior abdomen.

"Well, you can sure see everything now," Father pronounced sarcastically.

The peritoneal cavity was a pool of blood and the spleen, which was swollen four to five times its normal size, was split like a ripe melon down the center of its convex surface. Blood oozed continually like a spring from the depth of the wound.

I grasped the stomach and spleen and rotated them to correct the torsion. The huge vessels that conveyed blood back and forth to the spleen throbbed with each beat of the heart. Now that I could see how much blood was leaking, getting it stopped took on a new sense of urgency. My hands were shaking as I clamped the fanlike array of vessels that proceeded from the base of the spleen and disappeared in the fatty layer surrounding the stomach.

"Open that syringe for me will you, Doris?" My voice was strained, my muscles tense. "We need to save as much of this as we possibly can."

Creating a well behind the stomach, I placed the syringe tip at the bottom and filled it time and again. Doris opened the blood pack in such a manner that she could hold the top end and still offer me access to the sterile bottom end. Each time I filled the syringe, I connected to the needle and emptied it into the blood pack. I continued until the pack looked like a gigantic engorged mosquito.

"What about all the rest of the blood that's in her tummy? Don't you have to do something with it?"

"So long as we can keep the blood flowing well enough to meet her short-term needs, she should be able to reclaim a lot of that free blood herself and get it back into circulation. Let's just keep the blood running—we sure don't want to lose her after all this!"

Why the telephone always seems to wait until all hands are busy, I don't know—but it does. It began ringing as Doris and Father were trying to change blood bags and continued until Doris finally ran to answer it.

It was obviously Dr. Walker. Doris gave him a blow-by-blow description of what had happened. I could picture the poor old guy sitting in his motel room worrying about Jessie, but time was wasting and I needed to get on with this.

"I need some suture material, Doris!"

She quickly hung up and rushed over, fishing the packages of Dexon from her pocket. One after the other, I tied off the vessels. The size of the veins was daunting enough, especially after the swelling associated with the torsion, but there was something about the splenic artery that commanded respect. I took extra care in anchoring my suture to the surrounding tissue and placed a second ligature about a quarter of an inch below the first.

"Just look at the way that big mother pulsates." I released the vessel and watched as it throbbed with each beat of Jessie's heart.

"My lands, yes," Doris crooned in amazement.

"There must be a bag of blood left inside that spleen," Father noted, as I severed the vessels.

"Easily. The spleen's a storage vessel for blood in the body, and this one's stretched way beyond normal capacity . . . What's her color like?" I separated the last of the mesenteric attachments of the spleen and carried it to the sink.

"She actually has a pinkish hue and we still have most of a bag to go with our transfusion."

"Grab one of those new disposable endotracheal tubes that came in last week and open it for me, please!" I hollered. "And open the surgery text so I can have a quick read."

Because torsions can easily recur after splenectomy, the literature stressed the need to anchor the stomach in its normal position by creating an adhesion between it and the body wall.

"What's the tube for?" Dad asked Doris in a hushed tone.

She shrugged and lifted her eyebrows.

"I'm making a hole in her stomach and blowing up the balloon on the cuff to pull it tight to the body wall. Once enough scar tissue forms around the tube, we'll deflate it and simply pull it through."

"Won't that leave a big hole into her stomach?" The tone in Doris's voice left little doubt that she found the thought revolting.

"Yeah, it'll leave a small draining tract to the outside, but that'll granulate in a few days after the tube's been removed."

Reading the procedure in the text a third and fourth time, I finally got on with it. As usual, it came down to common sense and observation of where the organ appeared best positioned of its own accord. Making a small stab incision where I wanted the tube to exit the abdomen, I drove a large pair of forceps through the muscle wall and incised over the bump in the overlying skin. Enlarging the tract, I pulled the tube through. With a stab incision in the stomach, the catheter was placed.

I blew up the cuff on the endotracheal tube and pulled back. The stomach sandwiched tightly against the abdominal wall. I finished suturing around the outside of the tube and congratulated myself on a job well done. I marveled at how complicated the author had made it sound and how simple it had really turned out to be.

"We're home free now!" Jessie was breathing steadily, she looked stable, and the surgery had gone so well that I could hardly believe it! "All we have to do is close her up and we're done."

It wasn't until I had placed the first suture through the peritoneum and the rectus abdominus muscle at the end of the flap and the base of the sternum that I realized I was in trouble. Cranking on the Dexon to try and tie a knot, I noted a good three inches of discrepancy.

"Oh no," I groaned. "Just look at how much those muscles have contracted!"

Grasping the end of the muscle flap with my gloved hand, I pulled toward Jessie's head with as much pressure as I could muster and still hold on to it. I pulled until my hands were aching from the exertion. Going back to my knot, I tried again to appose the ends of the muscle, only to find that I was still two inches short of joining them.

"Son of a bitch!" I hollered at the top of my lungs, as a pair of forceps bounced off the surgery wall. I suddenly felt very, very tired. I became conscious of the pain that throbbed in my head and the tightness that had developed in my neck. Standing back, I took a deep breath and let my head hang in an attempt to loosen the tension that had developed in my own muscles during the period of intense concentration.

"How could the muscle have shortened so much?" Doris broke the uneasy silence.

"You remember how hard I had to pull on that cat's leg the other day when we were doing the bone pinning? How I had to lever the two ends of the bones together? Well, the same thing's happened here—when the tension's taken off a muscle for any length of time, it shortens. We'll have to see if we can get around it somehow. How about you and Dad untying the hind legs and lifting her back end up? If you flex her forward, I may be able to put her back together."

Father and Doris flexed Jessie's body in the shape of a U while I reefed on the suture material and apposed the muscle ends.

"Just a little higher," I muttered. "Just hold her there now while I get a few more sutures in place."

As Doris and Father grunted with exertion, I managed to place one suture after the other until the ends of the muscles were pulled together.

"Can we put her down?" Doris's face was beet red. Her arms were shaking from exertion.

"Yes, I should be able to finish closing the rest of the incision without your help."

The remainder of the closure was pretty routine and, when I was finally finished, Jessie had a long row of sutures shaped like a horseshoe over the front of her tummy.

As Doris was cleaning up the instruments, I called Dr. Walker. He answered on the first ring, and I wondered if he'd ever gone to bed.

"Hello! Hello!"

"Yes, Dr. Walker, we've finished surgery, and Jessie's doing as well as can be expected."

"You were able to get the bleeding under control? It's stopped?"

"Yes, the bleeding's stopped and she's pretty stable. All in all, I'd say the surgery went well."

"Can I come and see her? I'd really like to be there for her when she wakes up."

I was hesitant because of the state of the room. "Give us a few minutes to finish up and it should be all right."

"Doris! Doris! We'll have to get things cleaned up a bit here—Dr. Walker's coming."

I had no sooner spit those words out of my mouth and filled the mop bucket, when he whipped around the corner.

"Oh my!" he croaked. "Is that blood all hers?"

"Yes, I'm afraid so. Her abdomen was just full of blood—we were lucky to be able to save and recycle as much of it as we did."

Dr. Walker took a long, deliberate look around the surgery as if taking a mental picture for posterity. The room could easily have passed for a poorly designed slaughterhouse. Doris had the instruments soaking in a crimson bath of water. The surgery table was plastered with blood that had run down and accumulated in congealed puddles on the floor. The blood-drenched drapes were piled in a laundry basket at the corner of the room. The floor had been tracked with red from one end to the other, and a set of bloody footprints led across the room into the reception area.

It took us the better part of an hour to make things presentable. By that time, it was eight-thirty and the first appointments were arriving for the day. Dr. Walker was perched on a chair in front of Jessie's kennel. He held her head in his hand and crooned a constant stream of platitudes in response to the whines she emitted with each and every breath.

"Does she have a lot of pain? She's usually not one to complain this way."

I thought about how poor Jessie's abdomen had to be feeling about now. The image of Doris and Father holding the dog's feet in the air and my reefing on the muscles made me hesitant to say no.

Doris struggled by, dragging a reluctant yellow Lab toward the kennel room. As he heard Jessie's wail of complaint and got a whiff of the surgery room, he planted his feet and tried digging his way back to his owner. Doris looked at me in despair and exhaustion, and I scooped him up in my arms.

"Lead on, McDuff," I joked. "How 'bout if you open the kennel door for me?"

Father was loading the last of the dirty laundry into the washing machine. Doris quickly opened the kennel door and I deposited our unhappy visitor inside. He looked around frantically for an avenue of escape, then let out a mournful wail and began scratching at the bottom of the door. We all started laughing at the same time. We would not soon forget this night!

"Well, Pop, did we have a good time on our day off?"

Father opened his mouth, then slowly shook his head and went back to loading the washing machine. Doris sighed deeply and retreated to the reception area to sign in and collect another patient. A new day had dawned and there was nothing to do but to dig into it.

Jessie went on to make a miraculous recovery. After the second day, I discharged her to Dr. Walker with the understanding that when they got home, she be examined by her own doctor. Jessie's veterinarian was an old friend of Dr. Walker's. They had been in constant contact, so the vet was well aware of the dog's progress.

That afternoon I carried her out to the Lincoln Continental. Dr. Walker had contracted a local carpenter to build an insert so that the entire area behind the front seat could be made into a bed for Jessie. The whole surface, including the seat itself, was covered with pillows that he'd just purchased to make the ride more comfortable for his precious dog.

Ten days later, I got a call from Jessie's veterinarian.

"Dr. Perrin, I'm calling to update you on the progress of your recent patient, Jessie Walker. I just removed the endotracheal tube from her abdomen, and I can't believe how well she's looking."

"Great! We were very impressed with Dr. Walker and Jessie while they were here. I'm certainly glad to hear that they're doing so well."

"I have to tell you that you make me feel a bit dated."

"What makes you say that?"

"I've never heard of the technique you used to tack down the stomach, and I've certainly never seen anyone make an incision quite like that."

"Well, if it makes you feel any better, the surgery was cook-booked from *Veterinary Clinics of North America* and I'd certainly never use that approach again—I had a devil of a time closing her up!"

We both had a good laugh, and I was about to hang up when he began again.

"I don't know exactly how to say this, but do you mind if I ask you about your fees?"

I flushed and my heart picked up its pace. Fees have always been a touchy subject for me, and I tended to be defensive when someone even hinted that my services might not be worthy of the fee that I charged.

"Dr. Walker was upset with the fees? Three of us were up all night working on her, and I tried to make the bill as reasonable as possible."

"This really is none of my business, Dr. Perrin." He was struggling with his words. "If we didn't have a good rapport on the phone I wouldn't mention it, but Ralph's a good friend of mine and he did ask that I bring it up."

"Okay, fine. What did he have a problem with?" My heart was pounding, and I felt as if I were behind Rayfield's boat being catapulted out of the wake one more time.

"Ralph practiced dentistry for over thirty years himself, and I've been at it for twenty-five. When the bill for Jessie's pillows came to thirty-eight dollars more than what you charged him for your services, he thought you ought to know!"

"I don't follow you." My jaw flopped open in disbelief. "You mean he didn't think I charged enough?"

"Let's just say that he would have paid three or four times that amount if I had done the procedure here. Ralph was shocked at how little you charged but didn't want to insult you by saying so!"

There was a long period of silence, as neither of us knew what to add. Finally, he closed by saying, "Thank you very much for taking such good care of my patient and my client—they're both more than happy with your services."

I listened to the dial tone for several moments after he hung up. I've since learned that, at such times, the only solution is to have a good laugh. Somehow, I couldn't even manage a smile.

My Kids

y belly was sore from leaning over the false front. The fascia board was rotten; nail heads poked out in an irregular fashion. Several times, I recoiled as one drove into my ribs. My shirt was filthy and riddled with puncture holes.

I reached anxiously over the edge to scrape at the last of the huge scrolls of peeling gray paint. I was sick of this job. Soon I could start smearing on the white latex. Doris kept telling me that new paint and wallpaper hid a multitude of sins, and I couldn't wait to cover this ugly building. I had been here for two months and still didn't have the courage to hang out a sign.

"Can you help me, mister?" I looked down with a start. I had been so engrossed in attacking that final square of stucco that I hadn't noticed what was going on in the street below. The boy was plastered with blood; the dog in his arms looked more dead than alive.

"I'll be right there! Just give me enough time to get down the ladder." I tossed the scraper onto the irregular surface of the tarred roof and squeezed my frame through the hole that offered access to the apartment below. I quickly descended the ladder and ran down the stairs to the office.

"Boots got hit by a car! We were up by the Dairy Queen and a guy ran right over him. He never even stopped!" I looked at the innocent face, at the limp body that he held in his arms, and rushed them into the clinic. I slipped my arms under the dog, and the boy reluctantly relinquished his burden.

"They told me at the Dairy Queen that you were a vet . . . Is he going to die?" Intense blue eyes burned into me as I ran my hands over the pup's body. Open wounds gaped everywhere; his right ear was half torn from his head. The upper thigh of his right leg was shortened, and his leg dangled at a grotesque angle. His tail was hanging by a shard of skin. Blood dripped steadily from the stump and from his nostrils. The dog's chest rattled with each breath he drew.

"I don't know, son. We'll do what we can." I quickly assembled an intravenous administration set and shaved the dog's foreleg. I plunged a catheter into the cephalic vein; as a slow reflux of blood appeared, I connected the fluids. Turning on the oxygen, I slipped a mask over Boots's nose.

"I don't have any money, mister." The boy's wet-eyed gaze was intense; he spoke with a maturity beyond his years. "I have no way to pay for what you're doing."

"We'll work something out."

"We have no money. Mom never did like Boots—she'll be furious." Tears trickled down his cheeks. He stood silently looking at the lifeless body of his friend. He shivered, then looked away and lifted an arm to wipe at his tears.

Boots's gums were white. I grabbed a penlight and examined his eyes. His right pupil was the size of a pinpoint, the left one ten times its size.

"What does that mean? Why is one so much bigger than the other?"

"He's been hit on the head, and his brain is swelling. When the pupils are like that, it means one side of the brain has more pressure than the other."

I grabbed a vial of a potent steroid called Soludelta Cortef and pushed down on the rubber stopper that mixed sterile water with the white powder in a lower chamber. I drew the solution into a syringe and slowly injected it through the port of the intravenous set.

"Is that sort of like a concussion?"

"Yes, Boots has a concussion, and he's in shock."

The dog lay unresponsive as I cleaned up the lacerations on his head and shaved away the hair on the wound margins. I had the muscle layer closed and was suturing the skin when he shivered and started whining.

"Does he feel that?" The question was matter-of-fact, the boy's handsome face impassive.

"He doesn't know where he is right now. I can't tell you for sure, but I don't think he feels any pain yet."

I continued shaving, scraping, and washing Boots's wounds. As the hours passed, his gums began to pink up; his whines became more constant; and, occasionally, he made a move that suggested a conscious effort. The remainder of that afternoon was spent huddled over the surgery table with Boots. Another Sunday was fading into the record books.

"I'm going to be in big trouble with Mom. She hates Boots—keeps telling me to get rid of him. But he's my friend. I can't let anything happen to him."

"We'll do the best we can for him, but I want you to know there's no guarantee that he'll be normal. We'll have to keep him here as he recovers, and if all goes well with his head, he'll need surgery to repair that broken leg."

"You won't tell Mom, will you?"

"How can you keep her from knowing? She'll notice that he doesn't come home with you."

"No, she won't—not if you don't tell her! Mom doesn't notice much of anything. It'll be fine if I just stay away from her."

I wanted to question him further, but the look in his eyes brought me up short. An uncomfortable silence ensued.

"Have you lived in town for long?"

"We just got here last week. Mom and Andy were talking to a guy in a bar back in Calgary, and they found out that they could make lots of money picking fruit here in the orchards."

"So has it been hard work?"

"Haven't tried it yet. Mom went to Welfare, and they gave her money for the place we're in. She keeps saying we're going to try it soon, though."

The pup paddled slightly with his right front foot. The boy's eyes met mine as we both searched for a way to continue.

"My name's Dave Perrin."

"Mine's Brian Gallagher." He hesitantly reached out and shook my hand, then smiled and returned his gaze to Boots.

The boy stayed with me throughout the afternoon and into the early evening. By the time Brian reluctantly said good-bye, Boots was looking more stable, and his pupils were almost equal in size. It had been a long day. I bedded the dog down in the kennel and went upstairs for something to eat. I was totally preoccupied with Brian. He seemed like such a nice young lad—how sad that things were so rough for him at home.

It was after midnight when I checked Boots for the last time. His IV was running fine. I changed the bag and gave him an additional injection of steroids. I'd hoped that he would be conscious by now but, other than his sporadic whining and an occasional paddle, he was still gone to the world. I was hoping for a miracle.

My mind was whirling when I finally got to bed. I lay staring into the darkness listening to the sounds of my new residence. There was the characteristic intermittent hum of the directional sign for the City Center Motel as the arrow blinked on and off. Engines raced and tires squealed as a steady stream of cars roared up and down the street. A semi hit the pothole in front of the clinic and responded with the usual metallic clatter. A boisterous crowd of drinkers chattered their way from the front steps of the Creston Hotel to the parking lot behind.

I had moved to town two weeks before. The two fellows who had occupied the apartment before me had been evicted after a raucous party left the place in a shambles. I missed the solitude of West Creston, but I knew moving here was the practical thing to do. I would soon be occupying the entire building. Anthony had decided to close his barbershop and devote all of his time to teaching music. He was going to work from his home and was already hauling away the contents of his side of the building. I couldn't wait to have the additional room; I didn't know how we had been making do until now.

The phone woke me at five-fifteen. It was Herb Hurford—Tsolum Farms had a cow down with milk fever. I threw on my jeans and rushed downstairs. I could see Brian in my mind's eye—his long blond hair, his brilliant blue eyes, his look of gentle innocence. Was his dog alive? Was he conscious?

I hadn't bothered turning on the lights. Flinging open the kennel door, I peered into the gloom. Boots was sitting on his sternum, his head hanging dejectedly.

The dog was in the land of the living. I was elated! Running to the waiting room, I flicked on the lights and rushed back for a closer look at my patient. His eyes were almost swollen shut and what I could see of the whites was blood red.

I clapped my hands. "Boots! Boots! Over here, Boots!" Was he aware of me? Was he able to see? I couldn't tell.

It was nine by the time I got back to the office. Hurford's cow had responded well and was on her feet within a half hour of receiving the calcium. Herb had invited me in for breakfast, and Ev fed me along with her own troops.

I found Brian sitting on the floor next to the kennel. I could hear a murmur as he directed an incessant stream of banter at his dog.

"He was waiting outside the door when I got here," Doris whispered. "He hasn't stopped talking to him the whole time."

"Hi there, Brian. What do you think this morning?"

"He knows me, but he sure looks sad."

"He does, doesn't he? Go over there and call him."

Brian moved to the end of the kennel. "Boots! Over here, Boots."

There was just the faintest twitch of the dog's stub. He never turned, never changed his facial expression, but his tail twitched.

Brian hung around the office for the entire day, leaving the dog's side only when he was obviously underfoot. I checked Boots over shortly before leaving on a farm call. He was stable, but still not looking very perky. It was just before five, and Doris was getting ready to leave for the day.

"Don't know what to tell you, Brian. We'll just have to wait and see what happens. He's improving, but I have no idea what to expect."

The boy looked so sad today. I wanted to give him a big hug—to tell him that everything would be all right. That his dog would recover. That his family would be fine. That his life would be a bed of roses . . .

I drove to Alice Siding, where Wayne Keirn had lined up a small herd of horses for tube deworming and vaccinating. I was sure every teenage girl in the neighborhood who had a horse was there, too.

It was after seven o'clock before I was finished. There were still a couple of hours of daylight left, and I was anxious to get some of that white paint smeared on the outside of the building. I had bought the supplies weeks ago and every time I tripped over the rollers and brushes I was reminded of how much more presentable the clinic would look when it was finished.

I was still a block away when I noticed him leaning against the front of the building. At first I thought it was old George but, as I got closer, I could see it was Brian.

"Can I see Boots?" The boy looked lost, as if his entire life was here inside this building.

"Sure, Brian. Come on in. Do you mind if I do some painting? I was sort of hoping to get started tonight."

"Can I help? How else can I pay you for all you've done for Boots?" He looked at me sadly. He was struggling to hold back tears. "Mom found out about him—she saw me here when she was going to the bar. She made me tell her. She's really mad at me! She says she's going to come in and make you put him to sleep."

"You visit Boots. When you're done, come up and give me a hand."

I had painted a two-foot strip as far down as I could reach by the time Brian joined me. I was thrilled with the brilliant, clean look! What a contrast to that tired old gray.

Brian took over my roller as I set up another and went down to street level. With extensions on both applicators, we covered the entire height of the building. Working with Brian did wonders to loosen his tongue. I learned that he had an older brother named John. That his mother used to be real nice until she started drinking all the time. That he never knew who his dad was, but that didn't matter.

He went on about a pigeon that he'd found on the streets of Calgary. He talked lovingly of the bird that would do anything for him. He choked up when he described how Boots had eaten him, but it wasn't the dog's fault because there wasn't any food.

He talked of how he and John gathered pop bottles. How they knew places in Calgary where they could find food in garbage cans that was almost as good as you could buy. How Creston was nice but hard to figure out; it would take him and John a while to learn the ropes.

It was after dark when I finally finished cleaning up the rollers and putting everything away. I let Brian out the front door of the clinic and thanked him for his help. He fidgeted, and I knew there was something bothering him. He started to leave, then blurted, "Can my brother, John, come with me tomorrow?"

"Sure, no problem."

His face broke into a smile as he ran off down the street. "See you tomorrow!"

They were both there when Doris opened the clinic door in the morning. "Your buddies are here!" she hollered up the stairs. I had slept in and had just gotten out of the bathtub. I hadn't even checked on Boots yet. What if the dog had died overnight and Brian was the one to find him? I whipped on my clothes and raced downstairs.

"He knows me, Dave!"

Both boys were crowded around the open kennel door. Brian beamed as the dog licked precariously at his fingers.

"I'm John." The tall, thin boy sprang to his feet and offered me his hand. "Thanks for helping Boots." His hair was blond too, but darker than his brother's, and curly—long and curly. I could see similarities—like the big blue eyes—but never would have guessed them to be brothers.

John's smile slowly faded and he looked self-conscious. "You don't mind my coming, do you? I don't have anything to do at home."

"Don't mind your coming at all, John. Have you guys eaten yet this morning?"

Without a moment's hesitation, John replied, "Yeah, we ate already!" Brian gave him an odd look, then returned to fussing with Boots. Before I left for a herd health appointment, I got the boys started painting. They were a fantastic pair; they worked well together and bantered constantly back and forth. They may well have been brothers, but they were good friends first.

I was pleasantly surprised to see the first coat on the front of the building when I returned. John was busy scraping away the loose paint on the side.

"Good job, you guys! You ready for something to eat?"

Brian's eyes lit up, and he was about to respond when John interrupted. "We're not hungry—we ate lots this morning."

I noticed the look of disappointment on Brian's face. The boy was hungry, and his brother's denial could do nothing to change the fact. "Come on, let's make lunch."

I had visited the co-op on Saturday for a shopping spree, and my refrigerator was uncharacteristically loaded with goodies. I fixed salami and lettuce sandwiches and plunked them on a plate in the center of the table.

"Dig in, fellas!"

That was the last time I ever had to prod them to eat. From that day forward, it got increasingly more difficult to keep food in the fridge. Boots gained ground on a daily basis and, by week's end, it was obvious that his recovery was going to be complete. Brian's mother had never bothered to come in; I could see no reason not to continue with treatment.

I had run out of paint, and the boys were taking a few days off from the drudgery. I was on my way to pregnancy-test a few cows in Lister. Still in town limits, I drove up Sixteenth Avenue. By the Crestonian Apartments, a roaring fire had been built on the sidewalk, and two boys stood facing it. I thought it was strange but continued by until one of the boys turned sideways. It was John!

Backing up, I pulled into the drive and stomped over to the pair. "What in the world do you think you're doing? You're in town—you can't light a fire in the middle of a sidewalk."

I kicked the fire apart, sending everything from dried hedge clippings to broom handles flying onto the lawn. A badly singed, unopened tin can rolled down the sidewalk.

"Do you guys realize what you were doing? When that can got hot enough, it would have exploded all over you!"

Both boys cowered, and I immediately wished I had been more tactful. John shrugged. "Sorry, we were just trying to cook some beans."

"What do you mean, cook some beans? You can't have an open fire in town like this. Where do you live? Why don't you cook in the house?"

"We live here. That's our suite over there—number one." John pointed sheepishly to the open door at the end of the walk. I entered the dark apartment and fumbled for the light switch.

"There's no electricity. That's why we're cooking on a fire."

I looked at them in bewilderment. "Are you serious? You guys aren't stringing me along about living here?"

"We sleep right there." John pointed to the sleeping bags that lay crumpled in the corner.

"Where's your mom?"

"The bar's open. Mom and Andy left an hour ago."

I wandered around the apartment in disbelief. The bedroom was a clutter of open suitcases and clothing scattered everywhere. My God, what an existence. I hated to see anyone live like this, never mind my Brian and John!

"Does this guy with your mom work? Can he do anything?"

"Andy always talks about being a carpenter," John offered. "But he hasn't done anything like that since we've known him. He can't even read a map. We ended up in Revelstoke on our way here."

I cringed. My mind was going a mile a minute trying to think of some way out for the boys. Maybe if I could get this guy a job, he could put them all on their feet. Maybe all the guy needed was a break. If he was really a carpenter, he could do well in Creston.

What was I doing? This was absolutely none of my business. I had stewed over this all day and had finally made up my mind. The door of the Creston Hotel shut behind me. I looked around, then slowly wandered toward the bar. It was midafternoon and the tavern room was almost empty.

A drunk sat talking to himself in the corner. Half a dozen guys in work clothes, whom I recognized as loggers, surrounded a table by the door. A young man with a cue in his hand hooted as his friend missed a shot.

It didn't take a genius to spot Mrs. Gallagher. She sat alone in the far corner with her back to the wall. She was dressed in tight black slacks and a loose yellow blouse. Her eyes half closed, she was mumbling to herself. Her head was tipped forward, and the blond wig that perched on her head was twisted to cover part of her face. Jet black strands of hair stuck out from beneath it. Why couldn't middle-aged women accept a few gray hairs?

I took a step toward the table, still wondering what I was going to do. The door of the lavatory swung open and out walked the man I was seeking. He was short and squat, probably in his early sixties. He strode unsteadily down the hallway, skirted a few chairs, and sat down next to the woman. His clothing was disheveled, his black-streaked gray hair greasy and ungroomed.

"Are you Andy?"

"That's me. What can I do for you?"

"I'm the vet from across the street. Brian and John told me you do carpentry work. Would you like a job?"

My gut instinct told me that this was not a smart move. Everything about Andy turned me off—his general appearance, his body language, his poky way of moving. He would be the last person I'd ever hire if I were looking for production, but I had to try for the sake of the boys. Surely a few bucks in Andy's pocket would filter down to a better situation for the family.

On his first day of work, I rushed in from the parking lot, anxious to see how much progress had been made in my absence. The door was open and I stepped over the threshold. The lights were off; the air was thick with fumes!

"Holy smoke!"

"Holy smoke, indeed!"

I could see Doris's silhouette through the smog.

"What in the world's going on here?"

"That idiot you hired rented a chain saw to cut the hole through the wall. He came looking for a pencil. When I went into the back room to do up the instruments, he was scratching lines on the wallpaper . . . A few minutes later, he started that saw—scared the daylights out of me!"

"I bet it did!"

"I got out here just before the lights went out. He must have hit a wire because there were sparks flying everywhere!"

"Where did the old fool get to?"

"He said he was going to Creston Hardware to get a flashlight so he could see to finish the job."

"Great!" I closed my eyes and took a deep breath of the acrid air. This was more than I'd bargained for. I had my doubts about his skills as a carpenter, but this was ridiculous. The man was devoid of common sense!

"Where in the world did you come up with this guy? He came in here this morning asking me if we had a hammer. What kind of carpenter doesn't even have a hammer? He went down to the hardware store to get one and, a few minutes after that, Morley called to ask if he was working for you. He wanted to charge a bunch of tools and supplies to your account."

"What did you tell him?"

"I didn't know what to say. I figured you could always take it out of his wages if you hadn't agreed to it."

"Great!"

"I tried to call Gordon after the lights went out, but the phone wasn't working either. I was waiting for the loser to get back before I ran down to Veitch's office. Should I call BC Tel as well?"

Oh man, I could just hear Gordon now. He had his buddy Elden Schultz all lined up to help me with the renovations. I was never going to hear the end of this! Look what my save-the-world mentality had gotten me into.

"Maybe I should go down and ask him if he can have a look at this mess."

"You haven't got time. Just before Andy started cutting, I got a call from Alfred Wiens. He has a cow he wants you to look at. She calved five days ago and hasn't been doing well."

"Is that all he said about her?"

"He said she wasn't eating her grain and that she was losing weight. She gave him less than a gallon of milk this morning."

I quickly headed for the car. I didn't want to be around when Andy came back, and I damn sure didn't want to be here when Gordon arrived. Was he going to chew on me for this one! Why was he always right?

I dawdled along Highway 21 south. My clothes were impregnated with chain saw fumes, and I opened the window to get some fresh air. It was warm, and the rush of the air against my skin felt good.

I drove through the Indian Mission on my way toward the American border. Fields of barley spread out below, the crops already fading from green to yellow. Farther south, a dredging crew tore at the marshy bottomlands, leaving mounds of silt and cattails in their wake. Ducks Unlimited was expanding the wetlands in a continuing effort to keep the skies filled with waterfowl.

I reached the Rykerts border crossing, turned east past a tiny lake, then ascended the bench lands of Huscroft and Lister. Alfred and Hilda Wiens were a German couple who had been in the area for only a few years. Although their farm was antiquated and the facilities left much to be desired, they were good with their cows. I had often thought that if I had to come back to this existence as a cow, I could do worse than to have Hilda and Al looking after me.

I wasn't disappointed when their cow turned out to have a twisted stomach—it gave me a good excuse to be away. As I proceeded with surgery, I kept thinking about what was likely going on at the office. I was glad I wasn't there when Gord found that I had hired some fool drunk with a chain saw. He wasn't a very tolerant man when it came to incompetence.

Damn it anyway, how was I to know that Andy was going to be that inept? He could have turned out to be the find of the year. He said that he had done carpentry work all his life.

Any sensible man would have tromped right down to the hardware store and canned the old guy on the spot. If he was stupid enough to get himself into this fix, what would he do next? Gordon was going to kill me and, if he didn't, Doris would.

It was quiet as I walked up the street toward the office. I half expected to be welcomed by the roar of a chain saw. I slowly turned the knob and swung the door inward. The lights were on. I walked to the back room and deposited the surgery box on the counter. I could detect only the slightest trace of smoke, and I could see into Anthony's side of the building.

I ventured into the new territory. Doris was scrubbing the walls in the back room. "Where's Andy?"

"He went for lunch about half an hour ago."

"I see he finally got a hole through the wall."

"He'd still be at it if Gordon hadn't come along. Gord got here just as he was going to start up the chain saw again. He raised holy hell, then went home for his sabre saw. The old fool just stood there and watched as Gordon did the cutting."

I shuddered. I was never going to hear the end of that one.

"It took Gord a while to get the power back on. He said you owe him a bottle of scotch. He told me to make sure you bought Glenfiddich—not to let you buy any of the cheap stuff."

How I tolerated Andy past the first day, I'll never know. I kept thinking it would be good for the boys. He was pathetically slow at best, and his shift at the bar often took precedence over working at the office. I tolerated his interruptions; he seemed to start sawing or pounding the moment I asked a client a question. What really upset me was the way the clients looked at him. I'm sure they were wondering what rock he had crawled from under.

The passageway was finally framed in, and the benches for the waiting room were constructed. My hired hand was struggling to build a frame in the window for a huge glass fish tank that Dave Rayfield was building for me. Three times I watched him cut the same board. After each attempt, he tried it in place to see if it would fit. The first two times, it was too long. This time, it was a quarter of an inch short! Leaving an equal gap at each end, he pounded the board in place.

Applying a molding to the inside edge really had Andy stumped. He stared at the corner for several minutes, then wandered to the back to cut the strip. He was about to saw, when he hesitated and returned to the window. Holding his thumb at arm's length, he used his other thumb and forefinger as a marker, then retreated to the back room to transfer this measurement to the molding. Scratching away with a pencil, he poised to cut then hesitated again. He closed his eyes as if staring at a blueprint that had been stamped on the back of his eyelids, then retreated one more time to the front. Again, he moved his thumb back and forth as if measuring to the exact millimeter.

I couldn't take it one second longer. "I'm going to check on the boys, Doris!" I climbed the ladder to the roof. The boys had worked every day for a week, and the change that a couple of coats of latex made to the building was truly remarkable.

I laughed loudly when I saw the condition of my painters. John turned with a start. His face was smeared with paint that plastered down strands of his long curly hair. His arms and bare stomach were white. "How in the world did you get that big streak down your back?"

He broke into a broad smile. Brian strutted over, his roller still dripping paint. The smile and the paint on his face told the whole story. He was every bit as mucky as John; it was hard to tell who had won the fight!

Boots had been recovering remarkably well. His only permanent disability would be a bobbed tail. When it had become obvious that he was going to recover from his head trauma, I repaired his fractured femur. The surgery was uneventful and, by the time I discharged him four days later, he was hobbling on his injured leg.

The boys were excited to take Boots home. I stood on the corner and watched as they disappeared from sight. Brian cradled the dog in his arms, and all I could see from my vantage was the constant wagging of his stubbed tail.

At three o'clock the next morning, I was awakened by pounding on the kitchen door. Who in the world could that be? I pulled on my pants.

"The police are after us!" Brian was hollering at me through the glass before I could even open the door. I ushered them into the living room, and they collapsed on the floor. Brian set Boots on the carpet.

"What's this all about? Start from the beginning."

"I pushed her!" Brian blurted. "She was going to hurt Boots and I tried to stop her."

"You pushed who, your mom? Was she okay?"

"We don't know. She was so drunk, she just kept screaming at us—how she was going to have us arrested for beating her up!"

John stood wide-eyed and silent as Brian spoke. Always the protector, he interjected, "He didn't hit her—really he didn't. Mom just went crazy. I've never seen her that bad—she just kept screaming and screaming! The neighbors must have phoned the police . . . The cops pulled up with the lights flashing.

We ran away and a cop chased us, but we lost him in the log piles at the mill yard. I think he went back to the apartment."

"I didn't mean to hurt her! Really, I didn't."

"Settle down, guys—everything'll work out all right. The police won't arrest you. I know a fellow with Social Services. I've already talked to him about you guys. Let me call him. Settle down. Just settle down."

I put the boys to bed in the spare room and got on the phone to Ken. Within a few minutes, I got a call back from the RCMP. They asked me to keep an eye on the boys. Mrs. Gallagher had been hospitalized but, aside from being drunk and incoherent, there was little wrong with her.

The boys stayed with me for a week while arrangements were made for them to live in a foster home. They never saw their mother again.

THIS LITTLE PIGGY

URING HER FIRST FEW MONTHS, Doris had proved to be a great ambassador for the clinic. She knew almost everyone in town, was good at thinking on her feet, and could handle a lot of the clients whom I found difficult.

Right now though, the look on her face suggested she was floundering. She had answered the phone a few minutes earlier and, aside from saying hello and identifying us as Creston Veterinary Clinic, had yet to say a word.

"I think you'd better handle this gentleman, Dr. Perrin." She flushed and held the phone at arm's length for me to grab. "He seems to have a problem with a pig."

"Dr. Perrin speaking."

"Hi, Doc! How the f . . . are ya?" The voice was deep and booming.

"Fine, thanks," I replied, unhinged by the introduction.

Doris focused intently on my face. She was straining to follow the conversation.

"Well, I'm glad you are, because I'm not too great right at the moment! I've got this little friggin' pig that ain't got no asshole."

At that moment, I knew with a certainty that I was dealing with one of my classmates. There was no question about it! It was only a matter of figuring out which one. It sounded like something Carney would do, but I didn't think he could fake the voice; there was something about the quality that I just couldn't put my finger on. Wetstein? He'd try something like this, but there was no way he could do the voice either.

"You there, Doc?"

"Yes. Yes, I'm here."

"Do you think there's something you can do? This poor little bugger's blown up like a balloon, and she's quit suckin' her mom. She's just layin' off by herself under the heat lamp and shiverin'."

"So you've checked and you're sure that there's no rectum?" I was waffling now. This had to be a prank, but maybe I could play along for the moment.

"Yeah, I'm sure! The little bugger's completely smooth back there, and there's no sign of shit around her tail at all."

Doris was still staring at me, waiting for an answer to the mystery. I raised my eyebrows and shrugged my shoulders.

"So do you want to take a look at her, or should I just take her out and knock her on the head?"

"Who's calling, if you don't mind my asking?"

"This is Verna Levett. I've got a hog farm south of town."

"And she's the only piglet in the litter that has the problem?" I was still half convinced that someone was pulling my leg.

"Yeah, the others are all doin' good. They're lined up and suckin' on their mom. Just that one poor little bugger that can't shit!"

"Well, why don't you bundle her up and bring her in. Stick a hot water bottle in with her before you leave—we don't want her getting chilled."

"Who in the world was that?" Doris asked the moment I hung up the phone. "I've never in my life heard so many four-letter words in such a short period of time!"

"She said her name was Verna Levett," I muttered, making a notation on the day page. "She's bringing in a piglet."

"Verna, did you say? That couldn't possibly have been a woman's voice I heard!"

"She had me going for a while too, but I'm convinced that she's the real thing!"

Shuffling through the stack of records on the top of the filing cabinet, I began making notations. I had just finished musing to Doris that the pig should be arriving any time, when the door flew open and in strode Verna.

I'd been trying to visualize the woman that went along with the voice on the telephone; although I had difficulty focusing on an image, the person who entered provided no major surprises. Her face was full, her hair cropped at medium length and pulled back from her face with a headband. She was of average size and height for a woman, but the clothing she wore made her appear far stockier than she really was. Although it was a cool day for summer, she was more appropriately dressed for the late fall or early winter.

A heavy red flannel shirt hung loosely below her waist, partially covering a pair of gray woolen pants that appeared several sizes bigger than she required. Her feet were adorned in black rubber gum boots that had seen use in a mucky barn on more than a few occasions. Although her clothing was clean, the odor that wafted in with her suggested a recent pass through her hog barn.

"Well, here she is!" Verna affirmed, passing a cardboard box to Doris. "Poor little bugger anyway; I just hate to see an animal suffer like this."

Doris hesitated but stretched her arms out to receive the bundle. She carefully lifted the blanket that covered it to peer inside.

"Aw, isn't he cute?" Doris crooned at the bloated little critter that lay shivering in the box. "How old is he?"

"She's just a little over a day old," Verna responded.

"Let's get her on the table, Doris. She sucked all right at the start then, did she, Mrs. Levett?"

"Oh hell, yes! She was right up there with the rest of them as soon as she was born. I never saw a thing wrong with her until she started blowin' up and layin' off by herself."

I reached into the box and slid my fingers under the piglet's belly. She was indeed distended, and her general appearance suggested that she was in a great deal of discomfort. She oinked pathetically as I lifted her from the box. After making a few paddling motions, she closed her eyes and resisted no more.

"She feels cool." I felt a shiver course through her body.

Pressing gently on her abdomen, I checked in the region of the anal sphincter for signs of a bulge.

"A lot of times, the distal colon and rectum are normal but the baby has a sealed anal sphincter. It's simple to correct those ones by just making an incision where the rectum was supposed to be and allowing the feces to escape through the new exit."

"So how can you tell if that's what it is?"

"With those cases, we can almost always see the rectum bulging out. Then all we have to do is stick a needle in to make sure she has poop; if she does, we make the incision."

"And you don't see a bulge?"

"No, I can't feel any indication that she has a formed rectum. Sometimes, there's nothing more than a little ropelike string of flesh that comes through where the rectum should be, and it's completely solid with no cavity in the center of it."

"So what does that mean for her? Should I just take the poor little bugger out and do away with her?"

For all her gruff exterior and rugged language, here was a woman with a soft heart when it came to dealing with the animals in her charge. This pig was obviously more than a number in a ledger book. Verna's face softened as she looked down on the creature, and I could tell that she found the thought of killing it more than a little distasteful.

"Well, to be honest with you, that's the most practical solution if you factor in the value of the pig and the cost of doing anything surgical to correct it. But . . . it just so happens we don't have anything else to do at the moment, and it might be fun to see if I could do a colostomy."

"So what's that in white man's language?"

"It's a type of surgery where we make the poop come out under her tummy instead of from her bum."

"You can do that?"

"Yes, realistically the surgery would cost far more than the pig's worth, but I haven't done one before, and I'd like to give it a try!"

"Well, you do what you can then," Verna boomed with enthusiasm. "Let's give the poor little bugger a chance!"

"Okay."

"I'll leave her with you then." The door had almost closed when it swung open again, and Verna appeared once more.

"You know, it seems like such a shame," she hooted, with a smile that nearly split her face in two, "that with all the assholes in the world, you have to go to so much trouble to create another one!"

I knew from that moment on Verna was going to be a client I could relate to. As crude and loud as she could be at times, there was never any question that her animals were important to her and that she'd do her best for them.

We had a part bag of saline with dextrose left over from a patient that had gone home earlier in the morning. I changed the administration set and hung it up ready to use.

"Baby pigs have a devil of a time regulating both their glucose level and their body temperature until they are a little older," I advised Doris. "We'll get this drip started as soon as we have her anesthetized so we can stabilize her during surgery."

"Just out of curiosity, what's a little pig like this worth?"

"This pig healthy, with a functional rectum, would probably be worth twenty-five or thirty dollars."

"Oh, so this is another one of your get-rich-quick schemes, is it?"

"Yeah, something like that!"

I slipped the anesthetic mask over the piglet's nose. She resisted for a few seconds, reluctant to breathe the sweet mixture of halothane and nitrous oxide. Finally, she took a breath and then another.

Before long, her breathing was rhythmic and she was in a deep, relaxing sleep. Holding her in an upright position, Doris opened the piglet's mouth and pulled her tongue forward as far as possible. After several attempts, I was able to pass a tube through the constricted pharynx and down her trachea.

We packed hot water bottles under and around her in the surgery cradle to help keep her from losing body heat. Perched there, her distended tummy appeared more prominent than ever.

"Hold your fingers tight across here," I directed, crimping down hard at the base of the piglet's ear.

With gauze soaked in alcohol, I rubbed vigorously along the top and margins of the right ear until I raised a dark blue network of veins, the only access I was likely to have for the administration of fluids.

"Hold tight. They always look bigger than they really are, and collapse completely if you happen to miss them."

Doris maintained a steady compression as I slid the catheter through the skin and into the vein. I connected the intravenous tubing and started the drip.

"Okay, you can let it go."

Doris released her hold, and fluid began drip, drip, dripping through the chamber. We rolled the piglet over on her back and prepared her for surgery. I pulled her feet toward the four corners of the table and tied them in place while Doris scrubbed her tummy. I washed myself and pulled on a pair of surgery gloves.

After clamping on the side drapes, I made an incision most of the length of the abdomen, through the piglet's skin and down to the underlying muscle.

The pressure of the gas in her intestine was intense; I was cautious not to penetrate the abdominal wall and puncture the bowel itself. Moving to the lower end of the incision, I made a small stab wound and inserted the tip of my scissors. I pushed them forward toward the head and split through the muscle layer to allow gas-distended loops of gut to surge through the incision and out onto the surrounding drapes.

Retracting the bowels to the side, I searched for the rectum. All I found was a pink cord of tissue about the size of a pencil lead. It ran forward to be lost in the gas-filled bowel that surrounded it. Following it patiently, I finally found an area at the level of the distal colon, where the bowel suddenly ballooned many times in size.

"Look at that, Doris! See where the abnormal bowel starts? See it, right here?"

"Well, isn't that something." Doris maneuvered for a closer look. "Is that where you'll cut it off?"

"As close to here as possible." I applied traction and pulled the bowel gently toward the body wall. "But more likely here." I pointed to a location a bit farther up, where the distal colon pulled easily over to the abdominal wall. I drove a pair of forceps through the piglet's body wall, incised through the skin, and stretched the hole by opening and expanding the jaws of the forceps.

"Are you going to put it way down there?" Doris looked aghast as I worked at enlarging the hole and approximating the length of the distal colon.

"Yes, we need it dumping far enough ahead so that the manure doesn't scald her back legs, and far enough down so that it doesn't run over her side."

I worked away at the body wall and the colon until I was sure that I was amputating where I wouldn't impede the blood supply and where I had a minimal amount of functioning bowel to sever.

I passed a pair of hemostats through the tunnel in her side and clamped across the colon. With another set of hemostats adjacent to the first, I severed between the two and pulled the free end through the tunnel. Carefully tying all the vessels, I amputated it through the solid portion of the dysfunctional rectum.

Finally, I removed the forceps from the end of the bowel, spread it out, and sutured it to the surrounding skin. Gas gurgled out as I worked, and fecal material ran down her side and onto the table.

I changed my gloves and began closing the piglet's abdomen. The going was slow as I pushed in the gas-filled gut and sutured behind it. It was after five by the time I unhooked the piglet from the machine.

"What do you say to Chinese food, Doris? I'm starved and sure don't feel like trying to cook anything now!"

"Sounds good to me. Don't feel like cooking myself!"

Within a half hour, the piglet was up and moving. A constant expulsion of gas and straw-colored feces was doing wonders to alleviate her bloated appearance, and I was pretty confident of her ability to recover.

"I'll just give Verna a call and let her know that things went well. Then we can head out."

"Hello." It was the voice of a young man on the phone.

"Hello, can I speak to your mom, please?"

"Maaaaa!" he bellowed. "Come get the phone!"

"Hello!" It was the gruff voice that I remembered so well from this morning's conversation.

"This is Dave Perrin. I'm calling to let you know that the surgery on the piglet went well, and she seems to be recovering quite nicely."

"Oh great, Doc, it's you! So the poor little bugger's going to be all right then? Well, that's great news—sure glad I didn't have to do her in!"

"She's not out of the woods yet, but the way she's looking right now, I think we should be able to get her back to Mom in the morning."

"Well, isn't that something. It's amazing what you guys can do when you make up your mind to do it. Thanks for the good news. I'll be in to pick her up first thing in the morning."

What an upbeat situation. I hung up the phone feeling like an ambassador for veterinary medicine! It had certainly been worth going the extra mile even though it was obviously not economically justifiable.

"Come on, Doris! Let's eat." I followed her out the door. "You know, it's times like this that I know I made the right choice of profession. It probably cost me as much as the pig was worth to do that surgery, but it was the best money I could have spent as far as public relations go."

"You're probably right. Mrs. Levett seems like the type of person you want to stay on the right side of!"

We were halfway down the block when I started worrying about the piglet with just the hot water bottles and a few jugs of hot water next to her.

I came to a halt in the middle of the street. "You know, Doris, I think we better go back and set something up for that piglet so she's going to be warm enough. Newborn pigs are really susceptible to hypothermia. We've just given her an anesthetic, so she's even more vulnerable!"

Doris turned reluctantly in the direction of the office, and we bantered back and forth about what would be the best way to keep her warm.

"How would they stay warm if they were out on the farm with their mother?" Doris asked.

"There are a variety of different systems from warmed floors to heaters, but Mrs. Levett would probably just have a heat lamp hanging over them. They could come and go from under the light whenever they got too hot or too cold."

"Well, why don't we just hang a lightbulb over the piglet? Won't that do the same thing?"

By the time we got back to the office, I had decided that the forty-watt desk lamp would probably be adequate. It was just a matter of running an extension cord to the kennel and setting it up. I placed a woolen blanket in the bottom of a cardboard box, transferred the now mobile piglet, and lowered the flexible head of the lamp until it was directly over the edge.

"That looks like it should do the job, Doris. She probably would have been just fine, but I feel better now that we've rigged this up."

Dinner at the Club Café was every bit as good as we had come to expect. Doris was playing out as the meal progressed, and I was forced to finish off the rest of the fried rice and sweet and sour pork. It was almost two hours later that we wandered back to the office. Both as stuffed as ticks, we were certainly in no rush to get back to cleaning up the clinic. We plunked ourselves on the benches in the reception area.

"Boy, Mae and her husband certainly know how to put on a spread of Chinese food," I muttered, laying my head back against the wall and patting my belly. "I'm so stuffed, I don't think I'll be able to eat for a week."

"Me too," groaned Doris. "All I want to do now is go to sleep."

It was an afterthought that pulled me from my repose. I wandered into the surgery, casually opened the surgery kennel, and bent down over the box to check the piglet.

"Oh nooo! Doris, she's dead!"

I couldn't believe my eyes; there as rigid as a board lay the victory that just a few hours earlier had been so sweet. It hardly looked like a victory of any sorts now!

"What could have happened? She looked so good when we left."

"I killed her!" I felt numb.

"Oh, don't be silly," Doris rebuked. "You weren't even here, and you did everything you could possibly have done to help her."

"You're right, I wasn't here and, because I wasn't here, she died! I fried her, Doris! I put her in that bloody cardboard box, and she couldn't get away from the heat. I told you about how piglets can't regulate their body temperature, then I went ahead and fried the poor thing! I rushed back up the street to kill her with kindness!"

We stood staring at one another for several minutes. What could we say to lend meaning to this travesty? What could we do to reverse the situation and breathe life back into this pathetic blob of flesh?

"I can't believe I could have done anything that foolish," I moaned, picking up the remains of the little creature and setting her on the surgery table. "I'm having enough trouble trying to justify this to myself. How am I going to tell Verna?"

The look of concern on Doris's face was far from reassuring as I dialed the phone and held my breath. The very thought of telling Verna sent shivers up my spine. Delaying the inevitable was not going to make it any easier.

I was imagining the dressing-down and the four-letter words about to be hurled in my direction. The telephone had rung a fourth time and I was telling myself to hang up, when the same boyish voice answered.

"Hello."

"Yes," I blurted. "Is your mother in?"

"Maaaaa! Yeah, just a second. She was goin' to bed."

I shifted the receiver away from my ear just in time.

"Maaaaaa! It's the phone. Sounds like that new vet again!"

"Hello," came the gruff voice that I'd been dreading.

"Yes, Mrs. Levett, I am afraid I have some bad news—the piglet is dead."

"Well, son of a b . . . anyway! After all that work you put into her, I was looking forward to see how she grew out."

"So was I, Mrs. Levett."

Verna seemed satisfied that the piglet had died from complications of the surgery and, for a brief moment, I was tempted to say no more.

"I'm afraid I did a very stupid thing. We went out for supper, and I left a lightbulb over her to keep her from getting chilled. She overheated and died as a result of exposure. I should've left her enough room to get away from it. I just didn't think that a little bulb like that could possibly generate enough heat to cause her problems."

There was a long silence, and I waited for the inevitable explosion. I had no way to defend myself for my stupidity and could only fall back on a plea of ignorance!

"That poor little bugger," she muttered quietly. "That's sure too bad!"

"I'm certainly sorry, Mrs. Levett. I wish I had it to do over."

The silence resumed. I could think of nothing sensible to add.

"Well, Doc, you tried. It's a hell of a lot better this way than if I had to take her out and knock her on the head!"

PLUM '72

JUST HAVE TO GET an X-ray machine, Doris! There's no way I can keep going without it! I'm sure Muppet's got a broken pelvis, and there's something going on with her left hind leg. If I put even a little pressure below the knee, she squeals and squirms to get away from me."

"What're you going to do with her? Mrs. Morris phoned a few minutes ago wondering when she could take her home."

"Isn't this great! We have a client who's willing to pay for whatever's required for her pet, and all I can do is guess at what's wrong. I'm sure there's a problem with that tibia, but I hate to splint it if it isn't necessary."

"What should I tell her?"

"That I've taken Muppet to Nelson for X rays! I'll give her a call as soon as I get back. Hugh Croxall told me to come over whenever I needed anything. I'll give him a ring right now."

The trip over the Salmo-Creston highway was a breathtaking experience at any time of year but now, with the fall colors in full blaze, it was spectacular. Lining the gorge that confined Summit Creek, poplar and birch trees sporting orange and yellow leaves were everywhere. Their colors mingled with the yellows of the larches and the greens of spruce, cedar, pine, and fir. Farther up the pass, the mountains grew more sheer and their rock faces more prominent. The drop was ominous in places and, often, not even treetops were evident at the edge of the highway.

The incline steepened and I shifted to a lower gear. Muppet sat stoically staring out the car window. A Thunderbird overtook us and quickly left us in the distance. Muppet swiveled to watch the vehicle as it barreled by and stared after it until the car disappeared. We overtook a transport truck laden with lumber. Discharging a plume of thick, black smoke, it lugged its way up the steep incline. I swung into the passing lane, jammed the gas pedal to the floor, and ground on toward the summit. Several big rigs were parked at the rest stop next to Summit Lake, the drivers wandering around the perimeter of their vehicles checking tires and brakes.

The car accelerated rapidly the moment we reached the crest of the climb, and we were soon freewheeling down the other side. Before I realized it, the speedometer read over seventy, and I braked. A half mile ahead a transport truck burdened with wood chips descended slowly down the mountain, its Jake brake metering out a constant rattle. I slowed to a crawl until we rounded the corner, then swung into the opposite lane to pass.

I was halfway to Salmo. Rounding a gentle sweeping curve, I noticed something move near the edge of the road. I slowed and pulled to the far lane. A Dall sheep with massive curling horns hopped onto the highway and sauntered in front of the car. Several more stood hesitantly below the shoulder waiting for me to pass. I came to a complete stop and watched as the sheep grabbed a mouthful of grass. Unconcerned, he glanced in my direction and munched contentedly.

Passing through the village of Salmo, I followed the winding highway to Nelson. Hugh's clinic was on the north end of town, on the same highway that I had come in on. The door was locked and a closed sign was prominently displayed in the window of the waiting room. I rapped sharply on the door.

A powerfully built man in his early thirties strode jauntily to the door and unlocked the bolt. "Well, you made it, did you?" His voice was bold and forthright, his British accent almost lyrical. "I've got the machine all set up; just bring her on in."

We used large plates and took radiographs of Muppet's entire back end from the abdomen to her feet. Metal lids clanked and clattered in the darkroom, as Hugh shifted the films from the tank containing the developer to the one with the fixer.

"She has to have something wrong with that left hind leg," I hollered through the door. "She sure resents it when it's handled. My money's on a greenstick fracture."

"Could be. We'll soon know . . . So you were from the Trail area then? Is that how you started visiting at Pete's clinic?"

"Yeah, I was born in Trail and grew up in a little place called Casino. Pete started his practice my last year of high school."

"I went out there with Pete to castrate a couple of horses when I first arrived in the area," said Hugh. "Casino's way up the mountain the other side of the river, isn't it?"

"Yeah, that's it. My dad and a handful of other guys started it as a sort of cooperative back in the forties. They bought up land at the end of an old logging road and started building."

"Seems a bit isolated. I know Pete hated going out there in the winter. That's one heck of a climb up the final stretch."

"Isn't it ever! We loved taking toboggans down that hill and getting the snow so polished that the bus couldn't make it. It was a good way to get a day off school."

Hugh sauntered out, the X rays dangling from one hand. "Well, you're right!" He glanced at the film against the light from the view box. "There it is running all the way down from the tibial crest. Doesn't look like there's any displacement though." He lowered the ventral-dorsal view and held up the lateral view.

"A Thomas splint should handle that nicely," I opined. "Let's just have another look at the ventral-dorsal view. That pelvis doesn't look bad enough to need repairs, does it?"

Hugh held up the other X ray. A crack ran through the right shaft of the ileum, and there was a jagged line where it had pushed back and separated the pubis.

"Got to hurt like hell," Hugh observed. "But give her a few weeks and she'll be as good as new."

"Well, that sure eliminates the guesswork. I just have to get my own machine. I've called a few distributors to try and locate a used one, but haven't found anything in my price range yet."

"They're out there. This one came from the Nelson hospital—just happened to be there when they were taking it out."

I gathered Muppet in my arms and headed for the exit.

"You'll stop at the house," Hugh pronounced. "Pat's expecting you for supper."

I had planned on heading right back but, being a bachelor, I rarely rejected the offer of a home-cooked meal.

"Sounds good to me." I took Muppet outside, set her down on the lawn, and held my hand under her tummy. She balanced awkwardly on her right hind leg for a few minutes, then gingerly squatted for a pee. By the time I had her settled in the backseat of my vehicle, Hugh was waiting behind the wheel of his car.

I followed him toward Nelson, a picturesque old city on the west arm of Kootenay Lake. I was looking forward to a view of the elegant stone buildings that lined the main street but, before we entered the city, Hugh veered west toward Castlegar.

The highway followed the rocky banks of Kootenay River for several miles. We had just crossed a bridge at Taghum, when Hugh turned right into a high rock cut and swung onto a dirt road. I bounced along in his wake as he raced through an outcrop of massive fir trees. I could see clear blue water through the vegetation and slowed to gaze with appreciation across a rocky point that jutted out over the river. Hugh bombed on ahead.

I continued in the direction of the dust that hung lazily over the constricted roadway. It grew narrower, and I slowed my pace. Squeezing the car between a huge fir tree and a jagged rock wall, I stopped. Surely this wasn't Hugh's driveway! Had I missed a turnoff when I was sight-seeing? Couldn't have.

Putting the car in gear, I advanced slowly, hugging the rock face in fear of dropping a wheel over the edge. The road veered sharply to the left, and it was necessary to back up and maneuver further toward the river. I had no sooner negotiated the corner than the trail narrowed drastically. A rough-sawn two-by-twelve had been laid down to span a gap that fell off twenty feet to the river below.

I gingerly opened the door. It bumped against the rock face and I pushed with my feet to squeeze out the crack. Walking to the edge of the road, I shook my head in disbelief. The bank had sloughed into the river leaving a drop-off that was almost vertical. I ventured onto the plank and jumped up and down. Several beams had been wedged against rocks below to support the wooden crutch. It seemed solid enough but, man, that drop!

I climbed over the console via the passenger side to get back to my seat. Taking a deep breath, I pushed the stick into low gear and engaged the clutch. The front wheel climbed onto the plank, and I idled across it.

I rounded the corner into a huge open meadow and a driveway that passed through a grove of cottonwoods into a barnyard. A massive Chesapeake retriever and a pair of Jack Russell terriers suddenly materialized. Barking madly, the terriers ran on either side of the vehicle. I watched uneasily as they darted back and forth in front of me, dutifully announcing my presence. Muppet whined anxiously and strained to peek out the window. The road curved gently away from the river and abruptly ended in front of the Croxalls' house. The rustic stone building had been erected in the meadow to overlook the river below—a picturesque home in a postcard setting.

"So you made it, did you?" Hugh stood in front of the kitchen door, his hands planted on his hips, a mischievous grin on his face. "What kept you? I was about ready to start draggin' the river for you."

"What kept me? I had myself convinced that I'd taken a wrong turn. I wasn't looking forward to backing out. No one in his right mind would live at the end of a road like this!"

"You've got that right," came a voice from behind us.

"Oh, hi, Pat! Never noticed you. I was a bit distracted by that road. All I could think of was how cold that water was likely to be."

"Isn't that the truth; I see myself tumbling into the river every time I drive over that horrible plank. But you know Hughie!"

Pat was a slender, shapely woman with delicate features. With her lilting English accent, I had always pictured her as the lady of a manor, but today she was dressed in a baggy cotton shirt and jeans that tucked loosely into a pair of well-worn black rubber boots.

"That road's the only reason we could afford to buy this property," Hugh chirped. "Everyone loved the place from across the river, but not even the Realtor wanted to come down here to show it."

"I can understand why." I shivered instinctively as I looked back down the road.

"So is supper ready, Mom?" Hugh queried.

"Not yet! I've got the cow milked and the calves fed. That old ewe's limping as bad as ever tonight, and I better have another look at her. The chickens need to be locked in, too—we don't want to lose any more. Damned skunk's looking to get popped off one of these nights!"

"Well, you get along with your chores then, Mom. Dave 'n I'll rustle ourselves up a beer."

I ducked my head and stepped into the kitchen.

"Sit yourself down." Hugh pointed to a chair at the head of a long table and opened the refrigerator. "Bloody hell!" he hooted, getting down on one knee and rummaging through the bottom shelves. "There's only one left."

"That's no problem, Hughie, I have to drive home tonight and better not be drinking anyway."

He plunked down a water glass, poured half a dark ale into it, and pushed it across the table to me. "Still can't call this Canadian stuff ale. Haven't found one with enough body to it."

I nodded and sipped at my glass. Hugh tipped back the bottle and drained a good portion of what remained in the first go.

"So, you're starting out all on your own over there, are you?"

"Yeah, there are some days I really wonder what I'm doing but, for the most part, things are going well."

"You know, back home that's almost unheard of. There are so many established practices around that it's hard to make room for another one. Besides, new graduates in Britain need to work under someone to get enough experience to learn the ropes. When I graduated, I had never done surgery on a live dog, what with the SPCA and all."

"I guess I was lucky. Graduates from Saskatoon had a fair amount of practical experience; I had a job after third year in a busy practice in Alberta. I worked in St. Paul with George Bosniak. He was a good vet. By the time the summer was out, I had gotten a pretty good taste of practice."

"You went right there fresh out of third year, and he let you start working up cases?"

"Not exactly." I chuckled. "When I got there, George had been working alone for months, and he was about bagged. I'm sure he wished I was more useful than I was. I started out handing him things and cleaning up but, as the summer went by, I got more and more opportunity to get my hands dirty—hooked up lots of IVs on scouring calves, repaired a load of hernias on pigs, and did some calvings.

"I still remember showing up for work that first morning. There was a lineup of vehicles outside his clinic that stretched halfway down the block. It just amazed me—the volume of work he was expected to put through. What a hodgepodge! There were heifers laid out and straining, cows trying to calve, a prolapsed vagina hanging out here, a prolapsed rectum there—all kinds of sick calves, some barely breathing. There were even a few pigs thrown in for good measure.

"I had never met George before that morning. I found him in the back of a pickup wrestling with a huge, bloody mess protruding from the rear end of a heifer. How he got through the work that day was beyond me. He just plugged away on one case after the other until finally the last vehicle was gone and the final phone call was answered."

Hugh wagged his head as I talked, then drained the rest of his beer. "A lot of guys out there on the prairies have a pretty tough go in the spring."

"That's for sure; that's why I decided to come to B.C. Being around a guy like George was a fantastic experience for a rookie. He was a real diplomat with clients and patients and never seemed to lose his temper. I think what had the greatest impact on me, though, was watching the battle between his dedication to the practice and his desire to have some time to himself. After watching George, I made a vow that I would never allow myself to be overwhelmed by my practice."

"Yeah, sure! Tell me that in a couple of years after you've been in the racket for a while."

Hugh looked longingly at the beer bottle that sat empty on the table before him. Pushing his chair back, he opened the cupboard and hauled a gallon jug from beneath the sink.

"Have I got a treat for you." He grinned and authoritatively plunked the crock down.

"My God, what's that?"

"Drink up." He motioned to my few remaining gulps of ale.

"I've got to head over the summit yet tonight. I don't need anything more to drink."

"But this is plum '72," Hugh pronounced, as if describing a wine of exceptional vintage.

I drained my glass and winced as I watched the cloudy, brownish-yellow sludge spew forth from the jug.

He filled the tumbler to the brim. "Whoa! You are trying to drown me!"

"Oh hell! By the time Mom gets supper into you, it'll be all soaked up. Besides, the brew's not even a year old; it's just starting to work."

I peered into the glass. Miscellaneous chunks of debris still swirled in a quiet little eddy. I was sure I could see a big clump bobbing deeper in the glass, but the wine was so cloudy that it was hard to tell.

"I better get the barbecue warmed up for Mother," Hugh grumbled, taking his glass and heading for the door.

"Do you plan on using that turpentine to start the fire?"

"You damned Canucks—none of you have the slightest appreciation for good liquor."

While Hugh was busy, I surveyed the room. Character oozed from every pore. The old-fashioned kitchen had cabinets along one wall and a sink in front of a deep window that was laden with plants. The living room was one with the kitchen, with a stairway heading to the upper floor. A couch and two overstuffed armchairs surrounded a stone fireplace, which occupied a portion of the outside wall.

"I sure like these high ceilings," I commented to Hugh, as he wandered in from outside.

"I've always been partial to older style places. This one reminds me a lot of the houses back home in England."

Hugh sat down. Throwing his feet on a neighboring chair, he grabbed his glass of wine. "Pretty good stuff, this." He took a sip and maintained a straight face. "Haven't even filtered it yet," he bragged, holding the glass up to the light.

"Have you tried putting it through a kitchen sieve?" I eyed a large floating mass that I hoped was a piece of plum.

Hugh chuckled, then leaned back and took another draft. "So have you always been a whiz kid?"

"What do you mean by that?"

"Well, I can't imagine anyone starting his own practice his first day out of school; Pete tells me you graduated third or fourth in your class."

"That had more to do with the hours I spent studying than the brain cells I had working. I remember taking a letter of protest around to get signatures from classmates when the college decided to close the library at midnight. There just didn't seem to be enough hours to take it all in."

"Somehow, you don't strike me as the serious type. Had a few book-worms in my class too, but I wanted to have time for sports and a few glasses of ale."

"I guess I always had this thing about being big and dumb." I lifted the glass to my mouth to wet my lips. I grimaced as the dry, acrid liquid spread over my taste buds—what swill!

"How old are you now?"

"Turned twenty-five in June."

"Well, anyone who qualified by that age sure didn't waste much time along the way."

"Always knew I was going to be a vet. Don't ever remember making the decision—but always knew it. Not many people thought I had a hope of get-ting to university, never mind graduating. From the time I started school, I was always struggling to keep up; spent the majority of my elementary years in remedial reading classes. I know what it's like to be branded as one of the slow ones."

Hugh sat quietly with the glass cradled between his hands. He rotated it slowly, staring at what was probably a piece of plum floating at the top of the slurry.

"Had a terrible time with math when I got to middle school. Failed ninth grade math even though I worked like a hound on it. My old man tried help-ing me. He'd get so frustrated that he'd holler and pound his fist on the table—it just didn't sink in. They advised me to take vocational rather than academic training."

A peacock screeched outside, and one of the terriers barked shrilly. I glanced out the window. My mind drifted back to the meeting with my high school counselor, where he spelled out in black and white that I wasn't college material. He stressed to my parents that I should work toward an apprentice-ship at the smelter where I'd be able to learn a trade.

I remembered my father shouting at him. "But the kid wants to be a veteri-narian! He's wanted to be one since he was old enough to want to be any-thing; I'll be damned if I'll stand in the way. I'm not about to sentence him to a life of hell with the company!"

The session ended with the counselor shaking his head as he stared at my academic standings. He agreed to allow me to continue the struggle, and after much wrangling, he arranged for me to take both ninth and tenth grade math in the same year.

I lifted my glass and took a sip. Hugh interrupted my reverie.

"You must have done better in high school to get into college."

"Well yes, but things never seemed to come easy for me. I'd work like hell to get the same grades that other kids got doing next to nothing. I was a dogged SOB though; I was determined not to fail. By the time I graduated, my grades had climbed to C-pluses and Bs.

"The best thing that ever happened to me was working one summer for Cominco. Didn't take me long to figure out that I wanted something more. Crawling into empty vats with sand-blasting equipment in ninety-five-degree weather, loading bags of fertilizer into railway cars—it was a great way to convince me to stick with school.

"I put in a couple of years at Selkirk College in Castlegar; if you didn't consider my marks for math, physics, and chemistry, my grades really didn't look bad. I struggled through those courses with the barest of passes. I tell you, those classes taught me a new definition of misery. I hated every minute I spent studying those subjects!"

"Did you keep working at Cominco during the summers?"

"No, didn't have the stomach for it. Got a job with a logging company on the Anzac River north of Prince George. It was way out in the bush, and stacking lumber was a treat compared to working in the dust and grime at the smelter. There wasn't a lot to waste my money on either. Had no problem saving for the next year at college."

"So you got right into the vet college from Selkirk?"

"No, I applied but never had a snowball's chance in hell. Ended up going to UBC for a year. Boy, I'll tell you, that was a shocker for a small-town boy. I couldn't stand the crowds and the traffic. The worst part was losing contact with my critters—really missed my horses, and I had never been without dogs and cats for as long as I could remember.

"It was a good year for me academically though. I got into courses that actually interested me. From that year on, it seemed relatively easy to keep myself in the upper third of the class."

The kitchen door burst open and Pat came clunking in, her arms laden with buckets, all three dogs following close behind her. The moment the

Chesapeake stepped over the threshold, the Jack Russell terrier yipped and attacked him with a ferocity that surprised me. He jumped up and grabbed the big dog by his jowl. Dangling there, he swung like a pendulum.

"Jeremy, stop that!" Pat hollered. "Behave yourself for a change! Duke could eat you in one bite if he had a mind to."

Only after Duke backed out of the house did the little white terror release his grip.

"Boy, he sure is a feisty little bugger." The dog strutted into the kitchen. His head held high and his belly only inches from the floor, he walked with the self-assured swagger of a barroom brawler.

"He's death on anything that moves if he thinks it doesn't belong on the property," Hugh affirmed. "And he seems to have the notion that poor old Duke doesn't belong near the house."

Jeremy presented his front feet on Hugh's leg; Hugh bent over and scooped him onto his lap. The dog promptly curled up in a ball and went to sleep.

"That poor old ewe has a swollen foot again," Pat lamented. "I gave her a shot and kept her in the paddock. I couldn't see a puncture, but it sure looks sore."

Hugh took another draft of his wine. "Maybe we'll have to throw her down and have a look if it doesn't improve. Aren't you going to pour yourself one, Mom?"

"Is it as bad as it looks, Hughie?"

"It's coming along real good," Hugh insisted. "It's already got a bit of a nip to it."

Pat rummaged through the kitchen cupboards; pots and pans soon rattled their way to the top of the stove. Dumping a bucket full of freshly dug vegetables into the sink, she began scrubbing them.

"What happened after UBC then?" Hugh continued.

"Competition for seats at the vet college was fierce; my less-than-stellar performance at Selkirk hadn't helped my grade point average.

"I was on my way to a job in Ontario, so stopped in Saskatoon with the hopes of arranging an interview. It wasn't mandatory, but I thought it might help my chances. The receptionist made several calls and told me that no one from the admissions committee would be available to meet with me for the rest of the week.

"As I was leaving, a distinguished-looking gentleman asked if I was interested in becoming a student at the veterinary college. He had apparently overheard me talking to the receptionist. I told him I had wanted to be a vet for as long as I could remember and that I would get in there eventually.

" 'I'm sure you will . . . I'm sure you will. I'm Larry Smith,' he said. He shook my hand and spoke as casually as if he were part of the janitorial staff. 'Would you like to come to my office?'

"I was more than a little humbled when he opened the door with Dr. Larry Smith—Dean of Students boldly printed across the front of it. I chatted with him about my hopes and my experiences.

"As it turned out, he'd been waiting for the president of the University of Saskatchewan to arrive for a personally guided tour of the clinical facilities. Before I knew it, I was being escorted around the college in the company of the president and his wife with the dean as guide."

"Wasn't that a stroke of luck," Pat chimed. "You sure wouldn't have gotten that treatment from Hughie's dean, would you, hon?"

"That's for damned sure," Hugh pronounced glumly.

"I was in a bush camp near North Bay when I discovered that I hadn't made the cut. BC's quota was only five students and, as it turned out, I wasn't one of them. They mentioned that I was on a list of alternates—that I'd be called if other candidates dropped out. I never had much hope of that."

"So what happened then?" Pat leaned back against the kitchen counter.

"I was down in the dumps for a while, but I can't say I was surprised. I went through the remainder of the summer with the thought that I'd just have to slug it out and raise my grade point average enough to get in the next year.

"Toward the end of August, I got a call from my parents that they'd received a letter for me from the vet college. Someone had declined a seat, and I'd been selected as a replacement. I had less than a week to help wrap up the bear project in Ontario and get to Saskatoon before the term began."

"You must have been pretty happy!"

"I was ecstatic about getting into the college, and I was sure that Larry Smith played a big part in it. The fact that I was one of the last students in a class of sixty to qualify left me feeling rather insecure though; I was sure I was going to have to work harder than all the others to survive."

Pat smiled and moved to the table to sit down. She tried to pull out the chair but it wouldn't budge. Lifting the tablecloth, she peered underneath.

"Suzie, you run along now! I want to sit here."

Suzie, Jeremy's better half, reluctantly jumped to the floor and shuffled away. She shot an accusing look at Pat and meandered to the living room. She stepped onto a stool, then jumped over to the sofa. Walking across its full length, she hopped to a high-backed chair, circled a few times, looked reproachfully in Pat's direction, then lay down and curled up with her nose tucked into her tail.

"My first day at the college really shook me up. I thought it would be like UBC where you were given brief overviews of what to expect from the different classes. I remember dawdling along and arriving at the room assigned for the first-year class assembly with neither pen nor paper. I was expecting some sort of orientation speech and maybe a tour of the facility. What a shock when I found myself immersed in a lecture on gross anatomy by Dr. Horowitz. He put things in perspective when he said, 'We're already behind by two weeks, so we better get hustling.'

"That pretty much summed up my entire stay at college! I always felt like I was two weeks behind. I found the first year tough—couldn't wait to get through all that theory and actually get some hands-on experience.

"The vet college became a home away from home. If I wasn't in the anatomy lab dissecting a cadaver and gagging on the formaldehyde fumes, I was in the library trying to absorb the material that had been fed to us that day. I found the course material intense, struggled with anatomy and a few other classes. I survived and eventually got my feet under me."

"So what's all this about bears?" Pat put another pot on the stove. "How in the world did you ever get a job like that?"

I took a swig of my wine. "I applied to be a part of a student exchange program between Ontario and British Columbia. The program was eventually canceled, but somehow my application managed to find its way to the desk of a biologist in North Bay, Ontario. Mike Buss was looking for a student to do field work on a black bear project in the McConnell Lake area. The fact that I was six foot eleven and weighed two hundred and thirty-five pounds caught his attention, and he hired me.

"It was a fantastic job working in one of the most beautiful areas of Ontario. The first year, we trapped and tagged bears—weighed them and took all sorts of measurements. I got to hike all through the area to collect data about the habitat and the bears' feeding habits. I loved the work and Mike was a fantastic boss. As long as he got results and knew we weren't jacking around, he pretty much left us alone."

"You're sure nursing that drink," Hugh grumbled, as he poured himself another tumbler.

"Still got to try and get out of here without drowning." I took a draft to appease him. "Can't afford to be drinking much more—I can feel this stuff already."

"So what made you want to become a vet, Dave?" Pat asked. "Were you from a farm like Hughie?"

"Not really. Dad had three acres in the country, but you could hardly call it a farm. From the age of six or seven, if you were to ask me, I would have told you I was going to be an animal doctor. Almost every picture I've seen of me as a kid has me cuddling a puppy or a kitten or stretched out with an animal of some sort.

"Nothing ever seemed to deter me. My health wasn't the best when I was a kid; I was constantly sniffling and coughing. Both my mom and dad were heavy smokers, and I can remember from the earliest age being disgusted with cigarette smoke and certain that it was a big part of my problems. In grade six, my symptoms got worse and worse. I was constantly staying home from school with a cough and snotty nose.

"One week things really got bad. My face got puffy; my eyes swelled shut. Mom took me to a doctor. He had her wait outside and spent a long time asking me questions and going over my body for signs of bruising. In hindsight, I think he was trying to rule out the possibility of physical abuse.

"As it turned out, I was allergic to house dust, cigarette smoke, and a variety of weeds; worst of all, I reacted terribly to cats, dogs, cattle, and horses. My parents decreed there would be no more animals in the house, but they kept smoking like steam engines."

"Wasn't that the way of things back then?" mused Pat. "People used to take smoking so much for granted. They never gave a thought to the fact that you had to breathe all that smoke secondhand."

"The doctor never made much of a big deal about it either. I'd always slept with my cat curled up on the head of my bed. The doctor was adamant that I'd have to avoid critters for the rest of my life; I told him that would be difficult seeing as I was going to be an animal doctor. He thought that was pretty funny. He laughed and told me I had lots of time to reconsider my choice of a profession—I had other ideas.

"I vowed that I'd overcome the allergies. The tests showed my most violent reaction was to cats, so I spent more time than ever outside handling my own. I propped a ladder against my bedroom window, closed the door so my parents wouldn't find out, and encouraged her to climb in for the night. The symptoms slowly waned, and the restrictions of animals in the house went by the wayside."

"You better throw the steaks on the barbecue, Hughie," Pat suggested. "I've about got everything else ready."

"Medium-rare all right with you?"

"Yeah, sounds good to me."

"Hope these steaks are good." Pat lifted the lid off a pot and stabbed at a potato with her fork. "They're from a barren heifer we just got done in and we haven't tried them yet." She had finished chopping up the greens for a salad when Hugh returned with a platter full of steaming meat. I had become increasingly aware of my hunger as the kitchen gradually filled with the smells of supper.

"Don't waste too much time on that rabbit food, Mom," he chortled. "There's plenty of real grub here."

"Who's going to eat all that?" I questioned. "You've cooked enough to feed an army."

"You obviously haven't seen Hughie eat yet," Pat chuckled. "Besides, you must be getting pretty hungry yourself."

Hugh plunked a huge T-bone on the plate in front of me. It covered the entire dish and hung over both sides. Juice dripped from the overlapping edges, staining the tablecloth.

"That's enough for all three of us, Hughie—sure doesn't leave much room for anything else."

"Well, what else is there? The rest is just rabbit food anyway." He transferred an identical steak to his own plate and set the platter in front of Pat.

"Dig in," he ordered. "No sense in letting it get cold."

He sawed off a piece of fat and tossed it to the floor in front of Jeremy, who gobbled it down. The dog couldn't possibly have tasted it. Suzie's ears perked up. Trotting to the kitchen, she jumped up on the chair next to Hugh and extended her long nose until it rested on the edge of the table.

"So you think you need some too, do you?" Hugh gibed, tossing her some trimmings from the other side of the steak.

I attacked my own steak with a vengeance.

"Well, Mother, this heifer's a lot more useful here than she was out on the pasture. She made darn good steaks!"

"She sure did." I swallowed a mouthful and chased it with a gulp of wine. "And this hooch of yours is tasting better all the time."

"It's damned time you developed a taste for good wine." He grabbed the gallon jug from the counter and filled my glass. "You sure you won't have a bit, Mom?" Without waiting for a response, he filled her glass as well.

Pat took a sip and suppressed an involuntary shiver. "So did you ever play basketball when you were in school?"

"No. Sort of wish I had now, but I was always a bit klutzy when I was growing up. Living seven miles from town made it difficult to do anything after school. Dad was never much on sports, and I wasn't much on walking home after practices."

"That's too bad." Hugh swallowed a mouthful of steak, then leaned back and presented a hearty belch. "He'd have soon changed his mind if you'd gotten into the NBA—the kind of money those buggers make."

"Yeah, I guess so. Just a different era and a different way of thinking. Pop scraped through the Depression and isn't much on taking a chance when it doesn't appear necessary."

"What did your dad do for a living, Dave?" Pat asked.

"He worked at the smelter like most of the other guys in Trail. He was a forty-year man this year. He's a millwright now but spent most of his years as a laborer."

"So he's still in pretty good shape then?"

"Relatively—he got lead poisoning a few times and God knows what effect that has as you get older. When I was a kid, he had a hell of a time with his back and finally ended up having surgery. I can remember when I was eight or nine coming home from school and finding Dad lying in the middle of the road. He was in so much pain he couldn't walk any farther. Some of the neighbors loaded him up and took him to the hospital. He was in traction for a week before they shipped him to Vancouver for surgery."

"What about your mom, Dave—is she well?"

"Yeah, actually Mom's in better shape now than she was when she was younger. She had polio right after I was born and took several years getting back to normal. Always seemed to be a bit sickly the whole time I was in school."

Hugh tossed his bone to Jeremy and speared another steak from the platter. I had just begun to get enough worried off mine to make room for a potato and some salad.

Leaning back, Hugh belched again and fired a piece of fat to Suzie's waiting beak. Her nose had migrated several inches in from the edge of the table, and she was drooling in anticipation.

"What about brothers and sisters?" Pat inquired.

"I've got two sisters. One of them lives in Trail and the other lives back East. I was sort of the afterthought. Audrey is five years older than me and Kay's almost eight."

"So you were the spoiled one!"

"That's what Kay's always telling me. She grew up when my parents were really struggling, and things were pretty tough. She claims that she tamed Pop down and made it easier for both Audrey and me. She was a bit of a hellion, so she probably did."

"I think the first kid in the family probably does have it a bit worse," Pat agreed.

"Kay was nine or ten when my mother got polio. Dad was so busy with work and running back and forth to the hospital, I don't know how he handled it. For the most part, Kay pretty much ran wild with no one to look after her.

"When my aunt Polly finally came to help out, Kay wasn't too happy about it. Polly tells a story about how my sister distracted her long enough to load her sandwich with earthworms. Poor Auntie! She was horrified when the end of one of the critters wriggled from where she had just taken a bite."

"Your sister sounds like quite a character." Pat chuckled.

I took a good slug of wine, then went back to paring away at my steak.

"It's funny how childhood memories are. I can't recall my dad ever hitting us as kids, but we sure lived in fear of the possibility. He never used a straight razor that I can remember, but he always had an old razor strop that he hung on a nail in a prominent spot in the kitchen. All he needed to do to get compliance from us was to walk to that strop and give a bellow, and things strangely went his way.

"It was always a mystery where that strop suddenly disappeared to. One day, it just wasn't there anymore. Years later, my father pulled its charred remains from the chimney clean-out. All of us knew that it was Kay's doing. She never admitted, until after she left home, that she climbed up on the roof and dropped it down the chimney."

"Well, what's for dessert, Ma?" Hugh handed the remains of his T-bone to Suzie and leaned back with his hands on his tummy. Suzie peered around for the whereabouts of Jeremy, then retreated to the far end of the living room with her prize. "Drink up, Dr. Perrin. There's lots more here."

I had to admit the wine was getting easier and easier to swallow. I took another good draft and hardly noticed the lumps. Pat pushed herself from the table and grabbed some pot holders. She opened the oven door to retrieve the most delightful-looking apple pie.

"That looks good, Mom." Hugh perked up as the pie, still sizzling juice through the slits in the pastry topping, made its way past him to the kitchen counter.

Only seconds before, I would have sworn I couldn't eat another bite. As I watched the mound of vanilla ice cream slowly melt into the top of a massive piece of pie, I realized that simply wasn't so.

"How did you ever pick Creston to start a practice?" Hugh maneuvered a forkful of pie and ice cream toward his mouth. "I mean Creston's a beautiful place and I think it'd be a fantastic area to live in, but it's small and Keith Marling is already well established there."

I fiddled with my fork for a few minutes before I answered him. Driving it through the crust, I watched as the pastry crumbled and juice oozed onto the plate. I dragged some ice cream to the top, then scooped some up and popped it into my mouth. I lolled it around, savoring the tart of the apples and the sweetness of the ice cream.

"My grandparents retired to Creston when I was two or three. Every summer our family would go over for a couple of weeks to visit and help them keep the place from falling apart. I suppose the fond memories of those days had something to do with the choice.

"I made a quick trip home to Casino after my summer job in St. Paul and, as soon as I drove into the valley, I got the urge to stop at Marling's clinic and feel things out. I hadn't really started looking for a job yet, but the time with George convinced me that I wanted to live in a rural community. I wanted a small farm where I could have a few critters of my own.

"As it turned out, Keith hadn't been in the best of health and was considering selling the practice. He seemed happy enough that I'd stopped, and I hung around the clinic as he finished off his day's work. The longer I stayed, the more I started conniving about somehow managing to buy his place.

"At first it was just a neat idea. I mentioned it to my parents, but never made a big deal about it. My dad thought it a bit ambitious for someone who hadn't even graduated from college yet. I can remember lying awake in my room at home with all the things of my childhood surrounding me. From there it seemed too much to hope for—just too high a mountain to climb."

"I know you sure wouldn't have been able to do it in Britain," Hugh mused. "There's no way anyone in our class would have even thought about it."

I sat staring at the glass in my hand. I was finding it more and more difficult to focus. I looked into the murky liquid and reflected on the past year. After returning to college, I found myself looking at everything from the point of view of working in Creston. I focused on learning more about dairy because it was a big industry there. I was constantly toying with different ideas to swing the purchase of Keith's practice. I called him several times during the term and made arrangements to meet with him over the Christmas break to see if we'd be able to finalize a deal.

"Hello . . . Dave!" said Hugh. "What happened with Marling's clinic?"

"Oh, sorry . . . I talked with him several times and thought we had a ballpark figure for the purchase. I met with representatives of both the dairymen and the beef growers' associations—got really excited about finally being able to put some of the material I was learning into practical use on farms that I had actually set foot on.

"Negotiations with Keith continued off and on until graduation. By then, his health had rebounded, and his incentive to sell had all but vanished. When it was obvious that we weren't going to make a deal, I just couldn't let go of the notion of living and working in Creston."

I drained the remainder of my glass, took a deep breath, and emitted a heartfelt groan. I had toyed with the pie and ice cream until nothing remained but a shallow puddle of milk that refused to be scooped up with my fork.

"That was one heck of a feast, Pat!" I squirmed at the uncomfortable feeling in my gut and leaned back in an attempt to get some relief. Hugh lifted the jug and refilled my glass before I had a chance to protest.

"You keep that up and not only will I not be able to drive, but I won't be able to walk." I stood up with the intention of easing my way to the door, but my head was swimming. I was in no condition to drive!

"Drink up! Can't let all those good plums go to waste."

"I'm half cut already! The last thing I need is more plums." I couldn't believe it—I was plastered! "This is ridiculous, I didn't think this stuff was so potent."

"Maybe you better think about staying over, Dave," Pat chuckled. My ears felt warm; I was sure the rosy glow to my face was very evident. "After all, that is your third tumbler."

"I planned on being back tonight," I sniveled. "The owner of this dog was hoping to pick her up today or early tomorrow. I better make a call over and make sure there's nothing urgent going on."

As it turned out, the only call had been from Mrs. Morris. She left a message for me to contact her in the morning.

"Maybe it would be best to stay over. I'd better see to Muppet though; she's probably ready to pee and is bound to be getting hungry."

The little dog polished off a half can of dog food, and we soon had her settled in a portable kennel that the Croxalls kept at home for just such occasions.

Hugh grabbed his glass in one hand and the gallon jug of hooch in the other and headed for the living room. "May as well be comfortable." Plunking himself in a large overstuffed chair that molded to his body, he set the jug beside him within easy reach. I settled onto the old high-backed sofa next to the fireplace. Taking another draft of wine, I leaned back and took a deep breath.

"So, are you as busy as you hoped?" Hugh pulled a footstool a bit closer, then propped up his feet.

"Seems like I'm always on the run." I was finding my tongue a bit more difficult to manipulate. "Can't say I've seen much correlation between how busy I am and how much money I have to spread around at the end of the month though."

"Yeah, isn't that the case. It's tough getting used to actually charging for what you do—even harder to try and get something for all the information that goes over the counter in the course of the day."

"I know, it's hard to charge for my advice. Some days, if I didn't make a few bucks selling medication, there'd be nothing at all."

"Are you doing a lot of large-animal work? Dad still runs a dairy farm back in England and I sort of miss working with the cows."

"Yeah, working with the dairies is good. Really have something to offer those guys and feel good when I can help them improve their bottom lines. I can see a difference already on some farms! A few of the guys think I'm wet behind the ears though."

Suzie jumped up from the footstool to the end of the sofa. Walking casually over my knees to the arm, she hopped onto the back and slowly circled. Giving me a disinterested look, she yawned and stretched out. Within a few minutes she was fast asleep, her head laid back, her feet in the air.

The rest of the evening is lost to recollection. Our conversation became more and more disjointed until Hugh's head finally began bobbing. I vaguely remember his showing me to a room at the top of the stairs and my drifting off to sleep while the walls slowly rotated around me.

Roosters were crowing in the distance, when the cry of a peacock brought me into the moment. I reluctantly opened my eyes to see a torsoless moose with a massive rack staring down on me from the opposite wall. The room was bright with sunlight that streamed in through the window. My head was throbbing. My mouth was dry and my tongue felt furry. I closed my eyes, hoping that I could drift off and awaken with a clearer head, but morning was nigh.

I swung my feet to the floor. The room seemed reluctant to stay in focus. I'd never be able to look at plums again! There was a rattling sound below in the kitchen, and I could hear Hugh's and Pat's voices somewhere off in the fog.

I staggered to the bathroom and stared with disinterest at the shaggy-looking face that peered back from the mirror. I turned on the shower and opened my mouth to let the water flow through in a desperate attempt to remove the vile, stagnant taste.

"Oh my, aren't we looking chipper!" sang Pat. I had my eye on the chair at the end of the kitchen table and paid attention to nothing else until I had plunked myself on it.

"Your eyes look like pissholes in a snowbank!" Hugh added cheerfully. I watched as he bit the end off a sausage and sawed away at the steak that perched on his plate next to a pair of eggs.

"Grab some sausages and bacon there, Dave. Do you want me to fry you up a couple of eggs?"

"Oh no thanks, Pat. I don't think my stomach is up to anything. I still feel like I'm half cut."

"I wondered how you'd feel this morning. When I went to bed, the two of you were still out there swapping lies, and Hughie had brought out another jug so you didn't have to walk across the room for a refill."

I closed my eyes to the sight of Hugh loading his plate with more bacon. "I'll have just one more egg, Mom," he said.

The drive up to the Salmo-Creston summit was torture! I squinted continuously and nodded off several times as I struggled to focus on the road. I pulled over to the lake and looked with disinterest at the shining waters and the vibrant blue skies. Muppet sat contentedly on the backseat staring up at me. Her eyes were bright and her tongue lolled happily from her mouth.

"Maybe just a few minutes of shut-eye will do it, girl!" Maybe . . .

MEINE BESTE FREUNDIN

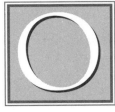"H NO," I GROANED. "There goes another Sunday!"

The phone was beginning to rule my life far more than I ever thought possible. I felt like letting it ring until the person on the other end gave up, but I knew from experience how guilty I'd feel.

"Hello," I answered hesitantly, half hoping someone had dialed a wrong number.

"Dr. Perrin, please. We have a person-to-person call for Dr. Perrin."

"Dr. Perrin speaking."

"Go ahead and deposit your money, sir."

I heard the metallic sound of coins striking a bell, then, "Hallo, Herr Doktor?"

"Yes, this is Dr. Perrin speaking."

"Heidi, she no gut . . . English no gut."

"What's wrong with Heidi?"

"Heidi sick!" He ran on for a good minute in German, leaving me no wiser than before.

"Heidi sick. How she sick?" I addressed him as if speaking to a child.

"Not eat for days. Very skinny! Not stand up."

"Is Heidi a dog?"

"Ja, dog!" His tone was indignant.

"Would you like to bring her in?"

"Ja, gut."

It was now nine o'clock and I'd hoped to get away from the office for at least a short while today.

"Can you bring her to the clinic right now?"

"Ja, gut. I come Gray Creek—no car."

"I'd appreciate it if you could get in as soon as possible."

I could see my day off melting before my eyes. I hung up the phone, realizing that I wouldn't be seeing him for some time; even if he could load the dog into his own vehicle, he'd be at least an hour getting here.

Gray Creek was forty-three miles from Creston on one of the most winding stretches of highway in British Columbia. To the sightseer on his way to the Kootenay Lake ferry, it was little more than a road sign on a very curvy and narrow section of Highway 3A. If he happened to be driving slowly enough, he might notice the quaint store and marina sandwiched between the roadway and the lake.

To the locals, Gray Creek was a community with a character and a history all its own. Until 1947, paddlewheel ferries had landed there making it an integral part of the Trans-Canada Highway. It had been the hub for miners who scoured the surrounding mountains for minerals and farmers who took advantage of the mild climate and shipping access to grow vegetables and fruit.

Now, it was a community, with a store and a network of dirt roads, that wound its way along the creek and through the rugged mountain terrain. The residents of Gray Creek were an eclectic group of persistent farmers, loggers, retirees, draft dodgers, hippies, and people who just plain wanted to get away from it all. I wondered how Mr. Schmidt fit into this picture.

I had been prowling around the office for hours waiting for his arrival. Here it was two o'clock in the afternoon, and I had still heard nothing from him—surely he'd have to show up soon. He could've walked to town by now!

I finally perched myself on the bench in the waiting room and stared out the window. John Shean, the tall, thin man who owned the Creston Hotel, was busily sweeping down the steps to the hotel entrance. Almost every day since I had moved across the street from him, I'd watched him push that same broom over those stairs. If this was a typical afternoon he'd finish the stairs, lean the broom against the building, then wander into the adjacent garden to prune back the fading roses. I watched intently as he worked his way down the steps, curious to see if he already had the pruner in his pocket. He had almost reached the bottom tier when a taxi pulled up in front of my building.

A stocky, leathery-looking man in his late sixties flung open the back door of the cab and strode toward my office. His movements were brisk, and the rap on the door was far from timid. Clad in heavy woolen clothing, he had the

175

look of a man who spent a great deal of time in the bush. Although his garments appeared well worn, they were clean and in good repair. The moment he entered, I could detect the distinct odor of wood smoke about him.

"Dr. Perrin?" He offered his hand. "Bruno Schmidt."

"Dave Perrin—glad to meet you."

His grip was strong; his rough, calloused hand pumped mine with an air of confidence and authority. He said nothing but stood with poker-straight posture, looking me up and down. Finally his eyes met mine, and he stared at me with an intensity that I found unsettling.

"I bring Heidi now?"

"Yes." I nodded.

Mr. Schmidt ducked into the back door of the taxi and emerged with a bundle swaddled in a heavy woolen blanket. Only Heidi's head protruded, but what I saw as she passed by me was distressing—her face had the look of a wasted and starving animal.

"Right on the table, Mr. Schmidt." I quickly guided him to the back room. As he folded the blanket down, I stared at the dog in disbelief. Mr. Schmidt's focus flitted back and forth from Heidi to me and, although I tried desperately not to show my emotions, he was able to read my thoughts.

"No gut," he said, directing his gaze away from Heidi to the floor at his feet.

Heidi appeared to be a golden retriever cross. Her hair coat had probably been reddish blond, almost copper in color, when she was healthy. Now it was dull, lackluster, a muddy brown. Every bone in her body stuck out; her abdomen was pendulous and ballooned. Her face and skull were totally devoid of muscle, and the prominence of the bones beneath her eyes and over the crest of her skull gave her a hideous appearance.

Mr. Schmidt watched attentively as my hands traveled over Heidi's emaciated body. She was lying upright on the table but possessed so little strength that she was having difficulty staying that way. The muscles of her head and neck were weak enough that she could hardly hold them up. As she shifted her lower leg to get more comfortable, she collapsed onto her side.

"*Gute Heidi! Du bist ein guter Hund!* Dad's girl, Dad's girl," he whispered, gently stroking her head.

"Has her color been like this for long?"

"Color?" Holding his hands out to his sides, he shrugged. His blank expression confirmed he had not understood my question.

I held Heidi's head in my hand and rolled back her lip. The mucous membranes exhibited the sickly orange of jaundice. The texture of her tissues was leathery from dehydration and long-term lack of nutrients, and her lip hung back like a piece of folded cardboard. I deliberately replaced it and raised her eyelid to reveal the same yellow-orange color to the whites of her eyes.

"Ah," he said, sadly nodding his head. "*Gelbsucht.*"

I lifted her tail and inserted the thermometer. Heidi lay with no change in expression and appeared not to notice the intrusion.

"When was the last time she wanted something to eat?" I moved my hand to my mouth to mimic eating.

"Eat, three days nothing." He pursed his lips and slowly shook his head. "Not eat gut, long time." Gesticulating with his hands, he pointed to himself, then motioned toward Heidi's mouth.

"Yes. Yes. You force-fed her. Did she ever vomit?" I made retching motions.

"*Ja, Ja.*" He nodded his head enthusiastically and went on with an explanation I didn't understand. Again, I nodded my head in acknowledgment.

Securing the stethoscope in my ears, I listened to the rapid pounding of her heart, then carefully checked her lung field. I could feel Herr Schmidt's eyes burning into me. He was waiting with anticipation for me to say something revealing and looked disappointed when I removed the apparatus and set it back on the side table without comment. I retrieved the thermometer and held it up to the light.

"Her temperature's more than four degrees below normal."

When he shrugged, I showed him the thermometer, pointed to the 101.5 and then to 99 and explained, "Normal here, her temperature here. See line here." I rotated the thermometer so he could see the mercury reflected by the light.

He nodded and let his gaze focus again on some imaginary spot on the floor.

With Heidi still lying on her side, I tapped her abdomen and watched in fascination as fluid sloshed back and forth like water in an unbaffled waterbed. Then, I slid my left hand under her abdomen and began palpating for what I suspected I'd find. It was huge, irregular, and occupied the entire anterior abdomen. I ran my fingers back and forth across and around it several times before I said anything.

"Mr. Schmidt, put your hand under here where my hand is. Put your other hand up here."

He looked confused by my instructions, so I took his hands in mine and placed them on either side of the dog's abdomen. I moved my hands back and forth together with his. From the look on his face, I could tell that he was feeling what I was feeling. He pulled his hands away from Heidi as if pulling away from a hot stove and, as I talked, he looked down at his spot on the floor.

"Cancer, Mr. Schmidt? You understand cancer?"

He lifted his eyes until his gaze met mine, then he slowly nodded.

"*Jawohl*, cancer."

"The tumor is involving her liver and extends as far up as I can reach. When cancer involves other organs like the spleen, the bowel, or the mesentery, we can operate to remove it, but when it involves the liver there's nothing we can do."

My words were falling on deaf ears. Mr. Schmidt no longer felt it was worth the struggle to try to understand me. I was looking at his face, his downcast eyes, his stooped shoulders, and wondering what to say next when there was a sudden change in his demeanor. A resolute, determined look came across his face.

"X ray! You have X ray?"

"Yes, I have X ray. But the tumor is so large and well defined, an X ray won't tell us anything we don't already know. I honestly think that with Heidi's symptoms and with what we can feel, doing an X ray would be wasting your money."

"X ray!" he said, jutting out his jaw. "X ray!"

"All right, we'll do an X ray," I replied in resignation. "Let's carry her into the other room."

Mr. Schmidt wrapped Heidi in her blanket and lifted her. She acted as if she were startled when he moved her—as though she'd been awakened from a deep sleep and wasn't quite sure where she was. When he set her down on the X-ray table, her head jerked up and down and her legs splayed out as she struggled for control.

"Let's just lay her on her side so she's more comfortable."

He looked at me with a blank expression and shrugged. *"Was ist los?"*

Lifting her myself, I motioned for Mr. Schmidt to remove the blanket, then set her gently on her side. She took a deep breath as I eased her onto the table; before I removed my hands, I felt a shiver run through her body.

After measuring Heidi's abdomen for thickness, I double-checked the technique chart for settings and calibrated the machine. I had only installed it last week and was still familiarizing myself with it. Moving the cone until it was properly positioned over Heidi's abdomen, I slid a large X-ray plate under her.

Mr. Schmidt sat quietly with his dog, stroking her head and occasionally bending down to whisper to her.

"We're ready, Mr. Schmidt." I handed him one of the heavy lead gowns that are worn to protect against radiation exposure when helping to position patients.

"Just put your arms through and tie like this." I demonstrated with my own. Mr. Schmidt slipped into the gown then returned to Heidi.

I exposed the first X ray with her lying on her side. Changing the plate and the calibration of the machine, I balanced her as best I could on her sharp, very prominent spine and exposed the view of Heidi from front to back.

Fifteen minutes later, I emerged from the darkroom carrying the film holders that suspended Heidi's still-dripping X rays. Mr. Schmidt's face was brimming with expectation, his steel-gray eyes focused to mere slits, his forehead creased with worry. He was intent as I carried the radiographs to the view box, held them up, and began studying them. He peered at them expectantly, then turned to focus on me.

"You see this shadow, Mr. Schmidt?" I pointed to an irregular, blurred line that extended from the top of the X ray to the bottom. "That's the outline of the liver. Normally it would be much clearer, but Heidi's so full of water that it blurs the contrast."

He didn't comprehend a word I had said. "Hold please." I handed him the film holders. "Book! I get book!"

Mr. Schmidt looked puzzled as I left but smiled for the only time during his visit when I returned with a radiology atlas that was written and illustrated in both English and German. I thumbed through the pages of the atlas to the X rays of the dog abdomen.

"See this line, Mr. Schmidt?" I pointed to the shadow in the book that outlined the farthest reaches of the liver. "Normal liver in front here." I indicated the outline of the last ribs on the X-ray photo.

"See Heidi." I showed him the same line on Heidi's X rays. "Liver very big, bumpy." The irregular shadow that delineated the edge of the mass went far beyond the margins of the last rib to take in the anterior third of the abdomen. Several large knobby lumps could be seen extending out from it. We were both silent for a long time, standing side by side staring at the shadows of Heidi against the light of the view box.

"Cancer," said Mr. Schmidt. It wasn't a question.

"Cancer," I confirmed.

His torment was evident. He knew deep down that Heidi's situation was hopeless but somehow still hoped for a miracle. Again, he spoke in German, his voice so low that I could barely hear him.

I shook my head and shrugged my shoulders to indicate that I didn't understand him.

"Operation!" he said forcefully. "Operation!"

"Oh, operation—surgery." For several minutes, I tried to think of some way to explain the gravity of Heidi's situation—that all of the symptoms indicated severe liver disease. That if that wasn't so, I could put her on intravenous fluids for a few days to see if we could build her strength enough to do an operation and explore the condition of her abdomen. How was I going to get through to him that Heidi's liver was beyond repair and certainly couldn't be removed?

"Cancer too advanced," I finally blurted, moving my hand back and forth over the tumor.

Mr. Schmidt rambled on in German. He shook his head to indicate that he hadn't understood me. The look on his face suggested otherwise.

"Too weak! Too sick! She would not survive the anesthetic." I shook my head emphatically.

"Put Heidi to sleep?" Mr. Schmidt queried flatly.

"I think that would be best for her. If she were my dog, that's what I'd do."

"Put Heidi to sleep."

I nodded. Mr. Schmidt turned away and walked over to Heidi. Taking her head in his hands, he whispered into her ear. I felt tears welling up as I watched him with his dog. I was about to take away what could be this man's only source of companionship. Going to the lock cabinet, I withdrew a bottle of euthanasia solution and filled a twelve-milliliter syringe.

I retired to the waiting room while Mr. Schmidt said good-bye to Heidi. Fingering the syringe full of liquid that would take Heidi's life, I reflected on how little college had prepared me to deal with such situations. Every day of my life was like a bloody soap opera. So much pain! So many decisions! So many types of people, each likely to handle the same situation in a different way! Who had made me God?

"Are you ready, Mr. Schmidt?"

He nodded and, putting his lips next to Heidi's ear, whispered to her. *"Meine beste Freundin, Heidi. Meine beste Freundin."*

I wiped her foreleg with alcohol and drove the needle into her vein. As I withdrew the plunger on the syringe, a jet of blood shot back into the clear liquid. I began a slow, deliberate injection. Heidi took a deep breath, exhaled gently, and lay still. That indefinable "light," which moments before had flickered in her eyes—that mingling of pain and love and desire to please—had disappeared.

Mr. Schmidt turned to me with a questioning look. He whispered softly in German to me, as if afraid to waken Heidi.

"She's gone," I whispered in return.

His face became a mask of pain and misery. His body convulsed, and he emitted the most tormented wail I'd ever heard. Throwing himself upon Heidi's body, he wept uncontrollably. I put my arm on his shoulder for a moment, then left him alone with his dog.

As I sat in the waiting room, I pictured Mr. Schmidt returning to a one-room cabin in Gray Creek and sitting alone in front of his woodstove. No radio, no television, no telephone, and now, no best friend. I closed my eyes, laid my head back, and let the tears trickle down my cheeks.

It was fifteen minutes later that a more composed Mr. Schmidt walked out to the waiting room.

"Taxi? Phone taxi?" He spoke quietly.

While waiting for the taxi to arrive, Mr. Schmidt was subdued. He paid his bill. While I prepared Heidi for her trip home, he sat in the waiting room with his head in his hands. I wrapped Heidi in her woolen blanket and slid her inside a large plastic cadaver bag.

"I'll carry her out for you," I said, when the cab arrived.

"*Nein, ich.*" He pointed to himself. "Thank you, Herr Doktor." He stared at me as if searching for something that was eluding him.

"I go." He stiffly turned on his heel and went back to Heidi. I opened the office door for him. Bill, the cabdriver, saw him coming with his burden. Maneuvering his bulky frame from the seat, he trudged around to open the trunk. Mr. Schmidt walked directly to the back of the vehicle, supported Heidi's body with one hand against the car and, with the other, opened the door. Without paying the slightest attention to Bill, he slid Heidi's body onto the backseat and followed her in. Looking only at the black bag on the seat beside him, he closed the door.

Bill stood for a moment by the open trunk and scratched his balding head. I could see he was considering asking the old man to move the body. He looked at me and raised his eyebrows. Finally, with a shrug of his shoulders, he closed the trunk.

I was in a somber mood as I wandered about the office putting things away and cleaning up. The best part of the day was now gone, and I was trying to decide what to do with the rest of it. I sprayed the exam table and X-ray table with disinfectant and, after washing them down, checked on the hospitalized patients in the kennel room.

I was leaving the office a half hour later when there was a knock at the door. To my surprise, it was Mr. Schmidt. Without saying a word, he entered and closed the door behind him.

Perusing the waiting room and the counter for something he had left behind, I asked, "Did you forget something, Mr. Schmidt?"

Resolutely, he walked to within a few feet of me and blurted, "Not baby!"

"Pardon me, Mr. Schmidt, I don't understand," I stammered.

He took another half step toward me, looked almost straight up into my eyes, and repeated, "Not baby!"

I could see that his mind was racing, that he was frustrated with his inability to communicate what was tormenting him. I couldn't imagine what would have been important enough for him to pay a taxi to drive him a good part of the way home and then back again! My God, what had gotten him this upset? I wondered if he had misunderstood something I'd said.

He spewed forth a torrent of German. I didn't understand a word of it, but the passion with which he spoke was unmistakable. In frustration, he stopped midsentence and raised his hands as if to tear at his hair. "*Verdammte Scheisse!*" he hollered.

Finally, with intense concentration, he took a deep breath and pointed to himself. "Me 30 . . . Germany . . . army." He looked intently into my eyes to see if I was comprehending.

I nodded, still baffled by what was going on, and he continued, "I fight . . . three years. Kill. I not cry! Not baby!"

That's what it was all about! Mr. Schmidt was frantic because I'd seen him cry. He didn't want me to think that he was weak—that he was a baby.

"Don't worry, Mr. Schmidt. I don't think you're a baby! I'd have felt the same way if Heidi were my own dog—it just showed me that you cared for her."

He wasn't the least bit placated by my words. Not only did he not understand, he was so distracted that he wasn't listening to me at all. As he was searching for the words to continue, I wondered how in the world I was going to get through to him.

"I fight!" He was shouting. He struggled for the words he wanted, then broke into German again.

My blank expression told him that I hadn't followed. He rapidly unbuttoned his shirt and pointed to a long, jagged scar that meandered across his abdomen.

"*Verwundet! Verwundet!*" He stared at me for some sign of comprehension.

"Wounded?"

"*Ja, Ja,* wounded! Not cry! Not cry!"

He spoke slowly and forcefully in German, willing me to understand. When he saw that he had lost me again, he shook his head and rolled his eyes.

"*Krankenhaus, Krankenhaus.*" Suddenly, his eyes lit up and he pointed to the sign stenciled on my window. "Hospital, hospital! Three *Monate, hospital.*"

"Three months in hospital," I affirmed.

"*Jawohl, ja,* three months."

The charade began once again. He repeated the same thing several times, putting his hands together and moving them towards himself. When he saw that I was not getting it, he said, "*Meine Einheit, meine Einheit,*" searching for the word from the ether that would convey his meaning.

"Company?" I guessed. "Your unit?"

"*Jawohl! Mein Bruder . . . Mein Freund . . . Einheit . . .*" He waited for me to comprehend.

"Your brother and your friend were in the same unit," I suggested, getting into the flow of the conversation.

"*Ja, ja, Bruder, Freund,* same *Einheit . . .*" He looked more serious than ever as he continued, "*Einheit* go Russia." The very mouthing of the word "Russia" was difficult for him.

He stopped—not fishing for words this time. He just didn't seem to be there. I stood only two feet away from him, not wanting him to go on torturing himself, but not wanting him to stop telling his story either. His voice was almost a whisper when he carried on.

"Russians no gut." His voice droned on in his native tongue, but this time he seemed not the least bit concerned that I wasn't following. I recognized a few of the words he had used previously and tried desperately to make sense of what he was saying. The only thing I was able to pick up on was his change of tone. He was subdued—completely detached.

Finally, he whispered, "Russland hell . . . Many Russians fall. *Freunde* die." Then as though waking from a trance, he punctuated with, "Not cry—not cry. *Die Kompanie . . .* Russians . . ." He made rapid forward movements with his hands and motioned dramatically to indicate a circle. His face was the personification of agony as he clenched his fingers together and obliterated the circle within.

When he continued, he spoke with reverence. "Many die. Many prisoners."

After a long pause, he said, "I prisoner . . . I prisoner."

He began to speak in German, but caught himself. "Work hard . . . Prisoners die . . . no food. Eat roots . . . eat bugs . . . flowers."

He paused for at least a minute as if recharging. His voice was barely above a whisper. "Winter hell; prisoners die."

"*Ich,* like Heidi," he said pointing at himself. "*Mein Bruder* die. *Mein Freund* die. Many prisoners die."

He looked up into my eyes and said in a hushed tone, "Not cry . . . Pile . . . dead . . . wood," he indicated, crossing his arms to show again and again that he stacked up the bodies like cordwood.

"*Bruder . . . Freund . . .* " He lost me again as he went on in German but pointed to his head and placed one arm over the other, indicating that he stacked his brother and best friend head to head. He talked on rapidly, his arms and hands gesticulating. He was obviously approaching some sort of climax.

He could tell that he had lost me again and, laboriously, patiently, went through the motions of pouring from a container, then slowly said, "Gasoline." Motioning upward with his hands, he alluded to a big fire. "Germans on fire! Germans on fire!"

He paused and looked down, then almost inaudibly whispered, "*Viel Rauch, viel Gestank.* Not cry."

He looked up into my eyes for a minute without saying anything. His face had lost the look of tension, the urgency. Finally, he smiled and once again extended his hand.

"*Danke, Herr Doktor.*"

"Good-bye, Mr. Schmidt." I watched him march, ramrod straight, to the waiting taxi.

BLOOD BROTHERS

HE REMPLE BOYS were a handsome pair—tall, blond, blue-eyed. As near as I could tell, they were identical twins. I never really knew which one I had just come into contact with. Their father ran a small hog operation in Wynndel, and I had dealt with them a number of times as they came in to discuss problems pertaining to their father's animals.

They were literally beaming the day they brought a bouncy yellow Lab puppy in for vaccination. I found it somewhat unusual and gratifying that teenage boys could be so responsible and openly demonstrative of their love for that ball of yellow fluff. They doted over his every move, handing him back and forth from one to the other while they waited for their turn to be seen.

Doris got their case history as I finished up in the exam room; I could see the boys showing off the pup to her as if exhibiting their firstborn son.

"So you have a new baby," I said, as they proudly brought him back and gently deposited him on the exam table.

"We have! Paul and I went over to Nelson and picked Buddy up yesterday. We wanted to get him in and have him checked out and vaccinated right away. They told us we have two weeks to have him examined by a vet and make sure he's all right. If you find anything wrong, they said we could have another dog."

I had been presented with the opportunity I'd hoped for—I now knew which one was Paul and which one was Barry. As long as they didn't change positions, I would be able to call them by name. The boys watched attentively as I examined their new friend—both peering over my shoulder as I checked his eyes, ears, and oral cavity.

"Fat chance that we'd take him back even if there was something wrong with him now," Paul commented, "so make sure you don't find anything!"

"He's got a really good bite." I showed them how well the upper and lower arcades of the teeth meshed together in the front. "That's very important for a hunting dog."

"You don't have to tell us how good Buddy's teeth are," Barry said, extending a hand that was covered with scratches. "They seem to line up really well!"

I palpated the pup carefully to rule out hernias and other congenital abnormalities, then listened to his chest and the thumping of his heart.

"Heart and lung sounds are good," I said to the boys, who watched my every move. "It looks like you have chosen a happy, healthy puppy."

I plucked a thermometer from its disinfectant bath. As I applied lubricant and inserted the thermometer into the puppy's rectum, the boys exchanged glances, and Paul slowly retreated to the waiting room. Barry smiled from ear to ear and shot his brother a look that had some special meaning attached.

"Temperature's normal," I pronounced.

Grabbing the two vials of vaccine that Doris had laid out on the counter, I popped the cap from the needle and plunged it into the vial containing the liquid diluent.

"This is the part that you've been waiting for, Paul!" his brother hollered. "You better hurry up, or you'll miss out on his shot."

I rehydrated the vaccine, then quickly did the vaccination.

"You missed it, Paul! We come here and pay all this money and you missed it," Barry taunted.

Paul gazed out the waiting room window in a contemplative fashion, ignoring the barbs that Barry was hurling in his direction. He said nothing as his brother handed him the dog and went about settling their account with Doris.

I next saw the brothers when they brought Buddy in for his second vaccination. I presumed that the boys were in the middle of a disagreement of sorts, because they were both rather sullen, and there was no chatter or fussing over the puppy. One of them brought Buddy in while the other sat glumly in the waiting room.

"Well, how's he been doing since the last time we saw him? Have you had any problems with him?"

"He seems to be doing fine. He's eating us out of house and home and is growing like a weed."

I examined the pup in silence and was just mixing up the vaccine when the brother that I deduced to be Barry hollered to the waiting room. "You better hurry up, Paul, you wouldn't want to miss the shot!"

"You not too fond of needles, Paul?" I asked, as he directed his gaze out the window and away from the pup.

Paul was about to answer when his brother did it for him. "Paul's a real boob around needles. He always faints at the sight of them. If he were back here, he'd faint for sure. He always does when we get needles at school. He usually doesn't even make it to the shot—he faints in the line when he sees the needle."

Paul opened his mouth as if to respond but closed it again.

"That's why he sits out there," Barry went on. "He doesn't have as far to fall if he's close to a chair."

Paul continued his impassive stare out the window in obvious anticipation of what was coming.

"It's the same at the farm," Barry went on. "Show Paul a drop of blood, a scalpel, or a needle, and we end up scraping him off the ground. I can remember when we were kids and we went to the circus, there was a guy who could pop his eye right out of his socket and into his hand."

"My Lord," interjected Doris, "that would be enough to make me faint, too!"

Paul rolled his eyes, knowing that he was really in for it now. His brother was on an all-out rampage.

"He fainted right in the middle of the crowd in front of everybody—just toppled like a great big tree." Barry illustrated the fall with his hands and emitted a big "Crrraaassshhh!" for emphasis.

I didn't see much of the Remple boys or Buddy over the ensuing six to eight months. I had passed them on the street corner once or twice and noted that Buddy appeared to have grown into a strong, healthy specimen. One Saturday afternoon, we had just about finished with our morning appointments, when one of the boys arrived.

"Just wanted to make sure that you were here before we brought him in," he started. "I know you're supposed to be closed already. Buddy's cut his foot. We were running him out on the dike when he went into the ditch on the side of the road and came back limping and bleeding all over the ground. Of course, Paul had to leave him all to me because he can't stand the sight of blood. It was bleeding pretty good too, so I covered it up with a sock that we had in the truck and wrapped some duct tape around it."

Barry ran back outside and returned within a few minutes with Paul and Buddy following close on his heels. Buddy appeared subdued and hobbled with a pronounced limp. The sock dragging with each step, he left a trail of blood on the floor. Paul's movements were slow and deliberate. His face was ashen, and he focused his gaze on the ceiling to avoid looking at the blood that seemed to be all around him.

"Paul's been a real hero today," joked Barry, as he led Buddy to the examination table. "He's seen more blood today than ever before, and he's still on his feet!"

Doris's eyes grew bigger with each step Buddy took into the room. Every time he put his foot to the ground, he left behind a pool of blood that soaked into the carpet.

"Let's get him on the table quickly, Barry, or Doris and I'll be here all night washing the carpet."

Barry quickly bent down, scooped the dog up, and placed him on the table. Buddy struggled for a moment as his feet slid on the stainless steel surface but soon settled into his master's arms. Gently pushing him on his side, I grabbed his right front foot, cut the duct tape, and pulled off the blood-soaked stocking.

"We need you back here, Paul," Barry mocked in a loud voice. "It's time to get a look at the cut. You wouldn't want to miss out on that for anything in this world!"

Paul remained in his chosen seat, staring sullenly out the window and refusing to give Barry the satisfaction of a response.

"That's a boy, Buddy," I crooned. "This isn't going to hurt too much."

The dog had a nasty gash running from the front of the main pad to the very back, literally severing it in two and exposing the pale pink tissue. The sulcus of the pad was packed with clotted blood, and the wound was wide open and full of dirt and bits of grass.

"Man, Buddy, you sure did a number on that foot of yours!" I wiped away debris from the outside of the wound with a piece of gauze. "You must have found a big piece of glass out there."

"How serious is it?" Barry asked, looking tentatively over my shoulder at the gaping wound. "Will it heal up all right, or is he going to have a limp for the rest of his life?"

"As you can see, the wound's pretty deep, but it's not involving either a joint or a tendon. When it heals there should be no reason for a limp."

"Oh my," said Doris, arriving with a stainless steel bowl full of water, "that really is a nasty cut!"

I grabbed a three-milliliter syringe from the counter, filled it with lidocaine, then put a bottle of Bridine and a stack of gauze sponges within easy reach. Buddy was being most cooperative and lay quietly in Barry's arms. Blood oozed steadily from the wound margins and kept up a steady drip, drip, drip onto the surface of the table.

I started by scrubbing the blood from around the edge of the paw and worked my way into the crevices between Buddy's pads, trying to remove the majority of the gross contamination first. The water in the bowl was taking on a deep crimson hue and a considerable amount of blood was accumulating in a gelatinous mound on the table. Barry had stopped talking and was no longer as attentive as he had been at first. I noticed that it had been a few minutes since he had hurled any torment in his brother's direction.

"Could you get me another bowl of clean water please, Doris? I want to give the cut itself a real good scrub before we freeze it."

I had just refocused the surgery lamp to get a better view of the wound when I noticed that Barry was indeed looking peaked. His face was pale and his grip on Buddy seemed far less firm.

"Are you all right, Barry? You look like you should maybe sit down!"

"No, don't be silly! It's Paul that can't handle this stuff. I'm just fine."

He struggled to perk himself up and even managed a feeble smile but, by the time Doris arrived with the fresh water, it was painfully obvious that he needed some air.

"Doris, you better hold Buddy for us; Barry isn't looking too good!"

"No, no, I'm fine," he responded, glancing furtively in Paul's direction.

"I'll just give you a hand while the doctor freezes his foot," Doris said, tactfully moving in next to him.

I returned to cleaning up Buddy's wound but was distracted by Barry's wan complexion. He was about as white as he could possibly be; beads of sweat were forming on his brow. I spread the wound wide open and poured Bridine soap to its depth. Making a pass with a gauze sponge, I removed a piece of grass and two small chunks of gravel that persistently clung to the severed pad. I swiped at a gob of dirt on the opposite side, and all hell broke loose.

The artery had been sealed off by the pressure of the wrap but when I was cleaning the clot dislodged. A jet of bright red blood erupted like a geyser from the base of the wound, hitting me on the forehead and covering the surgery lamp with tiny red droplets. Instantly, I grabbed a pair of mosquito forceps to clamp the vessel, but not before blood had sprayed like a mist over the edge of the table onto Barry's hand and arm.

One look at the boy said it all!

"Paul, get in here! Quick! Take Barry out of here!"

Barry relinquished his hold on Buddy and struggled to pull himself to an erect position. The look in his eyes told me that he had lost total contact with reality. I made a dash to get around the table and support him before the inevitable fall. He made no attempt to cushion his descent. He fell over from full height and crashed on the floor, his head hitting with a frightful crack.

Paul and I reached Barry at the same time. He was out for the count, his face completely drained of color.

"Is he still alive?" asked Paul, with the faintest hint of a smile. "Boy, he sure keeled over, didn't he?"

"He sure did, and he really whacked his head."

By the time I got back with a cold towel, Barry had opened his eyes. Paul was standing over him with a wicked grin.

"Welcome back, brother," Paul crowed. "You don't look so good!"

He helped his twin into an upright position and soon had him sitting in the waiting room with his face in his hands. Doris and I were able to get on with suturing Buddy's foot. By the time we applied the bandage and returned the dog to the waiting brothers, Barry had recovered some of his composure. Although he mentioned having a slight headache, he didn't appear too much the worse for wear.

The brothers paid their bill and were on their way out the door when Paul turned to me with the biggest smile. "Dr. Perrin, I want you to know how much this day has meant to me—it's certainly one that neither of us will ever forget!"

The import of that statement was not lost on Barry, who responded with a sheepish smile.

Then Paul launched his parting shot. "Dr. Perrin, from your perspective, would you say that Barry toppled over like a great big tree?"

Both boys stood framed in the door, one chagrined and one triumphant.

"Yeah, Paul. Now that I think about it, that would describe it quite well—he toppled like a great big tree!"

THE TROUBLE WITH COWS

HE RAIN FELL CONTINUOUSLY in the form of a fine drizzle. The flimsy cotton gown that covered my body was soaked through and clinging to my skin. My hair was saturated. Rivulets ran down my face onto my back and chest. Droplets formed on my nose and hair; I frequently had to lean back and shake my head to dislodge them, lest they fall onto the surgery site or into the heifer's abdomen.

The cold of early morning crept into my body; as I began to close the uterus, I shivered convulsively. I kept telling myself to hurry, to get this over, but there was no way my numb fingers would cooperate. Only by plodding along methodically, driving and tightening one suture after the other, did the surgery progress.

By the time I finished closing the abdomen, the morning had eroded, and I felt about as spry as the critter looked. My back was stiff from bending over her; I found it difficult to stand erect. Stumbling to the surgery box, I picked up my shirt and vest and struggled to force my arms through the sleeves.

Considering the circumstances, the surgery had gone remarkably well. Going into it, I would have bet on a dead calf—how happy I was to be proven wrong. The Charolais cross heifer had been bred by accident and was calving at just seventeen months. Although the owner recognized she was pregnant and was anticipating difficulties, he assumed she was still several weeks away from delivery. When she didn't show up for morning feeding, he began a search of the rambling hillside where the cattle ranged. He found her at the back of his property. She had been laboring for most of the night.

I hadn't been enthused to hear that the animal was somewhere on the mountain a half mile from my vehicle and power. We trekked uphill on a narrow cow path that meandered next to the fence line. It was slick, and the overhanging bushes were dripping with water. We hadn't gone a hundred yards before my coveralls were soaked through. Water penetrated the inside of my boots, and I could feel the chafe of my jeans against my legs.

We reached the end of the trail and thrashed through the bush for a couple of hundred yards before we spotted her. She had chosen to calve in a small clearing at the base of a big rock outcrop. Steam rose from the heifer's back in the chill mountain air. Exhausted from straining, she lay with her head along her side, making an occasional weak effort to push.

I could see neither the head nor the feet of the calf extending beyond the vaginal lips. All that was visible was a sheet of dark, discolored membrane and a firm, rounded object that would prove to be the calf's tongue.

It didn't take a genius to see that a cesarean was the only option; a trek down the mountain was necessary to retrieve my surgical supplies and water. By the time we made the return trip, I was drenched. I laboriously shaved the heifer using nothing more than a razor blade, then finally got on with the surgery.

It was one of those procedures where every step had been a struggle but now that it was over it all seemed worthwhile. Just watching that vigorous newborn calf as it steamed in the late morning air gave me the energy to get on with cleaning up my mess.

When I warmed enough to move my fingers, I milked the heifer and fed the meager ration of colostrum to the calf by stomach tube. She would probably need the next few meals that way, but her tongue should return to normal size within a day and allow her to suck on her own. Her mother still looked rough but unless I missed my guess she'd be up and around in a few days.

This had been a difficult day from the start. Most of the appointments on the book this morning had yet to be done! Doris was doing her best to pacify clients but as the emergencies stacked up she was becoming frustrated. Luckily, two of the appointments were in hospital surgeries that we could do at our leisure—contingent, of course, on there being leisure time before the day was over.

I had just cleaned up from the cesarean and sedated a rambunctious little spaniel for neutering, when the phone interrupted again. Doris was struggling to pack the large-animal instruments, but she wasn't making much headway. I watched her expression as she talked on the phone and surmised that our day was not getting any smoother. Adjusting her glasses, she took a deep breath and turned to me.

"Dan Hurford's on the phone. He has a cow he's really worried about. Do you want to take the call now, or would you rather phone him back?"

"I'll take it now. How about holding Jake for me?" Yes, this was going to be one of those days!

"Hi, Dan, what's up?"

"Number 202 looked a bit off this morning at milking. I wasn't too concerned about her at the time; just jotted her number down for you to look at her tomorrow. I walked through the barn a few minutes ago to check for heats and found her stretched out in a stall. She looks terrible! I had a heck of a time getting her up. When I did, she staggered and dragged her hind feet all the way to the sick pen."

"How long's she been milking?" I was going through a mental checklist of possibilities.

"She's fresh about three and a half weeks now and was really coming into her own for milk until today. She's squirting out manure like water, and her eyes are terribly sunken. If you don't get here soon, we'll be doing a postmortem on her for sure!"

"I'll head out right away. Doesn't sound like we can waste any time!"

It was raining when I left the office, not heavily, but steadily—the type of rain that over twenty-four hours is a real soaker. I started the car and turned up the radio. The CBC was interviewing the outgoing president of the British Columbia College of Physicians and Surgeons. They were discussing cutbacks in the medical field—how Canadian standards of care were on the decline.

The good doctor went on at length about the difficult conditions that his colleagues were forced to work under, about the inadequacies of both surgical facilities and emergency rooms. According to him, they were dealing with a true crisis, and the poor physicians were struggling to cope. I thought of this morning's experience and wondered how he would view his own working conditions if he'd had the opportunity of kneeling next to me on that soggy hillside, a fine drizzle falling onto his surgical field. I couldn't help but feel that a day with me might change his perspective considerably.

By the time I drove across the flats and turned down the lane to the Hurford farm, the rain had become slush, and a residue of ice was building up under the wiper blades. This time of year, the weather couldn't quite make up its mind, and an hour one way or the other made the difference between rain or sleet or snow.

I reluctantly stepped out of the car into heavy wind. Sleet whipped against my face, and I had to close my eyes to slits in order to see. I shivered as cold inched its way to the bone; I took a moment to adjust my scarf to cover my neck. Facing the wind, I stumbled to the milking room door and heaved it open. Dan was waiting for me in the coffee room, a bucket of water ready to go.

A few years younger than I, Dan was a dynamo. He was lithe and handsome, energetic, and determined to make his family farm one of the finest in the valley. Along with his brother, David, he did his best to keep up with the night life and often returned from a party just in time to fire up the compressors for the morning milking.

"Can't understand what's going on with this cow," Dan groused, as we walked to the sick pen. Shaking his head in disgust, he fumbled with the twine that held the side door closed. "I swear her eyes are sinking more by the minute!"

A big Holstein lay at the far end of the pen, her head stretched out in front of her. Her tongue protruded slightly, and she emitted a faint grunt with each breath. Her hair stood up in a disheveled fashion. Her tail was wet from diarrhea, and the straw beneath was covered with dark, undigested particles of stool.

"Do you think she'll be able to stand?" I asked.

Dan slipped a rope halter over her head and tightened the sliding knot under her chin. "She wasn't very steady when I put her in here a half hour ago, but she's always been strong-willed. She's one of those cows that works hard without attracting much attention."

Dan moved to her side and made a few quick plunges, driving the point of his knees into her rib cage. "Come on, girl! Come on! Get up! Get up!" He slapped her sides with the flat of his hands as he shouted. Number 202 made a halfhearted effort to rise, shifting herself only a few inches from the ground.

"Yeah! Come on, girl! Give it a try!" Dan urged, as she settled back to the straw. This time her effort was more determined, and she struggled to an erect position. Shaking violently and shifting unsteadily from one leg to the next, she appeared ready to fold at our feet. We stood one on either side of her to help keep her from collapsing sideways. Finally, she planted her feet and stood resolutely.

"Just can't believe how quickly this cow has gone downhill!" Dan shook his head in dismay. "She was milking close to a hundred pounds a day and looked fine at milking last night."

I began a methodical examination, as Dan stood by her hind end waiting to steady her if she moved. The cow's udder was devoid of milk, but felt completely normal as far as the texture was concerned. I struggled to get enough milk from each quarter to do a mastitis test and wasn't surprised when it tested clear.

Grabbing the fetid tail as close to the base as possible, I inserted the thermometer into her rectum and waited patiently. I had no sooner removed it than she sent a jet of watery, foul-smelling stool over her tail onto the straw-covered floor. Her temperature was only 99.1 degrees Farenheit—more than a degree below normal.

I took a quick listen to her chest. Her lung sounds were normal and, although her heart was pounding rapidly, I could hear nothing unusual. There were no sounds of rumen contraction on the left side, but no evidence of anything else out of the ordinary.

As soon as I moved the stethoscope head to the right side and flicked the rib cage, I heard it—the deep, resonant, high-pitched, ringing sound of an extremely distended organ. The textbook described it as the sound of a coin dropping into a metal milk can.

No wonder she was going downhill so rapidly! The cow's main stomach, the abomasum, was twisted off so that, although fluid could accumulate, it couldn't leave to be reabsorbed lower in the bowel. She was literally taking fluid from her bloodstream and depositing it in the gut.

"She's got a torsion of the stomach, Dan. We'll have to do surgery right away."

"How's that different from a displaced abomasum? We've had lots of cows with that, but I've never seen one this sick."

"That's because the circulation's still fairly normal when the abomasum's just displaced. It's more a problem of discomfort and the stomach contents not moving along normally. With a torsion, the circulation's cut off completely, and the cow goes into shock and dies in a matter of hours."

197

While Dan clipped the hair from 202's right flank, I ran a couple of bottles of dextrose and some dexamethasone into her jugular vein to help her failing circulation. I scrubbed her side, then went on to administer the injections that would leave her surgery site free from pain. I poked aggressively at the skin where my incision would go. Blood trickled from the series of puncture holes, but the cow gave no indication that my actions were causing discomfort.

Stripping to the waist, I began scrubbing my arms from the shoulders down. I hadn't warmed up from this morning's episode; repeating it now just didn't seem fair. What a shame to leave those warm clothes in a heap on the straw.

The only bright spot of undressing in cold weather was that farmers invariably sympathized with me. As he watched me scrub, Dan zipped up his sweater and pulled down his toque. He helped me don the surgery gown and gloves. Although little more than a thin layer of cotton and a thinner layer of latex, the covering made me feel better on some ephemeral psychological level.

I quickly made my incision. A pencil-thin red line leaked a fine stream of blood down the cow's side and onto the straw. I clamped a disposable drape to her side and was about to resume cutting, when she started sinking.

"No you don't, 202!" Dan hollered, giving her a jab in the ribs. "Stay up now, girl! Stay up!"

The cow hovered in a couched position then, with a bit of a struggle, planted her feet, locked her hocks, and stood firm.

"Good girl, good girl. Just stay on your feet. Boy, we're gonna be lucky to get this one done before she goes down."

Shifting unsteadily from one hind foot to the other, 202 swayed dangerously on several occasions. Each time Dan was there, jammed against her left hip to prevent her from toppling over.

Resolutely, I made a stab incision through the muscle, then extended it with scissors. I snipped through the peritoneal layer and heard the air rush in to fill the contracted area of her flank. Extending the incision in both directions, I reached into her abdomen and toward her head.

There it was, as huge and distended as an elongated beach ball. No question that it was the abomasum—there was the fatty, white mesentery around its outer edge.

"Well, are we in the right ballpark?" Dan's voice was playfully sarcastic.

"We certainly are!" I stood back and retracted the wound margins. "Come have a look!"

Slowly backing away from the cow, he stood for a few seconds to make sure she wasn't going to topple over. Satisfied, he came to my side and stared attentively into the abdomen.

"Boy, that's bigger than any we've ever had before. What about that color? It's almost purple."

"Yeah, if it's still the same after we deflate it, then we're in deep trouble. If it turns pink again, it means we still have circulation and she has a fighting chance."

I drove a large needle with an attached rubber tubing through the uppermost portion of the abomasum. A hissing sound emitted from the end of the apparatus, and the acrid smell of sour gas soon filled the air.

For the next ten minutes, we steadied the cow between us and waited patiently for the air to evacuate. Even with most of the pressure removed, poor 202 showed little sign of improvement. I reached into the abdomen and followed the contour of the fluid-filled organ to the location of the twist. The animal moaned in agony.

"You're sure doing something she doesn't like!"

I grasped the pendulous upper portion of the stomach and rotated it in a counterclockwise direction. The tension suddenly relaxed, and the organ fell into its natural position.

"Look out! She's going down!"

As if she had been shot, 202 crumpled to her brisket. My arms inside her, I dropped to my knees in a frantic attempt to keep her abdominal contents from boiling onto the ground. Dan's efforts to hold her up forced her farther in my direction, and her body flopped onto me with an oppressive force. Flailing with her hind legs, she pushed even harder toward me, literally pinning me to the ground. Jets of bowel pumped out with each bit of additional pressure.

"Oh, my God!" Dan was trying without success to bend the cow's hind legs and get them back under her. "Are you all right?"

"Not really!" My back and calves were screaming with pain. "Try to get her to roll the other way!"

Pulling madly on the manure-sodden tail, Dan fought to pull her onto her other side. The effort only made the cow more determined to push with her hind legs and grind her incision into the dirt. Great mounds of bowel accumulated in the dam created by my chest and arms. I was tempted to simply push myself away and let the bowels spill out onto the straw.

"The legs, Dan! Get the legs!" She struggled again and forced more bowel into the pile building in my arms.

Wrestling with her, Dan battled until both hind legs were jammed under her abdomen. As I heaved on her vertebrae, Dan levered her head and pushed mightily on her right front shoulder. At first, it seemed that we were attempting the impossible but, ever so slowly, the cow gave up to crumple onto her side. I followed forward with my burden of bowel. Surprisingly, the drape and my surgery gown had protected it from being fouled with straw and manure.

"Will you look at that mess." Dan stared at her in disgust. "Should I get the gun?"

"Not yet." Struggling to straighten my cramped legs and balance the guts on top of her flank, I worked my hands out of her cavity and started pushing the bowel back in. Progress was slow at first, but eventually, the last of the intestine disappeared through the incision and into her abdomen.

Grasping the abomasum again, I brought it to the incision site. It was almost pink in color, and its wall appeared to have already contracted considerably. I located the portion of the fatty mesentery that looked very much like a pig's ear, pulled it into the incision, and began suturing it into the closure. Tacking it in the suture line was meant to hold the organ in place, preventing the possibility of a future displacement.

Surprisingly enough, the remainder of the surgery was pretty routine. Granted, it would have gone much faster if I hadn't been soaking wet and cold from all the peritoneal fluids. The incision closed nicely, and there had been a minimum of contamination to the abdominal cavity.

Before I left, I pumped ten gallons of hot electrolytes into the cow and injected antibiotics. Dan was convinced that she was a tough cow and was going to make it. I was hoping he was right.

"For heaven's sake, Dave," Doris exclaimed, as I entered the office, "you're absolutely filthy! You'd better hurry and get cleaned up. Mrs. Reynolds'll be here any minute."

I deposited the surgery box and my dirty coveralls on the counter in the back room. Doris rolled her eyes and shook her head as she viewed the instruments and dirty laundry. Rolling up her sleeves in disgust, she plucked out the surgery gown.

"How did you get this so mucky? Were you rolling around on the barn floor?"

I opened my mouth to reply, then smiled and headed upstairs to wash and change. I looked longingly at the deep, old-fashioned tub. I was tempted to run it to overflowing with hot water, then submerge myself with only my nose sticking out.

I stripped off my clothes. My upper torso was coated with 202's blood in differing degrees of dilution. My arms were bloody and smeared with a few dollops of manure for good measure. My knees had taken on the pale green of the manure pack that I knelt on for the latter half of the surgery, and my upper thighs were covered with the same mixture of peritoneal fluid and blood that had done such a nice job of staining my underwear.

Kneeling in the bathtub, I splashed water onto my body. A shower would have been heavenly, but this spit bath was just going to have to do. The warm water sent paroxysms of shivering through me, and my flesh was soon covered with goose bumps. Slathering on the soap, I loosened the crusts of caked-on blood and splashed on handfuls of hot water. As good as it felt, it was only a tease; I kept visualizing the tub filled with luscious hot water.

I thought I had done a decent job of cleaning myself up, but the color of the towel after I dried suggested otherwise. I threw on underpants and a pair of jeans.

As I passed the refrigerator, I flung open the door to the same uninspiring scene that had driven me to the restaurant for yesterday's meals. The lettuce had gone beyond the usual stages of wilt and was well along in the liquefaction process. I gingerly picked it up, touching only the plastic bag that contained it, and flung it into the garbage. The cheese and bread were salvageable; they were only moldy. Mold was something that, as a bachelor, I was well schooled to deal with. I trimmed off the crust and a patch of green from two pieces of whole wheat bread and was diligently carving mold from the cheese when Doris hollered up the stairs. Mrs. Reynolds was here with

Gidgit, and one of the Ramseier brothers was back in about a sick cow. It was the third time one of them had been in this afternoon.

Stuffing the dried-out cheese sandwich into my mouth, I pulled on a pair of socks, grabbed a shirt, and rushed downstairs. Doris was busy talking with Mrs. Reynolds about Gidgit, so I choked down a bite of my sandwich, deposited the rest on the counter, and rushed out to talk to Mr. Ramseier.

"Yes, Doctor." Bob's gaze focused on my stocking feet. "We have this cow that seems to be lying around a lot."

"Is she off feed as well?"

"Well, she's been eating some . . ." Bob stared in fascination at my right foot. The big toe was sticking out in a rather exaggerated fashion. "The others are out there picking, and she just kind of wanders over and lays down like she's full or too tired to be bothered with eating."

"Sorry, but I haven't had a chance to get my shoes on yet."

"What's that?"

"My shoes—I just got back from a surgery in the country and haven't had much time to get on track here."

"Oh, sorry, your shoes . . . right."

"I'd certainly run that cow in and get her temperature, Bob. If it's over one hundred one point five, then we better have a look at her. If it's normal, give her a day or two and see what she does."

"Okay, I'll call you later and let you know." A funny grin crept over his face as he turned to leave. "And good luck with your toe!"

I rushed into the back room to pull on my shoes. Mrs. Reynolds watched me run by in my stocking feet, and I wondered if she had noticed my errant toe as well. She had recently moved here from Vancouver and still seemed out of place in this rural setting. I'd never seen her when she wasn't dressed as though she had somewhere to go. Recently widowed, she had purchased Gidgit to keep her company and satisfy her nurturing instincts. She and Doris frequented the same hairdresser and as they waited for me they went on about Tom's latest antics.

Although Gidgit had never been sick a day in her life, we were constantly seeing her for one thing or another. For a toy poodle, she was a delight to handle and seemed far more practical about life than her adopted mother.

I peered into the mirror in the back room and decided that my appearance was acceptable. I entered the exam room with my shoes on and my smock neatly tied up.

"If anyone else talked to me the way Tom talks to me," Doris was saying, "there's no way I'd ever go back." The fact that both women had biweekly hair appointments was a testament to Tom's winning ways.

"Dr. Perrin." Mrs. Reynolds smiled at Doris then turned to me. "Gidgit seems to be having a major problem with hiccups. She just about drove me crazy with them this morning."

"Does she seem fine in other respects, Mrs. Reynolds?" I bent down to stroke the immaculately groomed little dog. She sidled over to greet me, the fluffy poof on the end of her tail wagging boisterously.

"Oh yes, she's just fine otherwise."

As Gidgit jumped up to greet me, I lifted her to my chest. It was at that point that I first noticed the expression on Mrs. Reynolds's face. At first, I chalked it up to concern about Gidgit—or was it more?

I continued my examination while Gidgit licked at my face. I smiled at the pink bow that sat perfectly balanced on the middle of her head. She looked bright, and I had yet to detect anything that resembled a hiccup. Peeling back her lip, I examined her color and her capillary refill time. They seemed normal enough.

I pried opened her mouth and pushed her tongue down with the tip of my finger. The tonsils looked normal, and I could detect nothing unusual. I was about to ask Mrs. Reynolds a question, when I noticed again the look on her face. I was so distracted by her baleful expression that I completely forgot what I was going to ask.

I was dumbfounded. I glanced at Doris. From her vantage point behind Mrs. Reynolds, she crossed her eyes and held up her arm. Then again, in a less-than-subtle fashion, she pointed to her forearm and repeated the procedure of rolling her eyes. I gently put Gidgit down, then raised my arm and rotated it to look.

A "high water mark" of crusted blood decorated my underarm as though painted for dramatic effect. I looked sheepishly from Mrs. Reynolds to Doris and then back to Gidgit.

"Oh my, Gidgit, will you look at that! I didn't mean to bring along as much of my last patient as all that!"

I retreated to wash, while Doris went to great lengths to explain to Mrs. Reynolds just how hectic my day had been and how hard it was for poor Dr. Perrin to juggle large- and small-animal medicine.

The remainder of the afternoon flew by in a blur. It was getting on to eight o'clock by the time we had completed the last surgery and were waiting for the dog to recover.

"So, what do you say to Chinese food, Doris?" I rolled the dog onto his brisket, and he made a feeble effort to stand. "All I could scrounge for lunch was a moldy cheese sandwich and most of it's still sitting on the counter."

We had our coats on when the telephone rang. Doris shook her head despondently. Shrugging her shoulders, she picked up the phone.

"Yes, we are," she responded. "Yes, it's just been one of those days."

I had lulled myself into believing it was a social call, when Doris turned to me with a glum look. "It's Jeanette Evans on the phone. They're having difficulty with a calving. She says Bob Rogers came over to help but they still can't get it."

I took a couple of steps in Doris's direction, then resigned myself. "Just tell her I'll leave in a few minutes." Willie Evans was a practical, down-to-earth sort of fellow who had been around cattle most of his life. He had been with Bob Rogers for years helping with calvings and working the farm. If he and Bob weren't able to deliver this calf, there must be a problem.

"Did you ever get those large-animal instruments autoclaved, Doris?" I cringed at the thought of another surgery tonight.

"No, I got them washed and packed up, but didn't have time to sterilize them. For that matter, none of the other packs are ready to use either."

The weather had been miserable throughout the afternoon, and the roadway was covered with a couple of inches of slushy wet snow—terrible to drive through! The going was slow. I passed a vehicle traveling in the opposite direction on the Creston side of the ferry landing, and it sent rooster tails of slush spraying over my windshield. I pulled over to let my wiper blades catch up, then proceeded toward the West Creston hills. The road up the mountain was slippery, but I made it to Willie's driveway without much difficulty. I pulled into the yard and met Jeanette on the way over from the house.

I followed her to the clapboard structure where Bob and Willie were fussing over a large Holstein heifer. I was relieved when I saw the size of her. I had been dreading the possibility of another surgery. As big as she was, I was certain I could deliver the calf without trouble.

"Just can't seem to get those legs, Dave," Bob lamented. "Feels like lots of room but there's nothing coming but the tail, and we can't reach the feet to straighten out the hind legs. I think what we need is those long arms of yours."

"I sure hope you're right. Is the calf still alive?"

"Yeah, I'm pretty sure it's still alive," replied Willie. "I felt it move the last time I was in her."

I rolled up my sleeves and lathered my arms with surgical scrub. Soaping the vulva, I slid my hand into the heifer's vagina. She had lots of room in the pelvis, so once I got the legs straightened out, we'd be away. I directed my hand forward to feel the calf's tail and rectum. Bob was right; it was a true breech.

The trick would be reaching one of the calf's feet. After flexing the stifle and hock, I could bring the foot back and out through the vagina. With thirty-seven-inch arms, I was well suited for veterinary obstetrics. I hadn't run into many situations where I couldn't reach far enough to correct a difficult presentation.

I was following the calf's leg down from the stifle when I realized we had major problems. I could touch the inside of the heifer's abdominal wall and, further down, feel bowel slip between my fingers. I slowly withdrew my hand; from the look on my face, the boys knew we were in trouble.

"Can't reach it?" Willie's face was etched with worry.

"It's not that; the problem is that the uterine wall is split wide open. Unless we go in and sew it up, she hasn't got a hope."

Willie and Bob looked at each other, neither of them saying a word. Finally, Willie glanced at the cow and sighed.

"She was shaping up to be such a nice animal." He looked from the heifer to Bob, then back to the heifer again. "She's the easiest critter to catch—we can walk up to her darn near anywhere."

"What are her chances if you operate?" Bob asked.

"It'll depend on what we find when we get in there." I was trying to hedge my bet—this was a long way from a sure thing!

"We have to give it a shot!" Willie had a determined look. "I want to give her a chance."

"How well did you guys scrub before you went in to work on her?"

"Well . . ." Willie hesitated. "I washed myself with a bar of soap before I checked her the first time, and Bob here brought that brown soap that he buys from you. We've bin pretty careful."

"We'll start her on antibiotics right now. With that tear, bacteria can get directly into her abdominal cavity."

I went to the car and drew up a syringe full of chloramphenicol. Slapping her hip a few times with the back of my hand, I popped the needle into the muscle, attached the syringe, and injected the syrupy, clear liquid.

"Do you have a pressure cooker by any chance, Willie?" He gave me a puzzled look as I withdrew the needle from the cow's rump. "My instruments aren't properly sterilized. I'm sorry. We're usually ready to go, but I've been running with surgeries all day, and Doris didn't get a chance to do them up before I left."

"Just the one that the wife uses for canning."

"That'll do fine—a half to three quarters of an hour at steam temperature should do the job."

Willie took the instruments to the house and Jeanette fired up her pressure cooker. I'd finished clipping the surgery site and had the nerve block done when he came back with sandwiches and a pot of hot coffee.

"Boy, that'll sure hit the spot." I looked ravenously at the food. "It's been a long time since lunch!"

We had demolished the sandwiches and drained the last of the coffee when Jeanette arrived with the instrument pack. They were still steaming, and she had to carry them wrapped in a large towel.

"They're hot out of the cooker," she warned, "so watch you don't burn yourself."

I knew from the outset this surgery would prove to be far from routine. The bovine uterus consists of a body and two horns—as a fetus develops, it usually occupies one of the horns. When doing a cesarean, I always tried to keep my incision toward the end of the horn so that the uterus could be brought out through the incision, where it can be easily worked on. The tear in this cow's uterus extended well back into the pelvic region where nothing could be externalized. Everything would have to be done by feel.

I laid out the instruments and surgery materials on a bale of straw next to the cow, scrubbed her to my satisfaction, and was on my own final scrub when Willie couldn't stand it any longer.

"Good grief, man! If you worry away any longer, you may be needing a skin transplant!"

"I don't think there's much danger of that, Willie. How about your scrubbing up just in case I need some help to pull the calf out."

He pushed his jacket sleeves up past his wrist, then extended his hands toward Bob for soap.

"You better strip down more than that! You'll need to take all your loose clothing off. We don't want to expose this poor critter to any more sources of infection than we have already."

Willie winced as he pulled off his jacket and stripped down to his short-sleeved undershirt. As he scrubbed, I went ahead. Making the incision as far back on the left side as possible, I cut through the skin and underlying muscle tissue. I had just picked up the peritoneal layer and made a stab incision when I turned to grab the scissors. There stood Willie, hands on his hips, watching the surgery unfold before him.

"Willie! You're supposed to be scrubbed up so that you can help me if I need you."

"Well, I am!" There was a defiant look on his face. "How many damned times do you want me to wash?"

"It wouldn't matter how many times you washed; you're only as clean as the last place your hands have been. In this case, they're on your hips."

"Oh yeah, guess so." He held out his hands for more soap.

By the time Willie was scrubbed again, I was exploring the uterus to determine the extent of the damage.

"It's even worse than I expected!" I followed the rent into the pelvis. "The tear goes back as far as I can reach, then gets lost in the fatty area in the pelvic canal."

I reached into the abdomen and found the calf's head and front feet at the tip of the left horn of the uterus. Pulling up, I lifted the head and feet as close to the incision site as possible, then grabbed the scalpel and cut into the uterine wall.

Willie looked on in disbelief. "I thought you said she was all tore up inside? Why are you cutting another hole in her if she's already got a big one?"

"If I tried to bring the calf out through the hole that's way back there, I'd end up tearing the uterus even more. I'd rather make another incision and take the calf out where it's easy to suture."

Willie was at my elbow, anxious to help with the delivery. His hands clasped together at chest height, he watched as I manipulated the uterine wall over first one foot, then the other. Holding the feet in my left hand, I reached in with my right to guide the nose through the incision. Everything was lined up and coming nicely.

"Are you ready if I need you, Willie? Why don't you get the calving chains out of the disinfectant just in case?"

Before I could remind him not to let the chains get contaminated, he dragged them out of the bucket and dried his hands on his pants. Bob chuckled quietly, and I proceeded to extract the calf the best I could without help.

"You ready for the chains yet?" Willie asked anxiously.

"I think I should be able to manage without them." I extended the uterine incision another couple of inches. With steady traction, I pulled on the feet. We saw more leg, then the nose, forehead, and ears.

"Look! He's alive!" Willie was ecstatic, as the calf's eyes suddenly blinked open. I drew more and more of the black, white-faced calf from the womb. Once past the shoulders, all resistance ended, and the calf glided from the uterus to be deposited at Willie's feet.

"He's all yours." I eased him onto the barn floor.

Bob handed me the catgut suture material to close the incision, while Willie busied himself with rubbing down the calf. I quickly closed the wound with a single layer of sutures, then followed it with a second layer to fold the uterine wall over on itself and prevent leakage. I applied traction on the horn and rotated it slightly in order to get a better look at the damage to the uterus and cervix.

The laceration started at the level of the abdominal incision and disappeared in the abdomen as far as the eye could follow. "Have a look, Bob."

"That's quite a tear." Bob shook his head. "How in the world are you ever going to get that sewn all the way to the other end? Can you even reach that far?"

"It's going to be a challenge. I suspect I'll end up with a few holes in my fingers before all's said and done."

I tied the first knot, then began the tedious task of pulling together the wound margins. The first six inches was a breeze, but very soon the combination of pulling the uterus back, holding the wound margins in apposition, and suturing became onerous.

"I'm going to need help here. One of you'll have to hold the uterus while I suture."

"I'll give it a try." Willie pulled the calf out of the way and covered him with the towel. Daubing on a few drops of surgical scrub, he gave his hands a cursory rinse, then stepped up as if to grab the uterus.

"Whoa there, Willie! You need to wash up a lot better than that if you plan on helping."

"What do you mean? I'm clean! Look at these hands—if I wash 'em any more they're gonna melt."

"Back to the bucket, Willie! Scrub them for three or four minutes more at least."

Willie grumbled continuously as he lathered his hands and arms. When finished, he glumly stepped up to grasp the uterus.

"Just keep a slow, steady pull toward her head while I suture."

Traction on the uterus made a tremendous difference initially, and I closed the next bit easily. Time after time, I reached in, felt for the location of the next suture, then drove the needle through the wound margins.

Bob and Willie traded off as we struggled with the remainder of the tear. The more progress I made, the more difficult it became to place the sutures in the proper location. The needle found its way into the end of my finger as often as into the opposite side of the tear. My hands were raw and bleeding. Bob and Willie were impatient for the ordeal to end. Each time I reached again, they couldn't hide their disappointment.

Several times during the arduous process, Willie squirmed and twitched. He'd glance furtively in my direction, but invariably broke down and scratched madly at a different portion of his anatomy. Each time, he dutifully returned to scrub. By the time I no longer needed his services, he swore that he'd never wash again.

No matter how far I stretched or how hard I tried to finalize the closure, nothing was good enough! Left as it was, the suture line would leak fluid into the abdominal cavity, and the cow would almost certainly die from peritonitis. In desperation, I closed her abdomen, hoping that I would be able to suture the remainder of the wound through the vagina. If not, the whole effort would be in vain. Bob and Willie dressed themselves and watched in silence as I closed the cow up. They had been part of the struggle for the last three hours, and they were aware that I was less than happy with the outcome.

I was cold and miserable by the time I placed the final sutures. This was the moment I always looked forward to with great relish. The placement of the final skin stitches signaled completion! It was the time I got to put on my clothes and warm up; the time I threw my instruments into the box for Doris to worry about. Today, I had been robbed of that sense of completion; I was left with the feeling that this surgery would never end.

The next hour passed slowly as I struggled to suture within the confined space of the heifer's vagina. Countless times, I found the point of the needle by burying it within the flesh of my finger or thumb. By the time I called it quits, I was so fatigued that it was difficult to grip the needle well enough to drive it through the tissue of the womb.

"I think we finally have it closed off." I sighed and threw my instruments in a heap.

This procedure had ended with a whimper. Before going into veterinary medicine, I had thought of heroic surgeries as dramatic second-by-second battles where a life was saved or lost by one decisive act. And there are heroics in veterinary medicine; it's just that they are often lost in the mundane plodding that's necessary to achieve the glory. Looking back on this surgery, I'd say that it had all of the attributes of a heroic case. We started with a massive defect that would have meant certain death and ended with a cow that lived to be healthy and productive.

I later found it easy to be critical of my performance that day. Many of the tasks I was called upon to perform were difficult and rarely could I choose to deal with them when I was in top form. With this cow, I could have spent hours more fiddling here and tucking there, but I still wouldn't have been satisfied with the job.

When I finally got back to the clinic, I glanced at the clock in the waiting room—quarter to three. No wonder I felt so bagged! I threw the surgery box on the counter, plunked myself against the gas heater, and turned up the thermostat. There was a faint "whoof" as the heater ignited. Within a few seconds, the fan cut in, and I was bathed in a flow of hot air.

It felt so good to be warm and to be caught up with work. Nobody was waiting impatiently for me to get there. I focused on my breath and the slow rise and fall of my abdomen.

My tummy rumbled. I absently pictured the spread of Chinese food that I had missed out on this evening. I saw the steaming bowl of fried rice, the almond chicken, and the sweet and sour spareribs. I wondered if Doris had gone alone tonight, if she had continued down the street to Mae's.

If she had, it might still be there! I wandered into the lab and sure enough, there it was. My mouth watered as I bit into it. Heavenly delight. There was nothing like a cheese sandwich before going to bed.

My New Car

Y FIRST NEW CAR! I strolled out of the Volkswagen dealership clutching the keys and stopped to admire my purchase. I had ordered it in—a station wagon with a turquoise paint job. It had been one of the few vehicles I'd tried out that actually had enough room for me to sit upright without ducking my head. It wasn't fancy, but it had lots of room to carry my equipment, and something about it just felt right.

Although it had rained for most of the night, toward morning it had cooled off and started to snow. Huge wet flakes fell; the top and the hood of the car were already covered with a thin layer of snow.

I walked to the vehicle and opened the door. Ducking my head, I maneuvered my frame through the opening and settled onto the seat. Inhaling deeply, I relished the scent. There was something about the smell of a new vehicle that gave me a feeling of affluence.

Starting the car, I turned onto the highway toward town. I was going to have to be quick about loading my equipment. My appointment on the Hood farm was for one o'clock, and it was already afternoon.

I pulled into the lot at the back of the clinic and parked next to my old vehicle. I felt like a traitor abandoning it now! After six years of reliable service, I knew all of its little idiosyncrasies. I always seemed capable of getting it to perform, and hardly ever had it left me in the lurch.

It was with a great deal of nostalgia that I unloaded the drugs and tools from my old car. I looked at the little blue Teddy bear that sat on the armrest in the backseat and thought of that depressing Christmas I had spent in the hospital at Saskatoon—about how my classmate had brought me Teddy to keep me company. Somehow, I just couldn't take him with me—not now, anyway.

The cattle were bawling and milling aimlessly about the corral when I pulled up. Dempsey Hood already had the alleyway leading to the chute crammed with cows and, as I entered the yard, he signaled his assistants. They advanced with arms waving to crowd a dozen cows into the holding pen. A gray-haired man with hawkish features swung the gate closed and leaned against it until he was able to slide a bolt in place to secure it. The other man, a younger version of the first, climbed the corral fence and swung his leg over the top rail.

I quickly grabbed my palpation sleeve and worked my arm into the latex rubber cocoon. I was stretching the glove tight to my fingers when Dempsey approached. A stocky man, he was powerfully built. His forehead was deeply etched with frown lines, and he imparted an unmistakable intensity. "Well, we're about as ready as we're gonna get. Wouldn't you know that the weather would turn dirty like this. It was so beautiful yesterday—I was hopin' it'd be nice today, too."

His short-cropped blond hair was wet and plastered close to his forehead. Water trickled down his face, and he ran his coat sleeve over it to stem the flow. His red-and-black-checked flannel jacket was soggy, and the shoulders were covered with a thin layer of slush.

I looked up at the low-hanging clouds and the huge snowflakes and shook my head. "Doesn't look like it plans on letting up any time soon."

"Afraid you're right." He looked at the sky himself, then turned to the cattle. "Sure be glad when this is over. I'm going to miss the cows, but Mel here's offered me a price I can't refuse. He only wants cows that'll calve by April, so if it's all right with you, we'll use that as a cutoff."

"Sounds good to me. Guess we better get started." I plastered my hand with KY jelly and opened the gate to the squeeze. Slipping in behind a big Hereford cow, I lifted the sliding metal gate behind her and grabbed a tail that was sopping wet and covered with manure. As I inserted my fingertips into her rectum, she threw her head and flailed from side to side, making the ancient metal chute rattle and groan in protest. I forced my hand forward into the colon past the brim of her pelvis and expelled several jets of watery manure.

"The cows'll be plenty loose," Dempsey noted. "They're straight off pasture."

"So I see." I glowered in disgust as a gush of green slime ran down the side of my coveralls and onto the toe of my boot. The first cow—you'd think I could stay clean longer than this! Returning my attention to the big Hereford cow that still danced on the end of my arm, I directed my hand forward in search of a calf.

"She's pregnant," I affirmed, feeling a well-formed fetus bobbing beneath my hand. I grabbed the blue marking crayon from my pocket and ran a line over the soggy hair of her right hip. Dempsey stuck a pole behind her and opened the gate to release her. She charged forward and disappeared around the corner.

I ducked out of the alleyway as a small black, white-faced cow steamed forward. Determined to follow the Hereford, she charged over the pole at the back of the squeeze and struggled toward the open gate. Dempsey quickly reset the head gate, and it clanged shut, stopping her advance. She bellowed and strained to drive through. Thrashing past the tread at the back of the chute, she sprayed manure and muck into the air behind her.

A gob splattered the side of my face, and I reached my free hand to scrape it off. "Boy, you're really off to a good start!" Dempsey hooted. I stood back waiting for the cow to settle down, then walked in behind her.

Mel wandered forward to stand beside Dempsey. He looked at the cow with disdain. "Not much of a critter, is she?"

"Not to look at," Dempsey retorted. "But she weaned over six hundred pounds of calf, and I bet she's pregnant." He chuckled as I scribed a blue line across her rump and released her without further comment. Mel opened his mouth as if to speak, then thought better of it and returned to his post at the end of the chute.

We had put through twenty-five head, and we had developd a routine. Mel and his son, Dan, kept the chute full, with cows coming at an even pace. Dempsey ran the head gate and cut out the few cows that weren't in calf, and I waded around in their back ends for proof of pregnancy.

Mel was having difficulty convincing an old Hereford that she wanted to come down the chute. Wary of advancing further, she planted all four feet and pushed back against the cow behind her.

"Damned old crock anyway!" he hollered. Climbing up the rails of the chute, he whacked her with his stick. The old cow stood stoically with her eyes closed and refused to move. Mel reached over with his foot and goaded her along the spine—still no response. It wasn't until Dempsey gave her a jolt with an electric prod that she relented and waddled to the front.

I'd just gotten my hand into her, when Mel stomped up. "Doesn't matter whether she's pregnant or not! I don't want this one. She's old as the hills. Cut her out!"

Dempsey flushed. His blue eyes smoldered, but he said nothing. He watched as I finished palpating and scribed a blue mark across her rump. There was a tense moment as he stood staring at Mel, then he opened the gate and chased her in with the cull cows.

"Dan! Let's have some more cows. The vet's waiting on ya!" Mel turned his back on Dempsey and returned to his post. Dan had watched the confrontation with great interest and returned to his job with a smirk.

Huge wet flakes of snow continued to fall. The corral rails were white and slippery. The ground in the chute had become a sea of muck, and my coveralls were soaked and plastered with manure and mud. As I stepped into the runway behind the cows, my boots all but disappeared from sight, and even shifting my feet was an effort. Mel rejected two other pregnant cows—one that had the beginning of a cancerous eye and another that just didn't look good. Dempsey had acquiesced to Mel's demands, but each time his face looked a little more fiery.

"I'm going to run to the phone and see if the liners are goin' to be here on time," Mel hollered, after helping his son close the gate on the final dozen cows. We had been making steady progress and several times over the last twenty minutes I had looked at the remaining cattle thinking that the end was finally in sight. All but a half-dozen cows had been run through, when Dan hollered at Dempsey. "We won't be taking this brockle-faced cow either!"

Dempsey stomped over to the corral and crawled through the rails. I finished checking a Hereford heifer and struggled toward dry land. He and Dan were in the midst of a discussion. From the color of Dempsey's complexion, I could tell he wasn't happy.

"It's just an old pink-eye scar, I tell you!" Dempsey hollered.

Shaking his head, Dan straddled the top rail of the corral. He pushed his cowboy hat to his crown and affirmed, "No, Dad won't want that one."

Neither Dan nor I expected what happened next. One moment he was sitting on the rail, a cocky look on his face; the next, he was sailing through the air. He landed with a splat at the feet of the cow he had so adamantly rejected.

"You son of a . . ." he spluttered. Sprawled out flat in the muck, he stared up at the dynamo who stood over him—at his red face, his injected veins, his clenched fists—and fell silent. His eyes were as big as saucers. They revealed first anger, then frustration, then fear. He lay in the mud without moving a muscle.

"Do you want to run in those last few cows, Dempsey?" I interjected. "May just as well get them finished off."

"Yeah, sure," he muttered. He stepped over the young man and opened the gate. Dan struggled to free himself from the mire. Tears of frustration flowed down his cheeks as he grabbed onto a corral rail and pulled himself upright.

"Yeah! Come on!" Dempsey hollered at the cows that had been huddled at the opposite end of the holding pen. They churned for the gate, jostling Dan as he struggled to retrieve his partially submerged cowboy hat.

Dempsey and I finished checking the remainder of the cattle with neither help nor hindrance from Dan or his father. All the cows were pregnant, and Dempsey ran each of them in with the cows that were to be purchased.

I trudged to the house, my boots heavy and caked with mud. Finding a garden hose, I sprayed off as much of the accumulated muck as possible. I stripped my coveralls, slipped on a dry pair, and threw the wet ones in the back of the vehicle. This poor car wasn't going to smell new for long!

I left Dempsey's and headed to West Creston. The bypass had just been opened; the West Creston ferry was no longer in service. Willie Evans had been in this morning, and I had made arrangements to remove the stitches from the cow we had performed a cesarean on a couple of weeks earlier. Willie was overjoyed with her progress.

The car was far peppier than I was used to; I kept reminding myself to take it easy. Once off the main highway, the going was painfully slow. The four inches of snow on the road was slushy and pulled the car first one way, then the other. I turned onto the side road that wound its way up onto the West Creston bench. What a perfect day to try out this car! I needed a car that could get around in any type of weather.

216

Without the slightest hesitation, I whipped up the incline. The traction was fantastic with all of the weight over the rear wheels; it would take a heck of a snowfall to keep me grounded with this car!

I pulled into Willie's drive with a big smile on my face. What a treat it was to drive a vehicle that performed so well.

Willie stepped out onto his covered deck, still pulling on his coat. He lifted his foot up onto the railing and tied the laces of his boots. "New car, eh? Must be nice! Probably won't be able to afford to get you out here now. You'll be charging so much for all that shiny new paint."

"Feels good to know that I'm likely to get where I'm going without worrying about something falling apart." I clenched my jaw as soon as I finished speaking. A big smile spread over Willie's face, as he realized he had scored a direct hit. Why did I feel so defensive about buying a new car? Surely people didn't expect me to drive a ten-year-old vehicle for the rest of my days in practice!

"Must be nice." I could see that Willie was not ready to let go of the issue yet. "Wish you had waited a couple of months to do it, though. Still haven't gotten my bill for the night you spent out here."

My face was flushed, and I just knew my ears were the color of ripe plums. I plucked my suture scissors from the cold sterilization tray and followed Willie to the barn. "So, she's been doing fairly well, has she?"

"Yeah, she was pretty slow the next day, but I was surprised how quickly she picked up." Willie seemed ready to drop the subject of the new car, and I was more than happy to have him do so. He opened the barn door, and the big black-and-white heifer turned her head in the stanchion to look at us. Her mouth was full of hay; she continued munching as I walked up beside her.

A smile crept over my face as the bright brown eyes engaged mine. This job would be a lot easier if a guy had a good crystal ball. Who'd have predicted she would look this good a couple of weeks ago. Never say die!

The cow stood quietly as I snipped away at the sutures. The wound had healed beautifully. She was away to the races.

"Do you think I'll ever be able to get her back in calf?"

"It's hard to know at this stage, Willie. Most cesareans come back and get pregnant, but I've never had a cow as torn up as her before. I guess time'll tell."

217

I was floating on air as I left Willie's driveway. Who would have dared to predict such a rosy outcome? I wish that I'd known that night—it would have made everything so much easier to endure!

The sun poked out from behind the clouds; the valley lay before me under a shiny, white blanket. The river glistened a deep blue in contrast, and the mountains in the background formed a mosaic of white and gray and blue. Life simply didn't get much better than this!

I was crawling down the hill in second gear. The wet snow was terribly slick, and I was less than impressed with the car's steering on the downhill run. I was going to need some sandbags under the hood to get more weight over the front wheels.

I was almost to the bottom of the hill and eased the car into third gear. Only one more corner to go before I was again on level ground. I was not going more than twenty miles an hour when I started into the curve. I braked slightly and congratulated myself on keeping my speed down. The moment I touched the brake, the car took off like a toboggan! I came off the brake immediately and steered harder into the curve.

The next few seconds passed like slow-motion footage from a movie. The car was completely unresponsive. I watched myself slipping closer and closer to the edge of the road. I was traveling so slowly, I swear I could have stuck out my foot and pushed the front end straight. The wheels slipped gently over the bank. God no, not my new car!

It hung on the edge for what seemed an eternity, then slowly eased over onto its side and rolled down the embankment. My black kit box hit me on the side of the head and smacked into the windshield. The car rolled over gracefully twice, then came to rest on the driver's side next to a massive fir tree. I struggled to dig myself out from under the debris.

My new car! Not my new car! I sat there for a few moments trying to collect myself. Tears flowed as I was slowly forced to accept the reality of the situation. My head was throbbing and my shoulder was sore. I grabbed the cradle of the calving jack that was digging into my side and flung it into the backseat. I removed my seat belt and struggled upright. Standing on the driver's door, I opened the passenger door and climbed out of the vehicle.

I hollered at the top of my lungs. "Why my new car!"

Doris arrived at the office within a few moments of my calling her. Gordon and Ruth arrived five minutes later. I had been in anguish as I watched the tow truck pull my car back onto its wheels. Every time I closed my eyes, I could see the slow-motion replay of its demise. To this day, I swear I could have stuck my foot out to straighten it. Examining the tracks afterward, I determined the car had followed the edge for ten or fifteen feet, and it had been close to staying on the road. Why couldn't it have simply straightened out? Why hadn't this happened with my old car? Why me?

"Are you sure we shouldn't run you up to the hospital?" It was the second time Doris had asked me the same question. She was very worried.

"You've got a nasty bruise on the side of your head," Ruth interjected. "We better get you checked out."

"I'm just fine! If my car was in as good shape as I am, I'd be feeling a lot better about things. Wouldn't you know it? My first new car and I wreck it the first day out!"

Gordon and Ruth stood at the entrance to the living room looking down on me. I lay stretched out on the carpet with an overstuffed pillow crammed behind my back, looking dejectedly up at the light fixture on the ceiling, at its six bulbs and its smoked glass shades. My head was aching.

"Where do you keep your glasses?" Gordon pulled a brown paper bag from inside his coat pocket.

"In that cupboard over the sink, if they're not all dirty."

A few minutes later he handed me a glass full of an amber liquid. One whiff confirmed that it was Gordon's favorite, Glenfiddich scotch. With dutiful reverence, he handed glasses to Doris and Ruth.

"Here's to you!" He raised his glass and we all joined him.

I don't remember offhand how many times Gord refilled my glass. I do recall forgetting my aches and pains and feeling marginally less upset about my vehicle. I remember that Doris and Ruth were diligently trying to convince Gordon that it was time to go and let me get to bed. I remember standing up and my head hitting the light fixture.

The rest is a blur, but Doris says it was a miracle I wasn't cut to ribbons by the shower of glass that followed me to the floor.

THE FREELOADER

T'S A CRYING SHAME to have to destroy a dog like him, and I just can't do it."

"I know how you feel," I replied. "I absolutely hate putting an animal down unless it's suffering. Even then I ask myself why I should have the right to play God."

I was on the phone with Ben Fyfe, an RCMP officer based in Creston. The detachment was responsible for law enforcement along Highways 3 and 3A from Yahk to the Kootenay Lake ferry.

"Well, I'm going to have to bring this dog in for you to put to sleep! There's just no way I can deal with him. I had the big goof at the Crawford Bay dump for almost an hour and aimed at his head a half-dozen times. He gave me the saddest look, as if he knew what was coming, and I just couldn't pull the trigger!

"I brought him to my place thinking I could find a home for him, but he fights constantly with my own dog . . . I just can't handle it any more. They really got into it this morning and if I hadn't been right there handy, you'd have had some work to do putting one or both of them back together."

"Why don't you bring him in, and I'll see what I can do."

An hour later, he arrived at my office. His presentation was far different from the image that pops to mind when one thinks about an officer of the Royal Canadian Mounted Police. With his rounded, jovial features and tendency to carry a few extra pounds, I would have thought him more likely to be the local minister.

His cheeks were flushed and his eyes were downcast as he approached me.

"Sorry to put the burden on you like this," he said, slowly shaking his head, "but I just could not do it."

I had dealt with Ben previously on several occasions—once to vaccinate his own dog, and several times to treat abused or injured animals that he had come across in the performance of his duties. He always made sure that something

220

was done about the sick or injured animal that was unable to manage on its own.

"That's okay, Ben," I replied with a shrug. "I doubt that I'd have done any different if I'd been in your shoes. Why don't you just pop him into the office and we'll take a look?"

"I appreciate this. I've never been much on being an animal control officer, but that's supposedly a part of our official duties in outlying communities."

I followed him to the patrol car. A large, gray-black silhouette dominated the backseat. When Ben opened the door, the dog stood hesitantly on the edge of the seat before venturing onto the sidewalk. With his coloring and build, it was obvious that he was almost pure German shepherd. The only feature that argued was an ear that flopped lazily to the left side of his face, giving him an almost comical appearance.

Following the corporal, he walked calmly along the street and through the doorway of the clinic. But as he crossed the threshold, his demeanor changed. He panicked. Suddenly planting all four feet, he struggled to get back outside. Digging in his heels, the corporal dragged the desperate animal inside, and I closed the door behind him.

"He's obviously been in a veterinary hospital before. He picked up on the smell right away."

Ben stroked the head of the big hulk that quivered at his feet. "It looks like he's been well cared for until recently. But he's been running free for weeks down in Crawford Bay, and there've been a number of people calling in complaints against him. One woman has been organizing the campaign and has phoned practically every day for a week. Apparently, he's been terrorizing her poodle to the point where she can't let him out of the house. She's called in so many times that we just couldn't ignore her any longer."

"Come over here, fellow," I coaxed. "Come on! Get over here, you big lug—I'm not going to hurt you."

Keeping his belly firm to the floor, he crawled over to me and stuck his muzzle in my hand.

"There's a boy. You really are a nice fellow, aren't you?"

Encouraged by the chatter and a constant barrage of stroking, he raised himself to a standing position and took a hesitant step in my direction.

"There we go, fella. You're a fine-looking specimen, aren't you?"

He moved closer, leaned his shoulder against my leg, and extended his head for more petting.

"Well, it sure looks as if he's taken to you," Ben observed. "It took me two days to get to the point where he trusted me enough to let me pet him without cringing."

"By the look of things, Ben, you won't have to worry about my putting him to sleep any time soon. We'll keep him here and see if we can find a good home for him. I'd have as much trouble as you doing away with him."

Ben's face immediately broke into a broad smile. With a nod, he headed for his patrol car, leaving me with my reluctant visitor. After a few more minutes of handling, I coaxed him into a kennel. Although he was never really satisfied with life behind bars, he settled into a routine of lying quietly in anticipation of the breaks where he would receive attention and go for a walk on a leash down the alley.

There was a special chemistry between us from the very first moment we met and, as soon as he was released from the kennel, he would make his way to my side. I found myself being more and more particular about who we showed him to; I avoided people I just didn't think would be suitable owners for a dog of his nature. Nightly, I released him from the kennel and allowed him to come upstairs as I cooked my supper or sat in front of the television.

"I've got the perfect home for our star boarder," Doris chirped at the end of a particularly hectic day. "Mrs. Ross, from down the lake—you know— the lady with Sebastian, that big half St. Bernard, half German shepherd that we neutered a month ago. He got hit by a car last week and died out in front of their home; she's absolutely lost without a dog around the place. She can't come in until the end of the week, but she's asked me to keep this guy until she can get here. She says she'll pay his board until she's able to pick him up."

"That would certainly be an ideal home for the big lout," I admitted grudgingly.

"You sure don't sound overly enthusiastic about it," Doris noted, giving me a long look. "Are you sure you want to let him go? You seem to be getting rather attached to him."

"Of course, we'll let him go. How could I possibly keep a big dog like him around here?"

It was with a feeling of sadness that I slipped the choke chain over the shepherd's head that night and led him toward the front door.

"Are you sure you don't want me to call Mrs. Ross and tell her that he's already taken?" Doris asked knowingly.

"No, of course not. He's just a big nuisance around here, and he's taking up kennel space that we could use for other animals. We're full to the brim tonight and, if another animal comes in, I don't have a clue what we'd do with him."

The dog pulled happily on the lead as we made our way down the alley. Lifting his leg at all the strategic poles and on the more prominent corners of the buildings, he stopped here and there. Occasionally, he would drive his nose deep into a clump of dead grass or mound of snow, give a few decisive snorts, then move on to check out other spots that tantalized his olfactory senses. We were at the end of the alley when I took the lead off and, for the first time, allowed him to range freely on his own. Half expecting him to run off, I watched with my heart in my mouth as he ran ahead of me.

"Hey, you big lug, you! Come back here."

As though stung by a bee, he whipped around and came running back to me. Shoving his muzzle into my hand, he flipped his head a number of times to make sure my hand was on top of his head in petting position. He moaned as I rubbed his forehead and massaged his ears. Satisfied that he was in my good books, he trotted ahead to check out the rest of the neighborhood.

We were on our way back to the clinic when Doris came running down the alley.

"Mel Griffith just came in the door, Dave," she blurted between puffs. "He ran over his old Lab and it looks like the dog has a broken leg."

"Come here, you big mutt!" I hollered. "Your outing's over for the time being."

I snapped the leash onto the choke collar and headed after Doris.

"You're getting pretty trusting, aren't you? Don't you worry about taking him off the leash?"

"He seems to want to stay close; besides, it's not as if he belongs to anyone. No one would miss him if he took off."

"Are you sure about that?" Doris muttered over her shoulder. "Looks to me that you might be a bit upset if he left."

"Humph," I grunted

"Sorry to keep you here, Doc," Mel apologized, as I began examining his old dog. "I'd just stacked a load of empty boxes onto my trailer and was hauling them down to the shed for storage. I didn't realize that old Gabe had laid down in front of the wheel. I never thought to check for him when I took off, and I ran right over him with the trailer! He can't hear worth a darn any more and his reactions aren't what they used to be, so I guess he never even woke up until the tire went over him."

The old yellow Lab lay stoically on the table as I ran my hands over his body. His head was extended slightly, and it was obvious that he was not comfortable. His tongue protruded and he was panting as if he were hot. His gums were pink, and there was no evidence of bleeding anywhere on his body.

"Did he move at all that you saw, Mel? Or did he just lie there after it happened?"

"No, he was standing when I got to him," Mel assured me, "but he was holding up a back leg, and he didn't look very steady on his hindquarters."

I grasped Gabe's left hind foot and spread his toes; he let out a piercing whine and whirled to lick my hand.

"That hurts, does it, fellow?"

"Sorry 'bout that, Doc—guess I wouldn't make a very good assistant. If this hadn't been old Gabe, he might have nailed you."

"That's okay, I know he's in a lot of pain. Just see if you can keep him looking straight ahead."

By persistently manipulating the toes, I could tell that all but two of the metatarsal bones in Gabe's foot had been broken. Fortunately, the long bones higher in his leg seemed intact, and palpation of his knee and ankle didn't cause him discomfort. The opposite leg appeared to be in good shape, and no amount of poking or prodding elicited a response from the old Lab. The whole time I was working on him, he rested his head in his master's hands and soaked up the attention that was being lavished upon him.

I lifted the dog and extended both hind legs fully behind him. They were the same length and appeared symmetrical, but there was a definite tightening of his musculature, and he whined as though in pain. As I lifted him, the old guy stood fully on his front legs and tried to pull his back legs forward and away from me.

"How heavy was that trailer when you had it loaded, Mel?" I lowered Gabe to the table.

"Well, it was heavy enough." Mel shrugged. "But the boxes were all empty and probably didn't amount to much more than a couple hundred pounds."

As I released his hind legs, Gabe placed his right hind foot to the table and hunched in a position that resembled a three-legged sawhorse. His front legs were positioned farther back, so that they bore most of his weight. He was using his hind leg only for balance.

"From what I can see superficially, it looks as if the wheel just ran over his hindquarters. We'll have to watch him closely to make sure that he doesn't have a slow bleeder in the pelvis or abdomen."

"You think he's going to make it then and be able to get around all right? He's been a great dog. I don't want him to just lay around and be all crippled up."

"The way he's standing, I suspect a problem in his pelvis, so we better X-ray both his hips and that left hind foot. If the fracture in his hips was severe he wouldn't be able to bear as much weight on it as he is right now."

"Well, if you think he may have a few miles left in him, then you better get a picture of him and see what needs doing."

I administered some Demerol to diminish the old boy's pain, and by the time we got around to doing the X rays, he allowed us to roll him back and forth without complaint. His pelvis was in fact broken, but the location of the fracture and the lack of displacement suggested that it would heal well with restricted exercise. I applied a splint to Gabe's broken foot.

With Mel and Doris casually chatting at the surgery table, I tried to figure out how to rearrange the hospitalized animals so that everyone could be accommodated. There was no choice; the freeloading German shepherd was going to have to be moved so that Gabe could be properly bedded down for observation.

"What're we going to do with you, ya big boob?" I opened the kennel and gave him a pat. He sprang to his feet, wagging in expectation. "There's no place for spongers around here."

I stood back and he took a deliberate step down from the kennel, watching me continually for any sign of my disapproval.

"Come on out," I encouraged. "It's all right."

Wagging his tail, he danced around my feet, hoping for another walk.

"Come on, big fella." I coaxed him through the clinic and into the stairwell to my apartment. "You just wait here until I figure out what to do with you."

Closing the door, I returned to clean and ready the kennel for Gabe. He was still groggy from the sedation and within seconds of settling in the kennel, he stretched out on his side and went to sleep.

"Okay, mutt," I called up the stairwell. "You can come down here with us now."

The shepherd hesitated at first, then swaggered down the stairs and across the office to look up at the door.

"Not yet, fella—we've still got some cleaning up to do before we can go out for another walk."

"What are you going to do with him tonight?" Doris asked, as we wiped down the exam table and put away the leftover materials. "Do you think he'd start a fight with one of the other dogs or go after a cat if he had the opportunity?"

"I'm not sure, to be honest." I unconsciously looked over to where he was sitting. "Ben said he was aggressive with other dogs, but he hasn't really been bad with anything that I've seen."

Every hour or so, I ran down the stairs to check on Gabe. He lay stretched out in his kennel, snoring his way through the remainder of the evening. Only occasionally did he moan to protest the pain of his hip and foot. With each trip up and down the stairs, the shepherd trotted at my heels. Standing back a respectable distance as I examined Gabe and worked with the other patients, he showed only mild curiosity in the animals that were on the other side of the bars.

It was after eleven o'clock when I clicked off the television and made my final trip downstairs to see how Gabe was faring. He was resting quietly and, after checking the color of his gums, I closed the kennel door and went back upstairs. The shepherd followed me like a shadow every step of the way. He had been so mellow throughout the evening that I didn't give another thought to confining him from the downstairs area. I went to sleep with him stretched out on the floor beside my bed. He looked perfectly at ease, his breathing slow, deep, and regular.

I awoke to the sound of vicious barking from somewhere downstairs. Springing out of bed, I switched on the light and looked desperately around for signs of the German shepherd. He was gone! The clock on my dresser said it was 3 A.M.

"Damn it, anyway!"

That big lug of a dog must be downstairs beating up on the poor Lab. I pulled on my pants as I ran through the kitchen. Still fumbling with the zipper, I stumbled down the stairs in my bare feet. The sound of the barking intensified as I tore through the back room and headed toward the surgery. How could I ever forgive myself if that damned dog had gotten the kennel open and chewed up old Gabe?

A pattern of bright red and white lights flashed alternately against the wall of the surgery. My God, had I slept through this racket long enough for someone to have complained to the police?

When I rounded the corner into the kennel room, I half expected to see blood and carnage but realized the racket was coming from beyond. How in the world had that dog gotten out there? These doors were closed when I went to bed.

As I stumbled through the narrow passageway that led to the cluttered back room, I realized that something indeed was amiss. All I could see was the back end of the dog and, from the looks of things, he had his hackles up. Over the harsh racket of the barking, I could hear someone talking.

"It's okay now, boy."

"Here! Settle down now, you big lug!" I hollered over the din of his barking. "Easy now! Easy now! What's going on here?"

"Oh, thank God you're here!"

The big shepherd started wagging his tail at the sight of me. His hair, which had been standing almost on end, slicked down under the flow of my hand. He worked his nose under my palm and gave a couple of flips in search of support.

"What in the world's going on here?"

As if his job was done, the dark hulk wandered off toward the kennel room.

"My Lord, that dog just about tore the pants off me."

"Oh, it's you, Ben! What's happening?"

Ben walked cautiously to the door and peered around the corner, having gained a healthy respect for the critter that was now casually wandering around in the front office.

"I was driving down Canyon when I saw a guy running from this side of the street. He looked like he was in a real rush, and I had a hunch something wasn't right. I pulled over and had a look around, and that's when I noticed your back door open."

"Look's like the door's been kicked down." Shards of splintered wood still hung to the casing.

"I saw that and, when I went to step inside, I found out why the other guy left in such a hurry. That dog just about took my leg off, and he left no doubt in my mind that he meant business."

"Talk about a lucky break! This is his first night on duty."

"That was awful good timing on your part. When did you decide to keep him as a watchdog?"

"About two minutes ago."

"I thought that darned dog knew me," Ben muttered, "but there was sure no dealing with him out there tonight."

As far as I could tell, there was nothing missing. Other than the broken casing, not much damage had been done to the door. It didn't take me long to pound in a few nails to secure it for the night. The shepherd hung close to me as I facilitated the repairs, then followed on my heel as I wandered back to bed.

"Well, you big lug," I said, petting his head and roughing up his ears, "you sure paid for your grub this week. You could come in handy around here after all."

Rooting his nose under my hand, he moaned as I rubbed his forehead. He pushed against me and rolled his eyes in ecstasy.

"If you're going to stay around here, we'll have to come up with a name for you." He sat attentively staring up at me. "Lug . . . What do you think of that name, boy?"

His look of sheer satisfaction was his answer. It was obvious that as long as Lug received his quota of attention, he could care less what I called him.

MOUSE

HE SNOW WAS FALLING with a vengeance. The hood of the car, which I had just swept off, was already white. The wiper blades thumped back and forth as I peered through the swirling mass. I was late for my appointment at Basque Ranch. Ginger Ferguson was not the sort of person who appreciated waiting, and I'd hoped to be on time for a change.

I sat impatiently as a long string of cars followed a Greyhound bus and waited for it to turn off at the depot. A faded blue Ford pickup drove by, kicking up a blinding cloud of dry, whirling snow. Behind him, there was a long break in traffic.

I hit the accelerator and was almost fully onto the highway when something swished past the nose of my vehicle. Thirty feet behind the pickup, a snow-covered object was dragging on the end of a chain, plowing through the residual powder in the middle of the road.

What was that damned fool trying to do? Was this some sort of joke? I could have run into whatever he was dragging! Lug, in his usual spot next to me, craned his neck until his nose touched the glass. Painting a mosaic of slime on the windshield, he bobbed his head back and forth, trying to focus through the wipers.

The amorphous mass flowed as effortlessly as a toboggan over the snow in front of us. Not until I got directly behind the truck, did I realize that the object in tow might, in fact, be the carcass of an animal.

Couldn't be! What sort of sick person would drag a critter through town? I wondered if some sadist was getting his kicks. My hackles were really starting to get up at the driver of the truck, as I convinced myself I was in fact looking at a large dog.

"My God, that's Bill Hampton," I blurted. Could that lifeless form at the end of the chain be Mouse? I put the possibility out of my mind. It was just last week he had brought his dog in for his yearly checkup and vaccinations. Bill was a young carpenter and general handyman who lived in the Goat River bottom and worked part time for the school district. He was one of the gentlest people I knew; his dogs weren't pets, they were family members. He wouldn't intentionally hurt a gnat.

Honking madly on the horn, I was certain I could draw Bill's attention, but for some reason he kept on driving. The traffic finally halted in front of the Bus Depot restaurant. Convinced that Bill had figured out what was going on, I jumped out of the car and rushed to the rescue.

To my horror, I was looking down at a St. Bernard embalmed in snow. Mouse lay motionless, his pale blue tongue hanging limply. There was no evidence of life. The loop on his choke collar had collapsed and elongated but was still intact; the chain was as tight as a bowstring!

Grabbing the hair on the side of his chest, I heaved forward and dragged him toward the back of the truck. Just as I pulled on the collar to get some slack, the traffic light changed, and Bill drove away. The chain tightened like a hangman's noose, and I desperately ripped my hand free. Bill continued driving, pulling Mouse with him, and leaving me kneeling like a fool in the middle of the street. I jumped to my feet and ran down the roadway after him, hollering as I went.

"Bill! Biiillll!"

Just when it seemed that he was going to continue right through town, a woman on the sidewalk dropped her shopping bag and jumped into the street in front of him. The truck stopped.

Grabbing Mouse by the front legs, I slackened the collar, pulled it over his head, and threw him off the road onto the sidewalk. He was completely limp; there was no evidence of a heartbeat or respiration.

I pulled out his tongue—it was the color of day-old dishwater. His airway was clear with the exception of a bit of mucous at the back of his tongue. With my sleeve, I cleared away what I could and extended his neck. Placing the heel of my hand over the base of his heart and, alternately lifting his front limb and depressing his chest, I began attempts at CPR.

Bill jumped out of the pickup, took one look at his dog, and wailed, "Oh, Mouse, what have I done to you? Oh, Mouse . . . I'm sorry! I'm sorry!" Bill's face was ashen, his hands trembling as he held on to the side of the truck box. "Is he dead?"

Before I could answer him, a woman screeched at us frantically. "Quit fooling around! There's a vet just down the street—maybe he can do something!"

"He is the vet!" yelled the man standing next to her. "Leave him alone! Leave him alone!"

In the middle of a throng of people, I worked on Mouse for at least five minutes. Snow swirled in a constant barrage around us and my coveralls were covered with a layer of flakes. My hair was soaked and water dripped from my forehead and face onto the soggy carcass that I continued to harangue. I was almost ready to let him give up the ghost, when it happened. A thump! Just one, but a thump nonetheless!

"I've got a heartbeat!" A murmur passed through the crowd.

There it was again! And again!

Within a minute, his heart was beating regularly. He took a deep breath, then another. His front leg moved and then his hind. He opened his eyes—two pieces of coal in the head of a melting snowman. Gathering his legs under him, he made a feeble attempt to stand, then crumpled like a drunk.

"Let's load him up and take him to the office so I can get an IV going!"

We lifted Mouse into the back of the truck; with a bystander doing his best to keep Mouse from jumping up, Bill headed to the office. I arrived at my vehicle to find the traffic backed up for blocks. Gordon stood beside the car. His thinning hair was plastered to his forehead, and water dripped off the end of his nose.

"I tried to move your car out of the way, but you'd think that darned dog of yours had never seen me before!"

"Sorry, Gord, but he sure protects this vehicle." Lug was standing on the seat with his nose pressed to the glass, his tail wagging madly. The windows were steamed up, with the exception of those on the passenger side, which were covered in slobber. Wiping the windshield with my coverall sleeve, I made a quick exit onto the side street and reached the office shortly after Bill.

Mouse had overpowered the stranger who was holding him down and was bleeding on him from abrasions on both his front and hind legs.

Sure that the St. Bernard was in need of supportive care, I started an intravenous drip and loaded him up on bicarbonate to treat the buildup of carbon dioxide in his bloodstream. I gave him steroids to treat shock and ameliorate the effects of severe trauma and anoxia on his battered body. Even before I finished bandaging his wounds, it was plain that he didn't think much of the proceedings and was ready to check himself out of our establishment.

Bill hovered over his dog, whispering, "I'm sorry, Mouse, I'm so sorry . . ."

When the patient was finally in a kennel with his IV running, Bill had a chance to explain what had happened.

"Mouse had been running through the place next door, and my neighbor was rather choked with him. In order to keep the peace, I tied him up with a thirty-foot chain in the backyard. He's such a powerful dog, and he hated being confined so badly that he developed a technique of jumping off the top of his doghouse and breaking the chain."

Bill closed his eyes and shook his head in disgust. "The last time he broke loose, I was in a hurry to get to work, so I tied him to the back of my pickup. I wasn't the least bit worried about it because I was using the company truck constantly—hadn't driven my own in weeks. It just so happened that, this afternoon, Bob took the company vehicle and I jumped in my own. Mouse was curled up by his doghouse twenty feet away. I just never gave that chain another thought!"

"You mean he dragged behind the truck all that way?" I shook my head in amazement. "I would have thought it would have broken his neck or crushed his larynx, dragging him like that!"

"You'd think so, but you should've seen the way he launched himself off the doghouse. As luck would have it, I just bought that chain new a couple weeks ago. Maybe the old one would have broken with that much strain on it."

"I can't imagine how he lasted that long without air. He must've dragged for two or three miles, up the Archibald Hill and all the way along the Erickson back road—at least four or five minutes!"

Bill left the office shaking his head in disbelief—that it had happened at all, and that Mouse seemed to have survived it.

By the time I'd finished my farm call and returned to the office, Mouse had improved greatly. Just a few hours before, he had literally been dead. Now his kennel was rocking as he scratched and pawed at the door.

"Settle down, Mouse!"

"He's been carrying on like that for the last half hour," moaned Doris. "I think he's trying to tell us he's ready to go home."

Mouse had worked himself into a complete tizzy. His IV line was hopelessly tangled, and blood had backed up into it.

"That's done about all the good it's going to do." I opened the kennel door. "You don't look like you need that anymore, fella."

He wanted desperately to get past me, but every time he tried to evade me, I managed to block his exit. Finally, he sat resignedly as I removed the tape that held the intravenous line in place and pulled out the catheter.

"Grab me a leash and a big choke chain, Doris. After all those fluids, he probably has to pee."

I gingerly placed the collar around Mouse's neck, hooked on the lead, and stood back. He bolted past me like a freight train, heading on a course straight for the door. The next ten minutes found me being jerked first one way, then the next, all over the back alley. He yanked me from one marking post to the next. He didn't cough or gag; he never gave any indication that he was sore.

An hour later, I discharged Mouse. The last I saw of him, he was streaking down the snow-covered sidewalk, the leash straining and Bill dragging wildly along in his wake.

SUCH A GOOD GIRL

HE AFTERNOON BEGAN WITH A TRIP to the Ballman farm in West Arrow Creek. Theirs was typical of the hobby farms that dot the British Columbia landscape: ten- and twenty-acre slivers of grass carved from the surrounding forest, bordered by rock ridges, and often littered with boulders.

Jack was a local painting contractor who worked out and had as little as possible to do with the farm. His wife, Inez, absolutely loved her plot of ground and the animals on it. She was the secretary of the Creston Valley Beef Growers' Association and had been instrumental in its organization. She was constantly sending new clients to my door.

As I slowed the car, I caught sight of Inez's dogs milling around the back of an old log structure that floated like a boat at sea in the middle of the pasture. An unusual location for a barn, it was at least fifty yards from the nearest fence.

Inez emerged from the shelter, skirted a mound of decaying snow, and waved madly to attract my attention. She strode toward me, two barking dogs running before her. Lug perked up his ear and glared threateningly in their direction. A deep-throated growl was followed by several quick whines, as he twirled on the seat with excitement.

"I'm glad you could come so quickly!" Separating the strands of barbed wire, Inez gingerly worked her short legs through the fence and over the remains of a snowbank. "Jack's away at work, and I'm home alone with 'the boys.'" She motioned toward the still barking dogs. "Ushi's been worrying me for the last week. I checked her breeding slip and, according to my calculations, she should have calved three days ago. She was off by herself all day yesterday, and I checked her every two hours through the night. Her membranes were hanging out when I found her at seven-thirty this morning. I haven't let her out of my sight since, and she hasn't done a thing—hasn't pushed once in all that time."

"What type of bull is she bred to?"

Inez ran her hand through her graying sandy hair. "A Chianina by the name of Hannibal. He's supposed to be an easy-calving sire, but I haven't used him before. Who knows how big her calf could be?" Inez's voice trailed off, and her hazel eyes focused worriedly on the barn.

I grabbed my coveralls from between the seats, pushed Lug back from the door, and slammed it behind me. The younger of the two dogs cowered behind Inez's legs, growling as though threatened by my advance. The older dog tottered to the back of the vehicle. Emitting a low grumble, he lifted a hind leg, balanced precariously, and peed on the tire of my car.

Leaning against the fender, I pulled the coveralls over my shoes and stuck my arms into the sleeves. Just as I stretched to finish the job, the old dog woofed and stuck his nose into my crotch. Taking a sniff, he sauntered off in a disinterested fashion.

"Bruno! Where are your manners?" Inez scolded. "Don't worry about them, they're perfectly harmless. And he"—she motioned to the old dog who was now staggering away—"is just as deaf as a post."

I assembled everything I thought might be of assistance. Throwing the calving chains, handles, and soap into the bucket, I handed them to Inez.

"We'll need this bucket full of warm water. If you have another bucket, could you fill it with cold?"

"Maybe we could get her tied up first. I'd have had that done already, but she wouldn't let me close enough to put her halter on. She's halter broken and is usually a real pet, but today she doesn't want to cooperate. Between chasing her and coaxing her with the grain bucket, it took me an hour to get her into the corral. She had a spot over by that clump of trees all picked out, and she kept going back to it."

Shuffling the drug boxes on the backseat, I dug out my lariat and noted with chagrin the squashed and misshapen coils of rope. Flinging it onto the grass, I stretched it until I was able to wind it into recognizable loops.

With the rope over my shoulder and the calving jack and cradle in my hands, I followed Inez across the pasture. There, in the center of a log triangle at the back of the barn, stood Ushi.

"I'm afraid this isn't much of a corral. Jack isn't the least bit interested in farming, so I just do the best I can with what I can put up myself."

The corral consisted of logs stacked one upon the next with no posts holding the corners together. As far as I could see, no nails had been used in construction, and only long overlaps and the odd bit of plastic twine held the structure together. I could see why Inez was anxious to get Ushi tied up, considering the condition of the corral and the size of the cow. For a heifer, she was a huge animal.

"How old is she, Inez?" I stared in awe at the long-legged beast. "She's a massive creature."

"She'll be three on the third of May. She's from my foundation cow, Penny, and is fifteen-sixteenths Chianina. I'll be able to register her calf as a purebred . . . that is, if it's still alive."

Inez climbed gingerly over the corral rails and grabbed a rope halter from where she had left it on the top log. "Pass me that grain bucket, will you?"

Bucket in one hand, halter in the other, she advanced toward Ushi. "You're Mama's little girl, aren't you, sweetie? Good baby . . . Good baby . . . Come to Mama . . . Come get your grain . . . There we go, sweetie. You love your grain, don't you, girl?"

Ushi lowered her head as if interested in Inez's offering and took a step toward her. "There we go, sweetie." Rubbing the halter along the big cow's neck, Inez inched her way toward the head. "You just let Mama get that halter on you."

As though she'd understood the words, Ushi twisted her neck away and spun, hitting Inez with her hip and sending her, the grain bucket, and the halter sprawling to the ground.

Inez was near tears as she picked herself up. "She's always such a gentle thing to handle. She's never been like this before! Even when I got her in for the technician to inseminate her, I walked right up to her and slipped the halter on."

Ushi was not happy—not happy with being penned, not happy with the stranger who was too close, not happy that her owner was getting more distraught by the moment. Throwing her head, she took two quick steps toward the corner of the corral and flung herself onto the logs like a walrus leaping out of the water onto a rock.

I ran around the outside of the corral, managing to get in front of her before she tipped over the other side.

"Back girl! Back!" I delivered a solid whack across her nose with the flat of my hand. "Back you get!"

Ushi slid off the rails, twirled quickly, ran past Inez, and plunged headlong on to the corral rails of the opposite side. As they gave way under her weight, there was a sickening crack, and Ushi's body tipped forward until only her hind legs remained on the rails.

Fumbling with my lariat, I found a loop and threw just as the heifer got her hind legs free. "You got her!" Inez screeched with delight. "You got her!"

Sure enough, my loop was square on Ushi's neck. Planting my feet, I tried stubbornly to slow her retreat.

At first, I had her off balance and was able to pull her head to the side but within ten or twelve strides she had me following directly in her wake. She gained speed, and it was all I could do to keep up with her. In desperation, I made an attempt to get a wrap around a passing tree. There was a terrible burning sensation on the palms of my hands as the rope sizzled through them; then she was gone. We watched as Ushi disappeared into a draw at the other end of the pasture.

"How about your getting the water ready, Inez? We'll give her a few moments."

I was out of breath and my hands were on fire; it seemed like an ideal time to let Ushi settle down. I scooped some snow from a small mound and rolled the cool ball around in my hands. Perching on a nearby boulder, I leaned back to enjoy the warmth of the March sunshine.

Ushi was nowhere to be seen by the time Inez emerged from the house with a bucket in each hand.

"Just set the buckets down by the fence; we'll see if we can get her snubbed up first. I'll come back for them."

"Let's go over to that clump of trees." Inez motioned to a nearby spot where still-naked trees lined the pasture. "That's where we started out this morning."

"You know, Inez, with critters like her, it's sometimes best just to leave them completely alone so that they can get on with calving. Your being there all the time gives her something else to focus on and breaks her concentration."

"I couldn't do that! If something happened to that calf, I'd never forgive myself."

"Get yourself a good set of binoculars and watch her from a distance. That way if you see she's in trouble, or you see she's about to push the calf out, you can run over to be there."

"There she is!" Inez trotted in Ushi's direction without the slightest indication that she'd heard a single word I'd said.

We reached the brow of the hill to find Ushi in a gully. I had hoped that we would find her stretched out on her side with her calf pushed half out, but there she stood, head held high, ears erect, looking very much like a startled elk ready for flight.

"Maybe if I go get the grain bucket . . ." Inez's voice trailed off, as even she could see the futility of the suggestion. Her round face was skewed with worry; her lower lip trembled. "But what about the calf? How long can we leave her and still hope it's alive? It's been more than seven hours since she broke her water."

My gut feeling was that Ushi would calve on her own if we'd just get out of her hair, but I couldn't depend on it. What if there was a malpositioning? A simple problem corrected now could produce a live calf—if left, it might well result in a dead calf and a mark on my reputation.

"She's used to you, Inez. How about walking down there alone to see if you can get that rope wrapped around a tree? Maybe if you stay far enough back, she'll forget about the rope on her neck long enough for you to catch her."

While I sat down out of sight, Inez crept over the brim of the hill. Ushi watched Inez's approach. She lifted her head yet farther, then turned to confront her owner.

"Enough of this, girl." Inez took hesitant steps toward her. "Let's get that baby of yours on the ground."

The huge animal stood like a statue as Inez tried to maneuver behind her to get at the rope but every time she disappeared from the heifer's direct line of vision, Ushi would turn to face her. Soon the end of the rope was only inches from Ushi's heels with the rest of it wrapped in circles around her. She stood watching Inez's movements, raising and lowering her head to get a better view of the determined woman who just would not leave her alone. When Inez was almost close enough to touch the rope, Ushi trotted away out of reach.

"I'll give you a hand, Inez. She's obviously on to this game."

A spirited chase ensued over every square foot of the Ballman property. The game became well defined. We chased after the little knot on the end of the twenty-foot lariat, while the cow kept us from getting hold of it. We had all sorts of strategies for procuring that knot, but the heifer was too smart. Several times I actually held the knot in my hand for a few seconds, only to have it wrenched from my grasp by fifteen-hundred pounds of rapidly retreating beef. Not once during this entire episode was there any sign from Ushi that she was actually in labor; the only evidence of parturition were the ropes of membranes protruding from her vagina.

At the farthest corner of the property, Ushi's luck finally ran out. She arrived at the right angle in the fence at the same time as Inez and stopped for just long enough for me to run up behind her, grab the slack rope, and wrap it around a poplar tree. As she backed away from Inez, I gathered slack and took a couple of extra wraps around the tree. Ushi turned and retreated from me until she realized her predicament, then stood resignedly.

"You hold this and keep an eye on her while I go for the water." I handed the rope to Inez.

"I sure hope that calf of hers is still all right," Inez moaned. "I just have the terrible feeling that I left it too long."

Little had changed by the time I returned with the buckets. Ushi was hanging back on the rope, while Inez uttered a constant stream of platitudes about what a good girl she was.

Setting the bucket of cold water by the fence, I approached the gangly heifer from behind and gently scratched her tailhead. "Good girl, Ushi. There's a girl . . . good girl . . . good girl."

Moving my left hand slowly down her tail, I splashed some warm water onto her vagina. As if she'd been shot from a cannon, Ushi charged forward.

"Ushi! Ushi! Settle down, girl," pleaded Inez. "Settle down."

Around and around and around that tree Ushi lurched until she was snubbed as tightly as the lariat would allow. When she was literally at the end of her rope, I fished the container of soap from the water bucket, slathered it over her rear end, and scrubbed her quickly. Squirting soap on my arms, I worked it into a rich lather, introduced my hand through the vaginal lips, and pushed forward into the pelvis.

Ushi strained against the rope, bellowed as though her throat had been slit, and threw herself to the side. Turning in the opposite direction, she lapped the tree again, undoing herself as she went and getting farther and farther away from the tree.

"Did you feel anything?" Inez puffed, now out of breath from her laps around the tree in front of the rampaging heifer.

"The calf's in a normal position. Both front feet and the head are in the pelvis."

"Is it alive?"

"Didn't have long enough to find out!"

I jumped in front of Ushi and managed to stop her circling. Pulling tighter on the rope, I snubbed her closer to the tree and put another hitch to keep her from loosening it further. Scrubbing up again, I once more pushed into the vagina. Both of the calf's front feet were over the brim of the pelvis, and there seemed to be lots of room between the head and the mother's pubis. Grabbing the front foot, I spread the claws enough to cause a live calf discomfort and, sure enough, the foot was withdrawn.

"The calf's alive, Inez, and I think we've got enough room to pull it without difficulty."

I'd just soaped up the calving chains and was ready to place them on the calf's legs when Ushi blew up again. She charged forward and shook herself then, in a fit of defiance, pulled back, bellowed, and stuck out her tongue. She was pulling hard enough to cut off her airway; her tongue was taking on a distinct bluish hue.

"Give her some slack, Inez!"

Ushi was staggering from lack of oxygen, yet she still laid back on the rope, pulling as though her life depended on it. Inez had released most of her available slack and was clinging desperately to the remaining few feet.

"We'll have to loosen off until I get a half hitch over her muzzle." I grabbed Ushi by the nasal septum, braced my feet, and leaned forward until the rope was finally slack.

"Just a bit more and I'll get a loop over her nose so she won't choke herself."

"You can't have any more or we'll lose her!"

I'd just about gotten the half hitch over Ushi's nose when she shook her head and reefed backward. The rope slipped and tightened like a vise over the palm of my hand. I tried desperately to pull free, but Ushi's constant pressure held me firm. When I grabbed for her nose with my other hand, she was more determined to escape my grip. I was yanked helplessly in her wake as she jumped back and forth, shaking her head and bawling in a panicky attempt to free herself.

"Let go of the rope, Inez!" I hollered, as the pain intensified.

"We'll never catch her again if we let her go now!" Her jaw set, her lips pursed, Inez had drawn the line. She wasn't giving Ushi one more inch of ground!

Ushi lay back with her entire weight upon the rope, her breathing raspy and labored, her protruding tongue a sickly bluish-white. My hand, still ensnared by the rope, was now numb and about the same color as the cow's tongue.

"Let go of the rope!" I bellowed in rage.

"We'll never catch her!"

"Inez! Let go that f . . . ing rope!"

The rope suddenly fell slack. Ushi staggered back several paces and collapsed in a heap. I pulled my hand free. Surges of warmth and pain shot through it as I attempted to move my fingers. Ushi's breath was coming freely now, but she was still content to lie where she had landed. With sensation returning to my fingers, I quickly formed a half hitch and slipped it over the heifer's nose. Grabbing the end of the rope, I ran to a nearby birch tree and managed a wrap around the base of it.

Ushi got to her feet slowly, almost leisurely. As she turned her head in my direction, I took up the slack and got another wrap around the trunk.

"Come, take the rope again, Inez. You can tighten it up as she comes forward."

I grabbed the bucket and cleaned up Ushi's back end. After washing myself, I soaped up a calving chain, formed a loop with it, and manipulated it into the vagina. Ushi took a few hesitant steps then, and for the first time, strained against my entry. I quickly passed the loop over the calf's foot, tightened it, and followed it with a second half hitch. I repeated the procedure on the other leg. The entire time, Ushi was pushing against my presence.

"Good girl, Ushi," Inez encouraged. "Just keep on pushing!"

I attached the handles to the chains and began applying pressure. The calf slid forward easily to show feet and legs and tongue. I timed my pulling to the heifer's pushing, and soon a dark nose appeared, then a very dainty head.

"She's not even going to lie down!" Inez was beside herself with excitement, her eyes beaming anticipation.

With just a bit more pressure on the chains, the neck and chest were through. I dropped the handles and reached for the calf just in time for, with one more push, Ushi propelled it from her womb and into my arms.

"Why, the calf's absolutely tiny!" Inez exclaimed.

Laying it on the grass, I rubbed the infant's face and cleared some mucous from its mouth. As I cleaned its nostrils, the calf gave an explosive snort and shook its head.

I checked its anatomy. "It's a heifer."

"Oh, isn't that nice! I was sure she'd be having a bull. When they go over the due date like she did, they're almost always bulls."

"Give me one second more, and we can let Ushi have her baby." I scrubbed my arms again. "I'll make sure she doesn't have another calf in there. That one's small enough to be a twin."

A quick check revealed an empty uterus. There were no tears and Ushi wasn't bleeding. Gathering the calf in my arms, I set her down in front of her mother.

"I hope you like your baby after all this, girl."

The mammoth heifer stared in bewilderment at the wet little creature. The calf held up her head to check out her surroundings, and Ushi took a few hesitant sniffs. She jumped back as the baby attempted to stand and went sprawling, but immediately returned and started licking at her.

Ushi paid no attention whatsoever to me as I stepped up beside her to remove the loop from her nose and loosen the lariat.

"Didn't I tell you she was a beautiful heifer?" Inez chortled. "Ushi, you're such a good girl!"

THE CRUEL MONTH

HAT A WEEK! The pace of spring rush was more than I could handle. Hard to believe that when I moved to the Creston Valley I had worried that the cow population might not be large enough to support a veterinarian.

Thank God that most of the heifers had finally calved! I forgot what it was like to feel rested—to just be quiet and have nothing to occupy my mind. Not only were the days hectic, but it was a rare occasion when I actually slept the whole night through. There was always an emergency to roust me or some perplexing case that refused to vacate my mind.

I had looked forward to the weekend with the hope that things would slacken off, but Saturday was here and it looked like more of the same. Gerald Phillips called in; he had another milk fever. He was hoping that it wasn't a "funny one" like the case a couple of weeks ago. Funny was hardly an appropriate description; if it was anything like the last one, I wanted to run and hide!

The memory of Gerald standing in front of poor old Gert with the gun in his hands still sent a shiver up my spine. Gert was a huge old Guernsey, Gerald's favorite cow. She had calved without difficulty in the early morning, and he thought she looked fine until he couldn't get her to stand for evening milking. I treated her as a typical milk fever and was bewildered when she didn't respond to the administration of calcium.

I had come to expect instantaneous results from that magic potion! How many times had I arrived to a cow that was flat out and barely able to draw a breath. Invariably, the calcium would restore the flagging heart rate, have her shivering and shaking within minutes, and on her feet within the hour.

Gert perked up a bit after treatment; she shivered and took a pee. I left after giving her a second bottle under the skin, certain that she would soon be up and about. It was perplexing to be called back to her, even more upsetting to see her lying like a toad flattened on the highway, her hind legs stretched out behind her.

Cows were not made to lie like that! Although this was the first time in my career I had seen the presentation, I would come to view it with dread. I drew blood to send to the lab, then administered additional calcium. I was working toward developing a baseline on selenium, magnesium, and phosphorous levels in the valley. These minerals seemed to play a significant role in cattle health in other areas, and I was determined to get a profile on the local herds.

Gert was an enormous cow to argue with; even rolling her onto her side was a daunting task. By the time we'd repositioned her legs and propped up bales of straw to keep her upright, we were exhausted.

She never did improve. Each time I called in, it was more obvious that she was a "downer cow." Within five minutes of straightening her, she would invariably return to the toad position. In desperation, we tried using hip lifters, monstrous clamps that would fit well in any torture chamber. Tightened over the pin bones of the pelvis with a huge screw, they provided a means of lifting the cow's back end in the hopes that she would try to stand on her own. Gert simply refused to play the game; each time we applied the clamps, she hung pathetically, making no effort whatsoever to help herself.

Lab results revealed sky-high levels of calcium and magnesium, marginal levels of phosphorous, and low levels of selenium. I administered both phosphorous and selenium with no change in her demeanor. Five days of wrestling with misdirected legs, of struggling with hip lifters and belly bands led to naught. Each attempt to lift Gert found her hanging beneath the chains of the come-along like a sack of soggy grain. When it became obvious that she would never rally, Gerald sadly brought out the gun and ended the ordeal.

A postmortem revealed massive muscle damage to her hind legs, bruising along the entire ventral abdomen, and a liver that was so imbibed with fat that I could cut a line through it with my index finger. Samples sent to the lab confirmed that we were dealing with fatty liver syndrome.

Extensive research had proven that proper care for cattle during their non-milking period was vital. Feeding good-quality grass and hay high in phosphorous and low in calcium was the trick to preventing milk fevers. Keeping energy levels properly balanced so that the cows didn't get too fat was also part of the ticket.

Trying to convince Gerald to cut back on the groceries was not an easy task! As he approached sixty, a lot of the joy he derived from dairying came from spoiling his "girls." Gerald had wagged his head as I recommended cutting back during the dry period—his cows were just too fat at freshening—but I was certain he wasn't buying it.

I cringed when I got the first look at Jenny. She was a mammoth Holstein carrying far more weight than Gert. She lay stretched out on the straw like a whale tossed on the beach by a massive wave.

"Calving went fine, Gerald?"

"Never had a lick of trouble. She cleaned; her calf's as fit as a fiddle." His voice cracked. He hovered over me as I knelt by his girl, his intense blue eyes boring into me. A slender man with silver hair and sharp facial features, he had all the intensity of a hawk. "I was surprised to see her down this morning."

Jenny's heart sounded weak and distant. Her pupils were dilated, her ears and extremities cold. I palpated her udder for signs of heat and swelling, then struggled to get a milk sample from each quarter. The milk tested fine; there was no evidence of mastitis. She looked like a typical milk fever—I was praying she responded like one.

I administered a bottle of calcium, then ran in a couple of bottles of 50 percent dextrose. If there was ever a candidate for a fatty liver, Jenny was it! I hoped that flooding her with sugar water now would keep her from mobilizing fat as a source of energy. With any luck, that might prevent the rise in ketone bodies and the accumulation of fat in the liver.

I released the halter and looked on in disappointment as the cow tucked her head into her flank and emitted a long exasperating groan. "What do you think?" Gerald was no happier than I by her apparent lack of response.

"I hope we don't have another one, Gerald. She's awful fat. Have you had any other cows calve after Gert?"

"Yeah, sure. Floss and Tinker calved and they're milking good; Esther and Ilene calved around the same time as Gert and they're fine." Gerald stared at me sadly. I wanted to say something to ease his pain. Jenny groaned again. She looked for all the world like a milk fever cow that had yet to be treated.

I drove the seven miles from Lister to the office in a daze. Lug sat with his head on my lap. He always seemed to sense when I was down. My mind whirled around and around Gerald's situation. I hated passively accepting defeat—surely there was something I could do to make a difference! Doris met me at the door. Before she could utter a word, a plaintive wail emanated from the surgery. Lug's ears perked, and he trotted toward the sound.

"What is that?" It almost sounded like the bleat of a lamb, but . . .

Doris had been struggling all week with the flu. Her nose was red from blowing; she looked exhausted. "Alex Shopa was just in," she croaked. "Another of the heifers he bought in Alberta calved early—this one's alive. I've never seen him so upset; he fidgeted around here for a bit then left. He said he'd wait by the phone till you called."

I rushed to the surgery. Laid out on a blanket in front of the heat register was a calf that couldn't weigh more than thirty pounds. Its features were delicate, its hair barely half an inch long.

"I've never seen a calf this premature still breathing." The calf's mouth was open; its sides were pumping weakly. As I stooped to check it, it released another mournful bleat, then lay still. "Looks like I arrived just in time to administer the last rites. I'm beginning to feel like Dr. Death!"

"Don't be silly! Alex was sure it was too young to make it. He wanted you to have a look and see why it came so early."

Alex answered on the second ring. His voice was tense. I could picture him on the other end of the line listening stoically as I told him the calf was dead. His cigarette would be burning and hanging from the corner of his mouth. He would be squinting as the smoke encircled his head.

"This is the fourth abortion in the last two days, Dave. When the first one dropped her calf, I thought it was just stress from the shipping. Never even thought to call you."

"How big was that calf?"

"About the same size as the one you have there; it looked like it'd been dead inside her a few days . . . Never thought too much about it. Chucked it in the manure pile."

"What about the rest of your herd? Are they still eating well? Is there any coughing, any runny eyes?"

"Not that I noticed with the heifers, but now that you mention it, some of my own cows have started coughing, and I noticed a few with runny eyes."

"Darn! I want you to run the worst of those critters through the chute and get some temps. Have any of the heifers that aborted passed their membranes?"

"Haven't seen any cleanings; some of them have a bit hanging. What are you thinking?"

"Remember when I gave that talk on brood cow management? I told you about the problems the prairie guys were having with a virus called Infectious Bovine Rhinotracheitis—how there was a vaccine you should be using as soon as they calved again. You may be dealing with an outbreak of that in your herd."

"That's all I need."

"The only thing that doesn't go along with it is that calf's being aborted alive. My understanding has always been that they die from the virus infection and then are aborted."

"What am I going to do, just sit around and watch my calf crop evaporate? That'll make my banker happy!"

"You get started with the temps, and I'll get out there as soon as I can."

Within ten minutes, the waiting room was crammed with people and animals. Doris looked like death warmed over, and I hated myself for making her continue. It was after six before we herded the last clients out the door. Doris sat like a lump on the waiting room bench as I pulled on my coveralls.

"I'm going straight home to bed," she moaned. "I can't remember feeling so tired."

The streetlights were already on when I headed to the car. It was a clear night in March, and the temperature was dropping. The mud in the cow yards would tighten up tonight.

Alex was waiting for me by the back door of the old two-story house. He was uptight, his frown exaggerating deep, well-pronounced wrinkles. He took a long drag on his cigarette, then rolled it around between nicotine-stained fingers. Staring at the smoldering butt as if it contained the answer to his problems, he slowly shook his head.

"I don't like this, Dave. I don't like this one bit."

"Were the temperatures up?"

"Hell if I know. The thermometer I bought from you guys is in Celsius. I've never used anything but Fahrenheit! The ones that were coughing were mostly around forty; one was between forty-one and forty-two. Is that up?"

"They're up. That would be between a hundred and four and a hundred and six."

"Great . . . At least they don't look like they're slipping their calves. Maybe they'll just get sick and not abort."

"Maybe, but what usually happens is the cow gets the virus—just like we'd get the flu. Then the calf gets it from her. You hardly ever lose a cow to the virus unless they get pneumonia, but it seems that calves in the last three months are likely to succumb."

"That describes my whole bloody herd, Dave; they finish calving in two months!"

"Well then, we better get started. This'll be a lab diagnosis, so the quicker we get the samples off, the sooner we'll know what's going on. Let's check the ones that aborted first."

"I've got 'em in the holding pen; I set up a trouble light near the squeeze."

Four heifers milled impatiently about the corral as we approached.

"What temperatures were they running when you put them through?"

"I wrote 'em down." Alex dragged a crumpled cigarette package from his back pocket. Holding it at arm's length, he read, "thirty-eight point six, thirty-nine, thirty-eight point five, thirty-nine point two."

"I'd call those all normal; that'd be consistent with IBR. By the time they abort, they're pretty much over the infection."

Alex grabbed a rope and reefed on it. The sliding metal gate at the back of the squeeze screeched and rattled its way to the top of its guide. I climbed the rails of the corral and dropped to the other side. With one hand on a white-faced heifer's flank, I reached forward and tapped her on the side of the head. She reluctantly stepped away from the others, then headed down the chute. I ran behind her, banging the rails with a stick to herd her on. The end gate fell with a clang, and the head rack slammed shut.

The heifer squirmed and twisted her body in an attempt to pull herself free. She bucked and shuffled her hind feet as I pulled her tail to the side and began scrubbing her vagina.

"Does she ever stink!" Alex grabbed her tail. "You guys must be dead from the ass up to be able to work with this sort of stench all the time. Can't stand the smell of death."

I'd often thought the same thing when I was called upon to deal with rotten afterbirths and dead calves. I slipped my hand into a plastic glove, then applied more soap and continued my scrub. Rinsing my hand in clean water, I reached forward through the vulvar lips. It was a tight squeeze, and the heifer danced from side to side as I advanced my hand to the cervix. The muscular ring was already closing down, and I was only able to pass two fingers through it. I wrapped the rope-like placenta around my fingers and pulled. There was a tearing sensation deep inside her and the cord came out, a few patches of membrane still with it.

I withdrew, snipped some of the tissue from the sample, and dropped it into a jar of formalin. Leaving the remainder in the glove for culturing, I inverted it and tied a knot in the end. While Alex held up her tail, I drew a blood sample.

We put the heifers through one after the other until we had collected tissue and blood samples from all of them, then brought four cows from a holding pen behind the house. They looked bright but coughed the moment we started moving them. The old Hereford that led the group trotted through the open gate and milled around the corral. Her left horn stuck almost straight up like a giraffe's; her ears were high. A yellow ear tag displayed Number 82.

"Let's run her in first!" Alex whacked her on the rear end, and she flew up the chute. The head gate clanged shut as she drove the bars forward with her shoulders. The entire chute rattled as she struggled to pull herself free. "She's the craziest cow in the herd! Every year I swear I'm going to ship her, but every year she has the nicest calf and ends up staying."

I unhooked the trouble light from the beam overhead to get a better look at the old cow. She struggled violently and tossed her head in my direction.

"You watch yourself! She's a miserable old crock. If she can get at you, she will."

I leaned forward with the light, trying to direct it into her nasal passage. I could see that the membranes were red and inflamed, but she wasn't about to hold still long enough for a close look. A long white gob of snot hung from her nose and disappeared into the depth of the nostril. I gingerly reached forward to run my finger along it. She snorted and tossed her head; the mucous whipped through the air and landed on the leg of my coveralls.

"So much for your white-collar job." Alex smirked as I scraped the mess off. The old cow pushed ahead in the squeeze, tipping her prong horn forward in an attempt to prod me. I grabbed her nose across the nasal septum with thumb on one side and fingers on the other. She bellowed with rage and struggled to get free as I clamped down. The chute rocked, and I held on for all I was worth.

"Grab the light, Alex!"

He shone it into the old cow's face. As I slid my fingers into her nostril to wipe it clean, her eyes bulged from their sockets and tears rolled down her face.

"Look here, Alex. See these little white marks all over the inside of her nostrils? Over her muzzle? See how red and inflamed the lining is?"

"Yeah. What does that mean?"

"It's typical of IBR." I reached under 82's throat and firmly gripped her trachea. She coughed instantly and tears ran once more down her face. "She has an irritated windpipe as well."

Alex followed me to the back of the squeeze and held her tail up while I drew a blood sample. We ran the remaining animals through the chute in the dark, bobbing back and forth with the trouble light. All were running fevers, coughing as we worked them, and all had lesions similar to those of Number 82.

Alex looked dejected as I gathered my samples together. We stumbled toward the house, bottles clinking in my pockets. It was chilly and, except for a dog barking at the other end of Wynndel, the night was quiet. Alex's ever-present cigarette glowed as he took a deep drag. I could hear the sigh as he exhaled, smell the odor of burning tobacco in the cool night air.

"What the hell am I supposed to do, just sit out here and watch my calf crop disappear? There has to be some way to head this off!" We were sitting at the Shopas' kitchen table—it was after eight. Alex's wife plunked cups in front of us and filled them with steaming coffee. Much younger than her husband, Shirley was an active mother of two children. She focused worried eyes on Alex, then slipped into the chair next to him.

"I wish I could be more upbeat, Alex, but depending on the strain of the virus, you could be in for one heck of a ride. First thing in the morning, I'd like you to cut out the heifers you bought and all the cows that look sick—it may slow down the spread. I was just detailed about a new vaccine. They claim it won't cause abortion in bred cows but I've never used it before; every other vaccine on the market is contraindicated for use in pregnant animals."

Alex gave Shirley a mournful look. He popped the lid from a can of Player's tobacco and rolled another cigarette. Using the butt that still hung from the corner of his mouth, he lit up, then methodically ground the remains of the old cigarette into an overflowing ashtray.

"We've got to try something! I paid top dollar for a lot of the cows I bought this summer, and I stuck my neck out at the bank for those heifers."

I added cream and sugar to my coffee, then hesitantly took a sip. Coffee was not something I enjoyed. We had a pot on the go continually at the office, and it was only the last few months that I could stand to drink it when socializing with clients.

"What I'd like to do is call the vet college in the morning. I'll check with Dr. Radostits, the head of the large-animal department, to see what he suggests. He probably has a better feel for how this vaccine has been working."

"You better order some in! We've got to do something."

My mind was grinding away like a cement mixer on the way home. Cases that had been resolved months before flashed into my mind. For the better part of a year, it seemed that I could do no wrong—that so long as I persevered, I could drag any case back from the brink. The last few weeks had been a rude awakening. Was I slipping? Or was it just a string of hard luck? It wouldn't be so bad if it was just me struggling along. It really hurt to watch good people like the Shopas and the Phillipses in such a pickle.

It was after nine when I got back to the office. I was hungry, but I knew there wasn't a thing to eat in the place. I glanced at my watch—not much time left to get my samples off. For packing material, I found last week's *Advance* and dumped out the contents of a case of dewormer. I scratched out a history of events to accompany the Phillips and Shopa samples and hurriedly taped up the box.

I arrived at the Depot Restaurant hoping it would still be open. It wasn't, but the door to the tiny office at the back of the building was. I was relieved to see the clerk waddle toward me. She was short and squat—her face round, her gray hair bobbed short.

"You're at it late again." She looked tired and smiled feebly as she took the box from me. She wrinkled her nose as she plunked the box on the scale; I wondered if she was smelling something through the box, or if there was a rotten odor hanging on my clothing. "That'll be six dollars." I handed her a ten and waited as she made change and filled out my receipt.

I wandered down the street to see if the Kootenay Hotel restaurant was still open, but no luck. This was going to be one of those nights where I went to bed hungry. I dawdled home along the abandoned street and crossed aimlessly in front of the Daylight Grocery. The light was on, and I could see Mrs. Jackson wandering around near the back. I tried the door; it was locked.

Tapping gently on the window, I waited as she shuffled over and peered out. The door opened with a tinkling of the bell. "Good evening, Doctor. Having another late night?"

"Another late night and no food in the house. Would you mind if I did a bit of shopping?"

"You go right ahead." Mrs. Jackson tottered to the back of the store and perched on an old wooden stool. Her face was gaunt, her body thin and frail. To me, she always seemed sad. "I can't seem to sleep tonight anyway."

The place was bereft of almost everything one would expect to find in a normal corner store—no junk food, no cold meats, nothing frozen. It seemed that, as things were sold from the periphery of the store, they were never replaced. Only the display shelf beneath the dormer that gave the store its name had anything on it.

I wandered around the shelves perusing their meager offerings—a few cans of tuna and salmon, a lonely loaf of white bread. Poor Mrs. Jackson—her cupboards were almost as barren as mine!

I squeezed the bread only to find it hard, with the texture of stone-ground. I smiled at the thought of Mrs. Jackson buying it day-old at the Garden Bakery. I grabbed a couple of cans of tuna and some salmon, then reluctantly picked up the loaf of bread.

"Do you have any butter, Mrs. Jackson?"

"Sorry, Doctor, I'm fresh out." Her lips quivered as she spoke. I smiled at her and set down my purchase. With a pencil, she meticulously wrote March

12, 1974, in the outer column of her ledger book. Rotating the cans one at a time to find the price, she entered their sale. As she turned over a can of tuna, she looked in my direction. I glanced away as her shaky fingers picked off a price sticker from the Creston Valley Cooperative. I took a peek at the ledger—at the rows of meticulous notations, the most amazing penmanship. This was the first notation for the day, but there was the entry for the Garden Bakery—March 10, 1974. My bread was at least two days old!

The telephone was ringing as I entered the clinic. Lug was there with his wet nose to greet me. The recorded message clicked on, and I waited to see if it was something important. "Damn machine!" It was a man's voice. "This is Ron Missler. We have a dog that has been hit by a car. Please call us as soon as possible."

I picked up the receiver and shut off the machine just as he was giving his phone number. "This is Dr. Perrin here."

"Oh, thank God! I hate these bloody machines. Cindy's been hit by a car and we need help."

"I'm at the office now if you'd like to bring her in. How badly is she injured?"

"She's conscious. My son's on the side of the road with her; she's screaming in pain. She bit my hand when I tried to look at her, and I'm a bit leery of prodding her too much."

"Do you think you'll be able to get her loaded? If you're afraid of getting bitten again you can tie a piece of gauze or rope around her muzzle before you handle her."

"I'll manage, so long as you'll be there when we get there."

I rushed upstairs and dug through a stack of dishes in search of the can opener. I found it in the sink half submerged in a pot of water. Opening a can of tuna, I gagged a couple of mouthfuls down and chased it with a bite of bread. Damn, it was dry! I hurried to the fridge in search of mayonnaise—anything to lubricate it.

The pounding on the clinic door jolted me. I shoved another forkful of tuna in my mouth and rushed downstairs. Lug was on my heels, but I closed the door in front of him.

"Hello, Dr. Perrin. Thanks so much for seeing us."

I recognized Mr. Missler right away. The name hadn't rung a bell over the phone but the moment I saw him I made the connection. In his early thirties,

Ron was almost six feet tall, athletic, and youthful in appearance. He and his son had been to the office several times with a delightful yellow Lab. I had seen her for an initial health examination and then again for vaccinations.

On each visit, the child came in clutching the pup tightly to his chest. The love that ten-year-old boy felt for his dog was palpable, and Ron did everything he could to encourage it. Their visits were never treated as a grudging chore or an unwanted expense—more like a family outing, the bonding of a father, his son, and his pet.

"No problem, Ron. How's Cindy doing?"

"I'm not sure. She seems to have settled down a bit, but we're all stressed out. We had a terrible time loading her, and poor Paul's at his wits' end."

"Let's have a look." I followed Ron to the back of a blue Ford station wagon. The back door was open, and the boy was stretched out next to his beloved pet. Paul's long dark hair was caked with blood; his brown eyes brimmed with tears. His arms were wrapped around his dog, and he talked to her in nervous, squeaky blurps.

"It's okay, Paul. Dr. Perrin'll look after her. She's in good hands; she'll be as good as new." Ron reached out a bloodstained hand and gently pulled his son toward him. "Let Dr. Perrin have a look at her, son." The back of Ron's hand was discolored and swollen; serum and blood oozed from a pair of bite wounds.

"She really did get you."

"Poor thing. She was so frightened and in so much pain, she didn't realize what she was doing." Ron's eyes were focused on the dog as she puffed and panted through the tie that secured her muzzle. Paul rolled from the car and slipped his hand into his dad's.

I crawled in next to Cindy and rotated her head to catch a bit of light. She looked shocked; her membranes were pale. "Did she try and get up after the accident? Could she bear any weight?"

"She never really tried; we just kept her there on her side. She cried as soon as I tried to move her—that's when she bit me."

Cindy lay with her head at half mast. Protracted strands of drool hung from her mouth; her eyes were closed. A long gash ran across her forehead and behind her ear. Her left hind leg was uppermost and held at an unusual angle.

I lifted her eyelids one at a time; both pupils, though equal, were constricted. I ran my hands down her spine. Muscle tone appeared normal, and she responded with an increased pitch to her whine when I squeezed the tip of her tail.

Her front legs seemed fine, and gentle manipulation produced no evidence of discomfort. Her abdomen was relaxed; there was no distention. I clutched the toes of her left hind foot and flexed her tarsus; it moved freely without pain. Moving up the leg, I poked and prodded. I lifted it gently near the knee. There was a clunk deep in the hip; the dog screamed, then whirled to bite me. The side of her teeth grazed my hand, covering it with drool.

Paul buried his head in his father's back. He sobbed quietly, his shoulders rising and falling.

"There's either a fracture or dislocation in her hip. We'll have to treat her for shock and get an X ray of that back end."

I carried her in and deposited her on the surgery table. Within a few minutes, the intravenous was running; steroids and Demerol had been administered. Cindy's breathing became more regular, her whines more infrequent. After fifteen minutes, her circulation had improved—her gums had a pinkish hue. Paul had quit crying, but there was foreboding in his eyes. He stood glued to his father, clinging desperately to his hand.

I turned on the X-ray machine and measured the Lab's pelvis for thickness. I put on a lead apron, then slowly worked a large plate under her body. I had the Misslers leave the room, extended her legs as best I could, and exposed the first shot.

"I'm going to need help with this next one if you don't mind, Ron. Just slip into this gown and gloves and we'll roll her over."

I supported the hind legs while Ron rolled her on her back and held her in place by her elbows. We tottered back and forth as Cindy squirmed in discomfort. She lay still for a matter of seconds, and I pushed the button. The clunk of the X-ray machine was a welcome sound!

I left Ron and Paul to watch Cindy and retreated to the darkroom. I opened the cassettes and fumbled until I had them impaled by four corners on the racks. Lowering them into the developer, I plunked on the lid and set the timer. Three minutes to dig out new film and reload the cassettes.

The bell rang. After a few quick dips in the water bath to remove excess developer, I lowered them into the fixer and set the timer for six minutes. I squinted as I walked back into the lights of the surgery. The boy and his father looked expectantly in my direction. "The X rays'll be ready in five minutes."

I checked Cindy's color and winked at Paul. "She's looking much better." He managed a halfhearted smile but didn't look convinced.

The bell rang on the timer, and I retrieved the X rays. As soon as I lifted the films from the tank, I could see why Cindy was in such pain. Her hip was dislocated.

I pointed to the head of the femur, then moved my finger to the empty socket. "See how it's way out of joint?"

"How serious is that?"

"It's difficult to know at this point. I can't see any fractures. Most dislocations come along fairly well, but a lot depends on how much the surrounding structures were traumatized. It's all soft tissue, of course, and damage doesn't show up on an X ray."

We all stood quietly before the view box looking at the bones and the wide displacement of the head of the femur. Cindy squirmed on the table and groaned in agony. Paul looked at her and then at his father. "I want to go home, Daddy. I hate seeing Cindy in so much pain. I'm so sorry. I know you told me to keep her on the leash." He threw his head on his dad's chest and sobbed. "She was on the other side of the road. Why did she run out in front of that car?"

Tears were pooling in Ron's eyes. He ran his fingers through his son's hair and pulled him to his breast. "We'll never know, Paul. What's happened has happened. We can't change that now. Dr. Perrin will do the best he can do for her."

Paul gave Cindy a last hug. Ron wrapped his arm around his son's shoulders. "You have my number if there are any problems."

I could hear Paul's sobs as they retreated. Several times he repeated, "I didn't think she would run out in front of that car." The doors slammed, the engine started, and I was alone with Cindy.

Here I was again! Eleven o'clock on Saturday night—what to do? There was no way I could call Doris in—not tonight—not in the shape she was in. I could call Gordon, but I hadn't seen him all week. Damned if I wanted to call him at this hour.

I pulled up a chair and sat next to Cindy. A little voice told me to put her in the kennel overnight and watch her, to do the surgery when I was fresh and Doris was here to help. Tomorrow was Sunday. Doris had been lamenting about not getting to church in the last three weeks. I was bound and determined she would make it this time!

I got out my *Canine Surgery* and browsed through the index. I had done several dislocated hips in the last few months, but was always in search of that "secret trick"—the maneuver that pops the femur back in, first time, every time. It had taken me almost ten minutes of sweating and grinding and pulling to reduce the last one. It had finally gone in with a resounding pop, but I couldn't recall that I had done anything special to bring that event about.

The text claimed: "Reduction is accomplished by a coordinated series of manipulations designed to relax the thigh muscles, break down adhesions, slide the femoral head onto the brim of the acetabulum, and finally drop it over the edge into the socket." Sort of similar to my experience—sweat, grind, and pull until it pops into place.

I made up my mind. I'd put her under quickly and try and reduce the hip. Leaving her overnight was a cop-out; by morning all the muscles would be stretched, and the hip would be far less likely to stay in place. I had to quit sniveling and get on with it!

I laid out all the bandage material that I'd need and turned on the gas to the anesthetic machine. The nitrous oxide tank was up to pressure and the oxygen was half full—we were in great shape for a short procedure like this. I shut off the half tank of oxygen and tried the backup tank. The gauge zipped to the top—it was full. Switching back to the partial tank, I turned the dial of the halothane vaporizer to full open, and slipped the cone over Cindy's nose.

After an initial spate of whining and a bit of struggling, Cindy relaxed and drifted off to sleep. Her breathing was slow and regular. By the time I decided to intubate her, her jaw was completely relaxed. I opened her mouth and slid the tube down her airway. Lowering the level of halothane and nitrous oxide, I connected the tube to the machine, blew up the sealing cuff on the endotracheal tube, and tied it in place.

Rolling her onto her right side, I put gentle traction on the leg, rotated the lower portion inward, and pulled. There was a grinding sensation then a bit of a thump. I flexed the leg back and forth gently a few times—surely it couldn't have been that simple! The leg moved smoothly; there was no grinding.

I smiled—this was too easy. Rolling Cindy onto her chest, I extended her legs behind her. Sure enough, they were the same length! I gently shifted her back on to her side and grabbed a roll of tape. I had two wraps of Elastoplast around her abdomen. It was when I lifted her leg out from her body and flexed it that I felt it shift. It was just a fleeting sensation, the slightest bit of grinding when I moved the leg.

I manipulated the leg again; there was a terrible grating. Damn! It sure wasn't in now. It must have just been sitting on top of the pelvis somehow! I extended the legs again. There was a good inch and a half difference in their length. With a big sigh, I pulled her leg down and pressed on the head of the femur with my thumbs. Again, I got a halfhearted thump, and the leg flexed normally.

I didn't like the feel of this. Other similar cases had gone back with a resounding thump, and I had no doubt they were in. Was I not really getting it in place? Was the joint so badly traumatized that there was no musculature left to hold it? I placed my left hand firmly over the head of the femur and rotated the leg back and forth. It glided freely, had full range of motion. I was sure it was in!

I rolled her with the greatest of care, making sure to keep pressure on the hip the whole time. Sliding a plate under her, I exposed an X ray and gently rolled her back on her side. I pondered taping her and developing the film later. But what if it really wasn't in? What if I woke her up to find it just sitting above the joint somehow?

I took a step toward the darkroom. I hated to leave her unmonitored. I turned and checked the machine. Everything looked fine. I flexed the leg a few more times, trying to make up my mind what to do.

Dashing to the darkroom, I opened the cassette, mounted the film onto the holder, and submersed it in the developer. Setting the timer, I covered the vat and bolted for the surgery. Cindy was fine and I rushed back to reload the cassette before the alarm went off. I rinsed the film and slipped it into the fixer then headed back to Cindy. She was breathing regularly, looking so relaxed. I began to wish that I could just lie down beside her and sleep.

The alarm went off, and I retrieved the film. The hip was reduced, but the head of the femur didn't appear to be seated full depth in the socket. I leaned heavily on top of the head of the femur and rotated the leg back and forth. If there was a clot or some soft tissue in the bottom of the socket, surely that would drive it out!

I flexed the leg and winged it out slightly from the body. The text claimed that such positioning helped seat the femur more firmly in the socket. I had wound my way through the better part of a four-inch roll of Elastoplast when I felt it pop out again.

"Lord, help me!" Why did the tough cases always happen in the middle of the night?

This was the beginning of a struggle for reduction. Soon all the developing racks were in use; films dangled on strings in the water bath. Every time I reduced the hip, I X-rayed Cindy again. Invariably, I discovered it had popped out once more. Each time, I replaced it and tried again.

Finally, I had the hip reduced and taped in place. If it came out this time, I'd wake her up and go in at a later date to do an open repair. I was dragging my feet on my final trip to the darkroom. I pulled the last film from the rack and fired it into the garbage. I already had a half-dozen just like it dangling in the water bath. I stifled a yawn and waited for the bell to ring, then shifted the film to the fixer and headed back to Cindy.

I knew instinctively that I was in trouble! I had taken several steps toward her and not seen movement. I broke into a run and reached her in seconds. Her tongue was blue, her sides no longer moving. I looked desperately for signs of a heartbeat, then squeezed the chest over her heart. Nothing! There was no sign of life!

A cold shiver ran up my spine as I looked at the anesthetic machine. The blue gauge indicating the flow of nitrous oxide had not changed, but the green one for the oxygen read zero.

"Oh, my God . . . Noooo!"

I ripped off the connection to the anesthetic machine and breathed into the tube. Struggling with the valves, I turned on the reserve tank of oxygen and reconnected the machine. I closed the valves and started bagging pure oxygen. A minute had passed and there was no improvement in her color. Her tongue was still the color of clay. I felt over her chest—still no heartbeat! I put a hand on either side of her heart and started CPR.

Alternating the compression of her chest and the compression of the bag on the anesthetic machine, I struggled to regain some sign of life. Fifteen minutes later, I admitted defeat. I had killed Cindy!

I staggered to the waiting room in a state of shock. All I could see were Paul's sad brown eyes staring accusingly at me. I could see them filled with anguish, brimming with tears. I had killed his best friend! I had betrayed his trust.

"Oh, God! Why have you done this to me? When so many people don't care a damn about their animals, why would it be this one to die?"

I fell heavily on the bench. Tears flowed as if released from a huge reservoir. All the failures of the past week were heaped upon me. My shoulders convulsed, as sob after sob racked my body. I was the biggest screwup of a veterinarian who had ever lived! Why had I thought I could handle this on my own? Why had I thought I could be a veterinarian at all? I belonged at the smelter throwing bags of fertilizer into railway cars.

It was almost 1 A.M. when I phoned Doris. Her voice was husky; she was still half asleep. "Don't bother coming to work on Monday, Doris. I'm closing the practice. I'm leaving town." My voice was flat. I had made my decision. I was a failure—a complete waste of skin!

"What on earth are you talking about? Are you drunk?"

"I just killed Ron Missler's dog! The oxygen ran out on the machine, and I killed her."

"Oh, Dave . . . Why didn't you call me?"

There was a minute of complete silence.

"I'll be there in a few minutes."

"There's nothing for you to do. Go back to sleep."

"I'm coming right in!"

I stood with the phone in my hand staring at Cindy's motionless body. I felt numb. There were no more tears. There was nothing but a feeling of complete emptiness. I had to phone the Misslers. I picked up the phone, then hesitated. How do you tell a man that you just killed a member of his family? The dial tone gave way to an annoying bleating sound, and I hung up the receiver.

My mind was whirling. There was always a risk when anesthetizing an animal—especially one that has just been run over by a car. I didn't have to tell him that the oxygen ran out. He'd probably feel better not knowing the truth.

I dialed the number and waited in anticipation as the telephone rang. I always hated to give people the news of a pet's death, but this was different—never had I felt more complicity.

The phone rang a half-dozen times, and I fought the urge to hang up. "Hello." It was Ron. I could tell he was anticipating bad news.

My mind was whirling. "Ron, I'm so sorry . . . Cindy's dead." I hesitated before struggling to go on. "It's my fault. I was working alone. I shouldn't have been . . . I had difficulties getting the hip to stay in . . . The oxygen ran out on the anesthetic machine while I was developing an X ray. I tried to bring her back, but I was too late. I . . ."

"I understand, Dave. You did your best."

"I didn't do my best, Ron—Cindy shouldn't have died. I failed you and I failed Paul. I'm so sorry."

"I know this doesn't make sense, Dave, but Paul knew. He kept telling me that Cindy was going to die. I tried to reassure him. But somehow, he knew."

Doris came through the door moments after I hung up the phone. "What the . . ."

She stopped short of the surgery. The place was in shambles. Shelves had been whipped clean of instrument packs, the anesthetic machine lay on its side. With a look of amazement, she wandered about the clinic.

"How could you do this? You've worked so hard."

"It's over, Doris. I just can't take it anymore. I killed that dog as sure as if I took a gun and shot her. Every time I close my eyes, all I can see is that little boy and his big, forlorn eyes full of tears."

"You're not God, Dave!" Doris's voice quivered with emotion. "You're human and humans make mistakes!"

"I'm through with practice."

"Where'll you go? What'll you do? All your friends are here!"

I plunked on the bench in the waiting room with my head in my hands. Doris knelt down on the reception room floor and began piecing together the daybook. The binding was in one corner, the cover in another. Receipts lay scattered about the floor.

The phone rang. Doris tiptoed through the rubble to answer it.

She spoke in a muted tone. Hesitantly, she turned to face me. "It's Alex Shopa. He has problems with a cow calving. He tried himself, but says he can't get it."

I didn't answer. I was seeing aborted calves, cows lying like toads, mangled dogs . . .

"Dave, what should I tell him?"

I took a deep breath. "Tell him I'll get there as soon as I can."